Tele-Advising

Tele-Advising

THERAPEUTIC DISCOURSE

IN AMERICAN TELEVISION

MIMI WHITE

The University of North Carolina Press

Chapel Hill & London

© 1992 The University
of North Carolina Press

All rights reserved

Manufactured in the
United States of America

The paper in this book
meets the guidelines for
permanence and durability
of the Committee on
Production Guidelines for
Book Longevity of the
Council on Library
Resources.

96   95   94   93   92

5   4   3   2   1

Library of Congress
Cataloging-in-Publication Data

White, Mimi, 1953–

   Tele-advising : therapeutic discourse in
American television / by Mimi White.

      p.   cm.

   Includes bibliographical references and
index.

   ISBN 0-8078-2055-5 (alk. paper). —
ISBN 0-8078-4390-3 (pbk. : alk. paper)

   1. Television—Social aspects—United
States.   2. Television—United States—
Psychological aspects.   3. Rhetoric and
psychology.

I.   Title.

PN1992.6.W43   1992

302.23'45'0973—dc20   92-53623

                              CIP

TO JIM

Contents

Acknowledgments

Many people contributed, knowingly and otherwise, with varying kinds of support, to this book. The Pembroke Center for Teaching and Research on Women at Brown University provided the intellectual context in which the full dimensions of the project could be initially developed, along with a concrete opportunity to draft two chapters. Elizabeth Weed, Rey Chow, Shahla Haeri, and Kari Weil were ardent supporters and careful sounding boards for my ideas during my year at the Center. The Center for Twentieth Century Studies–Milwaukee offered further intellectual challenge and stimulation as my work developed.

Patricia Mellencamp, Patrice Petro, Chuck Kleinhans, Lynne Joyrich, Claudia Springer, Kate Kane, Margaret Morse, Lauren Rabinovitz, Bobby Allen, Kathleen Woodward, Pamela Falkenberg, Susan Lee, Linda Jenkins, Henry Giroux, Roger I. Simon, and Dwight Conquergood have all been generous in listening to, reading, and encouraging this work at various stages. Their input has been invaluable, and my strongest work comes from my interaction with them. Support also came from many colleagues at Northwestern University, especially those in the School of Speech, the Women's Center, and the Center for Interdisciplinary Research in the Arts.

Larry Malley and Iris Tillman Hill were both readily convinced that my idea for a book was viable; their interest and friendship are deeply appreciated. Kate Torrey, Ron Maner, and the staff at the University of North Carolina Press did a superlative job in taking the manuscript through the final stages of preparation and into publication.

James Schwoch has brought to this manuscript a profound knowledge of television, media culture, computers, and bibliography. He provided extensive support, including a willingness to sit and watch hours of *Home Shopping Club* and *The 700 Club* along with me—certainly service above and beyond the call of personal or professional duty, and more television therapy than anyone needs.

Introduction

Alf: Therapy for Aliens

The first episode of the NBC situation comedy *Alf* opens as an alien creature crash lands on the garage roof of a California suburban home after escaping from his own planet, Melmac, as it explodes in the wake of a nuclear accident. He invades an average middle-class family—husband, wife, two children (though a third is born in a later season), and a pet cat. As it happens, the head of the household, Willy Tanner, is an amateur radio enthusiast, and the garage is filled with an array of equipment designed to pick up all manner of electromagnetic radio signals (shortwave, ham radio, etc.). The crash occurs while Willy is tracking stray radio signals in space, hoping to detect some sign of life. The creature's appearance in the first minutes of the program's premiere episode is thus presented as the fulfillment of Willy's dream. His lifetime study of the universe, passion for radio, and belief in alien life forms are conjoined and rewarded when the Melmacian comes to roost on his roof. In fact Willy proposes that they name the creature who arrives "Alf," as an acronym for "alien life form." Later in the series we learn that Alf's real name is Gordon Shumway, but he is more than willing to adopt the appellation that signals his otherness to his hosts. This otherness is also embodied in his physical being: although a biped, Alf resembles a hairy aardvark.

Alf's appearance as the fulfillment of Willy's dream, the culmination of one chain of desire, is also a disruptive intrusion, enabling the weekly renarrativization of series television. An alien presence within the nuclear family, Alf introduces problems that must be negotiated repeatedly by Willy, his wife Kate, and their children Lynn and Brian. Alf's disruptive impulses are the result of a subjectivity that is fully informed by his familiarity with American-style consumer culture. Indeed the creature from another galaxy is so well versed in the patterns and products of contemporary American life that the problems he poses for the Tanner family are primarily transgressions of style and degree. In the context of the normative middle-class lifestyle of his hosts, Alf's problems are the result of his propensity for excessive consumption and his refusal to respect the limits of middle-class decorum. He eats too much, watches too much television, is overinvolved in the characters and situations he encounters in popular culture (including television, film, comic books, and popular music), belches too loudly at the dinner table, and yearns to eat the family's pet cat.

In a crucial sense, Alf is figured in terms that are usually associated with women and children in mass culture.[1] His lack of restraint and etiquette and his general range of tastes primarily align him with childhood, even though he is 229 years old in terms of the Melmac calendar and is a trained, professional pilot. Yet he is simultaneously, if less emphatically, associated with women. One of the structural constraints that leads to this association is his restriction to the Tanner home. An important premise of the program is that if government authorities and scientific experts learn of Alf's presence, his life will be in danger: he will be confined to a laboratory to be probed, studied, and possibly even killed. The Tanner home is defined simultaneously as his refuge and his prison. As a result, Alf is home all day long, like a housewife; and he does watch soap operas, along with almost everything else on television. His expertise in the feminine domain plays a prominent role in an episode where he becomes a sales representative for a cosmetics company that relies on home-based sales. He proves to be a success in this arena because he is able to use the telephone so well and to speak so effectively to the beauty concerns of potential customers—women—in promoting his products.

Alf's position in the family is thus unstable. He is figured as both a child and an adult, a male and a female. He is 229 years old, but his alien status and lack of restraint make it impossible for him to function as a patriarch. Moreover, there is already one head of the household—however weakly figured—in the Tanner home. At the same time, his behavior notwithstanding, Alf is neither a child nor a woman. In the program, he stands uneasily between these positions, sometimes providing parental-style support and advice to the children in the Tanner household and sometimes conspiring with them—or even outdoing them—in his childishness, subject to the parental authority of Willy and Kate. He regularly shifts positions, frustrating various family members by virtue of assuming a position at odds with them one minute and functioning as their ally and partner-in-arms the next. Most often, however, his excessive habits mandate the need for containment and control. Within this fictional context, the excesses of his behavior are all the more pressing because, as part of the very premise of the show, he is largely restricted to the confines of the Tanner home.

Even more than for the housewife or the preschool child, for Alf confinement to the home means that his contact with the outside world is channeled through the apparatuses of telecommunications—radio, telephone, and television. The fact that he is already expert in the basic forms and structures of mass culture, having watched American television programs on Melmac, helps him to believe he can make sense of life on Earth. Alf's strategies of social adjustment on Earth and his mode of personal expression via overindulgence are equally linked to American media and consumer culture. These two spheres—of social identity within the family and of consumption—are in turn associated by being affiliated with confessional and therapeutic strategies. Through the course of the program there are repeated conjunctions of the family, consumer culture, the media, telecommunications, and therapeutic discourse, so that over time these terms become interwoven and mutually implicating.

In the cosmetics sales episode, Alf causes a family financial crisis through his patterns of uninhibited consumption. He eats a week's worth of family groceries in a matter of days, and runs up the phone bill with long-distance calls ordering products advertised on late-night television, which he pays for with Willy's credit cards. When Willy demands financial retrenchment, Alf feels that he ought to contribute to the family budget in some way, although he cannot go out and get a job. By answering a magazine ad, Alf becomes a sales representative for a cosmetics company, selling the products out of the home, over the phone. Within a few weeks, Alf is named salesperson of the month, not for any actual sales but for placing the largest order for products with the regional office. Willy and Kate are livid when they discover that they are footing the bill, as Alf's inventory of cosmetics has been charged to Willy's credit cards. To make back their investment, they are forced to host a reception at which Alf's women clients can actually purchase the products that he has described to them over the phone. Much to Willy and Kate's surprise, the sales party proves to be a success, and they end up with a small profit. This is because Alf has done such a good job preselling the products over the phone; women have confided their particular beauty problems and concerns, and Alf has already told them which products they need. Thus Willy and Kate only have to stand around and exchange products for money. However, after this one-time event, Alf's business venture is put to rest.

Here the apparatuses of telecommunications are essential to plot development. Alf's overuse of the telephone and television, as well as his abuse of the consumer credit system, initiates a problem in the family that is effectively resolved through the same channels of communication and consumption. Using credit cards and the telephone to participate in consumer culture is both the cause of problems and the means of their resolution. Moreover, this connection underscores Alf's position in the Tanner family in terms that include economic relations (in which payment is deferred). However, the process of discovering the problem and its resolution also involves confessional and therapeutic interchanges, both between Alf and Willy and between Alf and the women he meets through his business. Twice Alf is forced to confess that he has used Willy's credit cards without authorization. Alf himself wins the confidence of women who then confess their beauty problems to him as an integral part of his business. He functions as an authority to whom the women must confess, a position facilitated by his own associations with the female sphere in the series. (It is perhaps unsurprising, in this context, that he also is seen to use the phone, television, and credit cards to excess, habits stereotypically associated with women in American consumer culture.) In this case, conventional, consumer standards of appearance, gender, the telephone, and confession are explicitly linked.

In another episode, Alf becomes involved with a blind woman. The relationship is initiated during a period when he is feeling particularly isolated and bored in the Tanner home. One night, he listens to a phone-in advice program on the radio. He hears a woman describing sentiments that resonate with his current state. She has recently moved to the area and is extremely lonely because she has no friends in the vicinity. Because she is blind, and unfamiliar with the area, it is hard for her to get out and about. In her loneliness, she says, she feels like an alien. Alf, feeling lonely because he is an alien, responds to her phone call. Over time, they become great phone friends, and the woman asks Alf to her house for dinner. The humor in the episode focuses on Alf's efforts to escape the Tanner home for the date. He enlists the help of Lynn to transport him to and from the woman's apartment even though he is not supposed to go out in public.

In this instance the phone-in radio therapy program, premised on confessional discourses, and the telephone provide Alf with essential avenues of contact for social identity outside the Tanner household but ultimately reinforce his place within the home. The visit to the woman is, initially, a one-time excursion. The woman's blindness provides the alibi for Alf's willingness to leave the Tanner home, since she cannot see that he is an extraterrestrial.[2] Furthermore Alf realizes that he cannot continue to go out in public, because to do so would both earn Willy's wrath and put him at risk of being recognized as an alien. Meanwhile, the subterfuge necessary to sneak him out of the house contributes to cementing his relationship with Lynn. Thus his position in the family, however unstable, is confirmed through the very act of getting away.

In *Alf* the world of aliens—usually the domain of science fiction—is not figured as an alternate world, or even as an alternate scenario within our familiar world.[3] Instead, alien culture is shown to be fully versed in networks of communications, consumerism, and therapeutic relations. While we commonly associate the media with consumer culture, the presence of therapy in this context is not just a passing or metaphoric concern. Indeed one of the first characters outside the Tanner family who is introduced to Alf, and is a continuing, semiregular character on the show, is a psychologist who is also a close friend of the Tanners. He is first introduced at a time when Willy and Alf are having particularly strained relations. The psychologist is brought into the home to observe their interaction and make suggestions to alleviate domestic tension. After this initial contact, he is periodically brought back into the family circle, as one of the few outsiders who know Alf, and for further consultations with respect to Alf.

Therapy/Confession/Television

Alf is only one among many programs on television that feature the simultaneous deployment of discourses on the family, the media, consumer culture, and therapeutic and confessional relations. The recognition of intersections and convergences among these discourses is not unprecedented at first glance. A large and varied body of scholarship has laid the theoretical and historical groundwork for initially recognizing the presence of therapeutic strategies on television. Psychoanalysis has elaborated, at once, a theory of symbolic relations, of familial and kinship structures, and of the process of the social and sexual inscription of human subjectivity.[4] Television has been widely discussed as the domestic cultural apparatus par excellence, anchored in the family and the home.[5] Consumer culture, American society in general, and certain television programs in particular have been characterized as therapeutic.[6] All of this work provides an important context for my study. Yet it hardly begins to account for, or anticipate, the pervasive production and deployment of conjunctions between therapeutic and confessional discourse, the family, and consumerism through the fabric of American television.

In this book I am concerned with identifying the deployment of therapeutic and confessional discourses on television in systemic terms and the ways in which these discourses are implicated in constructions of the family and consumer culture. In the process I also propose that contemporary deployments of therapeutic and confessional discourse produced through the television apparatus modify and reconfigure the very nature of therapy and confession as practices for producing social and individual identities and knowledge. Recognizing and understanding the connections between these modes also has important implications for understanding television's modes of address and the television viewer's relation to the apparatus.

In *The History of Sexuality* Michel Foucault discusses the importance of confession as an agency of truth and power in Western society. According to Foucault the theoretical model of confession subsumes a broad range of institutions and practices—including law, medicine, and education—in which, historically, religion and psychoanalysis figure most prominently.

> The confession is a ritual of discourse in which the speaking subject is also the subject of the statement; it is also a ritual that unfolds within a power relationship, for one does not confess without the presence (or virtual presence) of a partner who is not simply the interlocutor but the authority who requires the confession, prescribes and appreciates it, and intervenes in order to judge, punish, forgive, console, and reconcile; a ritual in which the truth is corroborated by the obstacles and resistances it has had to surmount in order to be formulated; and finally, a ritual in which the expression alone, independently of its external consequences, produces intrinsic modifications

in the person who articulates it: it exonerates, redeems, and purifies him; it unburdens him of his wrongs, liberates him, and promises his salvation.[7]

In Foucault's view the deployment of confession is inextricably linked to the production of sexuality, as a technology of the body and of sexuality, "for it is in the confession that truth and sex are joined, through the obligatory and exhaustive expression of an individual secret."[8] Further, confession is immediately understood as a therapeutic process, promoting expiation, a release of tension, or the narrative constructions of a psychoanalytic cure. This functional understanding provides the theoretical grounding for my association, throughout this study, of confessional and therapeutic discourse. Furthermore, this connection is subtended by confession as a structure of speech that enacts self-identity (the confessional "I") and the production of knowledge (the truth of identity as sexuality) within relations of power.

This book takes its lead from Foucault's theorization of confession but significantly revises his analysis in relation to contemporary media culture. In particular it proposes that confessional and therapeutic discourse centrally figure as narrative and narrational strategies in television in the United States and examines how this works in a range of programming. I understand confession and therapy to be privileged and prominent discourses in contemporary television, engaged by a variety of modes and genres. Problems and their solutions are narrativized in terms of confessional relations. Material prizes and personal advice are sought and won by those who demonstrate a willingness to confess on camera, in public. Self-identity and social recognition within familial and consumer networks hinge on participation in the process of mediated confession. Confession is at once the subject of programming and its mode of narrativization. Television viewers are engaged by the I-you structure of discourse, and may even participate directly as members of a studio or phone-in audience. Contemporary media technologies—broadcast television, cable, long-distance phone service—are brought together, proliferating the possibilities for, and the mediations of, confessional and therapeutic relations. In the process, television promotes a significant shift in the terms of the confessional transaction, transforming the very nature of the "truth" thereby produced.

Most immediately, the private exchange between two individuals—in a church or a doctor's office, for example—is reconfigured as a public event, staged by the technological and signifying conventions of the television apparatus. The couples who discuss their dates on *Love Connection* do not speak directly to the television viewer. Instead they speak to program host Chuck Woolery—one on stage with him, the other on a video monitor—in the presence of a studio audience, all taped for broadcast at a later date. These mediations are further regulated by the half-hour program format, the strategies of competition characteristic of the game show, the organization of the program around commercial breaks, and so forth. At the same time, the positions of confessor and interlocutor are both divided. Both persons who make up the couple must be present to speak the "truth" of the date; meanwhile, the program host, studio audience, and television viewer variably assume the role of interlocutor.

Through television, confession disperses and proliferates to the point where it turns in on itself, redefining its own conditions of expression. It now appears as a series of discursive positions in relative and unstable hierarchies of competing truths, powers, and judgments. The therapeutic function of confession in the case of *Love Connection* lies in the recognition of the couple as a social unit through their willing participation in the confessional reconstruction of their date. Self-identity as a couple is produced through their dialogic confession. Finally, in the (con)text of American television, all of these strategies and trajectories of discourse are circulated within networks of consumption and commodity exchange that include the couple, the television viewer, the celebrity host, the products advertised during the show, and the program itself.

The example of *Love Connection*, which will be developed more fully in Chapter 2, helps to illustrate the process whereby confession is reconfigured through its deployments within media culture. But this process is hardly restricted to a single program.[9] The nature of the mediations may vary, as may the strategies for multiplying positions within the structure of confession. Confession is repeatedly linked with consumer culture and social subjectivity, though the emphasis within and among these discourses is recast. For example, with its twenty-four-hour-a-day direct discount sales to television viewers, the Home Shopping Network immediately presents itself as a consumer service. The phone calls between individual shoppers and program sales hosts offer a continuous representation of typical viewer-shoppers who avow their own consuming habits in the context of familial relations. Thus the prominent consumer discourse is inextricably bound up in therapeutic interpersonal and social discourses that embrace individual shoppers, sales hosts, families, and friends, conjunctions that can only be achieved through the willing participation of home shoppers as confessional subjects.

The case of *Alf* is at once more obvious and more complex. On the one hand, therapeutic and confessional strategies of discourse occasionally provide the story material for the show, especially when the psychologist friend is brought in to help resolve Alf's most recent bout of uncontrollable loneliness, boredom, or general obnoxiousness; and, in conjunction with consumer culture and media technology, confessional and therapeutic discourses routinely play a role in plot development and resolution. On the other hand, the figure of Alf has proliferated as a consumer product. For a number of years, Alf was also a character in Saturday morning cartoons on American television. He is sold as a stuffed animal and a talking doll, and his image appears on T-shirts, lunch boxes, and other artifacts. In this case the appeal of the prime-time situation comedy *Alf*, with its therapeutic and confessional discourses, is not only linked to the networks of consumerism that inform all television viewing in the immediate sense but also implicates extended networks of television and product consumption.[10]

This study addresses some of the more prominent manifestations of the conjunctions of confession, family, and consumer discourses across a range of television genres and modes. As suggested above, television—with its particular institutional and signifying conventions—transforms confession in the very gesture of its production. An analysis of confessional and therapeutic discourse on television thus requires modification and rewriting of Foucault's theory. This revision includes consideration of postmodern and feminist perspectives that have centrally informed recent mass culture and television theory.

In line with these theoretical interests, the book offers analyses of a range of television programming to specify the different forms confessional and therapeutic discourse have assumed and to develop an understanding of the status of the therapeutic as a master narrative strategy of contemporary mass culture and of the nature of subjectivity thereby promoted. The analysis of television programs is not restricted to prime-time broadcast network programming. On the contrary, the study includes examination and analysis of network programs during several dayparts, various syndicated non-network programs, specific cable programs as well as some cable networks as a whole, and the Home Shopping Network, which could well be considered both a cable and a broadcast network. The analysis will include some consideration of institutional and demographic issues. But the major focus will be on the different ways television as a textual system and social apparatus constructs and implicates its own spectators as social subjects, often in explicit terms.

Confession and therapy are engaged toward finding one's "proper place" as an individual and a social subject, even as they are mediated through the apparatus of television. This proper place is overdetermined by family/gender relations and models of consumption. The study of the proliferation of therapeutic and confessional discourse also suggests that "communication"—understood as the injunction to participate in confessional discourse within the highly mediated channels of contemporary technology—has become a dominant paradigm of social, interpersonal, and commodity relations.[11]

Therapeutic Discourses and
Consumer Culture

The identification of a therapeutic ethos in American consumer culture has been made by a number of scholars. T. J. Jackson Lears, for example, has traced the emergent therapeutic ethos in advertising strategies during the first decades of the twentieth century.[12] He argues that in advertising the expression of the Protestant ethos of salvation through self-denial was reconfigured in favor of therapeutic self-realization. Leisure time, domestic space, and consumption were promoted as the social contexts for self-fulfillment and the sites for achieving physical and psychic health. The use of specific products became associated with health, beauty, and familial happiness. Therapy and self-improvement are thereby implicated in the very growth of consumer culture. Lears's idea of therapy focuses on the result, as well as the process, of participating in consumer culture. In the language of the advertisements he studies, one uses particular products—or engages in structured and regulated doses of play—to achieve specific restorative or curative effects.

Therapy can also be understood as a relation within discourse or as a particular strategy of discourse; therapy is understood as a means of generating narrative by setting in place a sequence of symbolic interpersonal exchanges. Over the course of the twentieth century, psychoanalytic theory —in its various versions of analytic and therapeutic practice—has been articulated as a specialized discipline within medicine and in the academy. It has also been rewritten in a wide range of professional and popular psychologies. In these varying contexts, a therapeutic cure is often ultimately less important than the process of therapeutic engagement itself. Strategies of negotiation to help people manage problems, emotions, and fantasies prevail over any final cure. And recognition, acknowledgment, and confession of these problems—even to oneself—play a crucial role in the process. In other words, therapy has come to refer to processes of negotiating and working through one's social subjectivity.

This understanding of therapy, which directly intersects with Foucault's ideas about confession, redefines therapy as a discursive practice and can be turned to account in analyzing the language of consumer culture and its productive force. On the one hand, evidence of the persistence of the advertising strategies described by Lears is abundant. Products are promoted as having the ability to transform our lives, alter our whole persons for the better, and renew our energies. At the same time, these therapeutic effects are mobilized as fantasies, setting in place trajectories of identification and desire.[13] From this perspective, no one really expects advertisements to deliver on their purported promises. Consumer fulfillment has less to do with any single product and its local effects than with the narrative fantasy it instigates. Indeed the value of advertising is that it sells these fantasies as much as it sells specific products; it provides a context in which buying products in general is associated with the lifestyle images and values that advertisements project.

The creation of this context enables consumption itself to proliferate even when individual products fail to perform in the specific or literal ways promised, or implied, by a particular advertisement for a particular product. Here the purported transformative qualities of a product are revealed to be an alibi and a lure propelling us to buy into consumerism as a system on a perpetual and ongoing basis, an activity and a process imbued with its own therapeutic value. Moreover, this version of the therapeutic ethos, whose ability to generate narrative extends beyond advertising (which nonetheless remains the paradigmatic text of consumer culture), pervades almost all modes of mass mediated culture that include a significant narrative or interpersonal discourse.

The confessional voice has played an important role in American consumer culture, including the print advertising Lears discusses. In early advertising, the ability of a product to cure one's ills was often demonstrated in a first-person narrative of some detail.[14] Confession magazines, which emerged in the 1920s, provide a further example of popular narratives in American mass culture assuming a confessional form. Of course, these magazines, like the advertising narratives, were authored by professional writers,[15] so the disjunctions between confession as a discursive mode and the authentic voices of speaking social subjects were enstated at the moment that confession appeared as a narrative strategy in consumer culture.

Lears suggests that "many women were victimized in new ways" by the therapeutic ethos of consumer culture, but he does not fully elaborate the historical context or implications of this insight. Indeed he suggests that "it is easy to exaggerate the sexual dimensions of hegemony,"[16] referring specifically to the sway of the therapeutic ethos. Recent feminist analysis of television and mass culture has more fully developed perspectives on how television has functioned as a cultural-social apparatus in relation to constructions of gender and consumer culture. Of equal importance, feminist theorists have pointed out the ways in which consumer culture, and particular popular cultural forms identified with consumer culture, are frequently discursively figured in terms of femininity.[17]

In "Melodrama In and Out of the Home" Laura Mulvey specifically identifies television as a domestic apparatus, intimately linked to the sphere of privacy, sexuality (itself repressed), woman as wife and mother, and consumption that is signified by "home" in the social mythology of urban bourgeois society. "Television," she writes, "arrived within the home, within censorship, for a family audience, tailored to front parlour size. It also challenged the previous, well-established separation between public and private by turning political events into spectacular drama acted out within the confines of the home. . . . It represents the triumph of the home as point of consumption of capitalist circulation of commodities."[18]

Patricia Mellencamp similarly aligns television with domestic consumer ideologies of the late 1940s and the 1950s: "Television was then (and continues to be) both an ecology— a repetition and recycling through the years—and a family affair, in the 1950s conducted collectively in the living room, with the dial dominated, in popular stereotypes, by Dad. A TV set was a status symbol, a rooftop economic declaration, and an invitation to other couples to watch."[19] She focuses on situation comedy as the genre that best expresses and enacts television's strategies of domestic containment.

Lynne Joyrich argues that television is an overdetermined cultural site where discursive connections are forged between melodrama and postmodern consumer culture, with important assumptions and implications in regard to issues of gender.

> The operations of postmodern culture—with TV as its exemplary mode—thus seem generally to involve the overpresence and subject/object confusion that have been linked to consumerism and "feminine" cultural forms. Dissolving classical reason, decentering identity, and abolishing the distance between subject and object, active and passive, that upholds the masculine gaze and the primacy of the male subject, postmodern culture threatens to draw all viewer-consumers into the vacuum of mass culture—an irrational and diffuse space coded as feminine.[20]

According to her analysis, the conventions and strategies of melodrama bring the possibility of a vision of clarity and meaningfulness to television, however provisionally. "TV melodrama, like its precursors in the theater and cinema, thus tends to deny the complex processes of signification and to collapse representation onto the real, assuring its audience of firm stakes of meaning."[21] Yet this assurance in turn raises questions of gender, since melodrama has historically been associated with female audiences.

As a contemporary form of melodramatic expression, historically identified with a female audience, the daytime soap opera has been television's most thoroughly analyzed genre in terms of gender and consumer culture.[22] Notably, it is recognized as the genre whose address to a female audience, especially to housewives, can be understood in institutional, demographic, and textual terms, enacting and confirming women's social identity as the primary consumers in the domestic sphere.[23] Feminist interest in the soap opera as a woman's genre posits a series of distinctions between daytime and nighttime programming as the foundation for more general arguments about identification, fantasy, pleasure, and ideology. In this context, daytime, melodrama, serial form, repetition, openendedness, and female viewers are aligned in opposition to prime time, drama, series format, progression, closure, and families. (This latter term implies a heterogeneous audience and assumes a prevailing male voice.)

This set of distinctive oppositions is at the core of feminist arguments that the daytime soap opera offers an alternative (and female) form of textuality to the dominant (and male) forms of prime-time dramatic series. While still ultimately in fee to patriarchal perspectives, the open textuality of the soap opera is variously associated with the rhythms of women's daily lives, patterns of daytime viewing, and models of feminine textuality. Through these strategies women are subject to ongoing construction as consumers of the soap opera itself as a genre and of the products advertised on soap operas.[24]

The elaboration of these perspectives on the soap opera very nearly coincides with the rise of the prime-time melodrama as a popular genre and with the incorporation of certain soap opera conventions by prime-time dramatic series.[25] These conventions include serial structure, multiple narratives involving a relatively large number of regular characters, and the deferral of closure. Certain of these characteristics even find their way into half-hour comedy programs. Without ignoring the theoretical and practical differences that inform television programming, especially among genres and dayparts, it may be necessary to reconsider our understanding of the specificity of the soap opera, at least during the past decade. Indeed, there are structural conditions of television programming that suggest the need for reassessment along these lines.

The regularity and repetition that inform most American television programming contribute to this process, as the weekly format and rerun schedule lead to ongoing development as much as or more than to definitive forms of closure. As a formal quality of a text, closure itself is a relative concept, especially in the context of dramatic series and serials that air on a weekly basis. In this sense it is possible to argue theoretically that most television programs share with the daytime soap opera the pressure of repeated regeneration of stories over time, even if on a weekly rather than a daily basis. Certainly, in distinction to films, for example, even series television is far more serial than not. One can watch characters (and the actors who portray them) age over time, change their interaction with other characters, or come and go from any given series.

To recognize this pressure to seriality—manifestly expressed in prime-time soaps and dramatic serial programs—is not necessarily to argue that all television is essentially melodramatic. Rather, to do so suggests that the structures and strategies discerned through feminist analysis of the soap opera may not be restricted to the soap opera as a genre. Rereading television in this way requires a provisional sacrifice of the theoretical supposition that female viewers have a place of their own within the television schedule in favor of recognizing far more dispersed and heterogeneous strategies of gender construction throughout the medium. These strategies encourage a continual renegotiation of multiple identifications in terms of class, gender, and history. Therapeutic and confessional strategies of discourse are one of television's tactics for this process of negotiation.

These connections between serial form, gender construction, identification, and confession began to be articulated in the context of writing on soap opera that included consideration of the genre's confessional and therapeutic characteristics. Here, women, and mothers in particular, are repeatedly situated as listeners and interpreters of endless interpersonal exchanges. This function is in turn specified in terms of the woman's role within the family. As Tania Modleski explains,

It is important to recognize that soap operas serve to affirm the primacy of the family not by presenting an ideal family, but by portraying a family in constant turmoil and appealing to the spectator to be understanding and tolerant of the many evils which go on within that family. The spectator/mother, identifying with each character in turn, is made to see "the larger picture" and extend her sympathy to both the sinner and the victim. She is thus in a position to forgive all.[26]

Along these lines, a number of scholars have noted that the soap opera is a form that moves into everyday life quite easily, via talk about programs that is dispersed through the workplace.[27] The position of the spectator/mother who assesses "all her children" is carried on through a discourse that is, among other things, confessional, involving an avowal of interest in soap opera deep enough to lead to engaging in ongoing discussion. In this context, the confessional transaction promoted by the soap opera is itself hardly stable. Modleski argues that in contrast to prime-time television, "in soap operas . . . the effects of confession are often ambiguous, providing relief for some of the characters and dreadful complications for others."[28] I am proposing the need to generalize this insight to other modes and genres of television, including prime-time dramas that may seem at first glance to offer an unambiguous therapeutic resolution to the problems raised in their narratives on a weekly basis.[29] In other words, a more systemic approach to television, encompassing a range of programming modes, reveals that the female viewer's place in relation to the soap opera is reproduced and dispersed through many other kinds of programming.

Postmodern Confessions

A consideration of therapeutic and confessional discourse necessarily raises the matter of psychoanalysis, and derivative forms of psychological and analytic practice. This is especially the case insofar as psychoanalytic theory has provided an important grounding for a great deal of feminist work in film and television. This includes ideas about language, subjectivity, spectatorship, and desire. Nevertheless, the idea of therapeutic discourse and confession as I am using it is hardly equivalent or limited to the body of psychoanalytic literature that has been so influential in film and television studies.

On the contrary, my focus is how television itself produces ideas about what therapy is and about the uses of confessional discourse within this context. In this sense I am interested in what might be called the institutional production of meaning, how the television apparatus has deployed confession and therapy in the context of contemporary culture. The programs I analyze are the product of a complex work of production, involving individuals, corporations, exchanges of money and labor, and so on, all focused on producing programs for the purpose of airing them on television for an audience. In this context, I am interested in how therapeutic and confessional discursive strategies carry possibilities for meaning, pleasure, and engagement for viewers. The modes of therapeutic discourse constructed through television and other media, fully implicated in consumer culture, participate in the production of social and cultural identities. Television programs not only transmit therapeutic strategies taken from the world of psychological theory and clinical practice but also construct new therapeutic relations.

With this understanding, my analytic approach draws on concepts that have been developed in the context of psychoanalytic theory, especially as developed in film and television studies. In particular, I am interested in the relation between discourse and subjectivity, wherein language and speaking positions are seen as contributing to the production of subject identity.[30] Foucault's work on confession conceptually intersects with this work insofar as the particularizing characteristic of confessional expression is that the speaking subject is also the subject of speech: "I" speak about myself. Moreover, elaborated through linguistic theory, an "I" in language always presupposes "you" as an interlocutor. It is on this basis that Foucault can argue that confession requires an interlocutor who is not a neutral sounding board. Rather, confession as a means for producing "truth" through a particular strategy of speech also links knowledge and power. In the traditional church confessional the one who hears confession has the authority to prescribe the means of atonement leading to expiation. In the traditional psychoanalytic situation, the analyst carries the weight of transference, but also the keys to interpretation. Of course, as I have suggested, and as is demonstrated in detail in the analyses of programs to follow, the deployment of confession on television produces a dispersed configuration of subjectivities and identities.

This emphasis on speech, subjectivity, and identification also refers back to the importance of the talking cure, as initially "discovered" by Sigmund Freud and Josef Breuer, wherein diagnosis and cure occur as patients talk through their problems and their past, tracing symptoms back to repressed traumatic memories. Any idea of therapeutic discourse premised on a confessional transaction necessarily evokes the talking cure; it is by no means coterminous with Freudian theory but participates in a more dispersed and generalized sense of therapy that pervades North American culture.[31] In discerning therapeutic discourse as a common strategy in television, the medium itself as a set of textual and institutional discourses is seen as contributing to psychotherapeutic dynamics. These dynamics reference Freudian theory, at least in its popular manifestations, while also projecting their own sense of contemporary therapeutic practice.

In other words, Freud's legacy is not restricted to a complex and multivalent range of academic theories and psychoanalytic practices; it is also implicated in everyday life and cultural knowledge. The modes of therapeutic discourse constructed through television (and other media) have an important status, producing social and cultural identities that may not follow directly from academic and professional ideas about psychoanalysis and psychology. In fact, I would suggest that the profusion of the therapeutic in everyday and popular media culture might be seen as one manifestation of a larger cultural interest that is paralleled in the academic sphere in psychoanalytic and psychological discourses. In this light, the two spheres can be played off one against the other, mutually interrogating and illuminating, without subsuming one within the other.

Television proposes modes of subjectivity that can be conceptualized as fluid and provisional, and yet simultaneously refer to conventional and fixed positions in terms of class, gender, and race. It is this simultaneous bind that is so difficult to grasp in any form except its local operation—through particular programs or moments of viewing. This is why the analysis of particular programs and genres is necessary as a way to get at the signifying logics of the medium. At once fixed and mobile, true and false, actual and simulacral, television's modes of representation and their attendant modes of subjectivity and reception require new ways of thinking about the subject in contemporary culture. This new way of viewing the subject is closely tied to questions about postmodernism and the role of television, among other media technologies, as the exemplary apparatus of postmodern consumer culture.[32]

The absence of a single master narrative is one of the primary definitions of postmodernism.[33] Popular conceptions of therapy thus might seem at odds with postmodernism, especially if therapy is defined in terms of cures and fulfillment, as a process with a coherent beginning, middle, and end—definitive closure on the heels of a narrative controlled from the top down.[34] Postmodern philosophy (and the system of American television as a cultural manifestation thereof) challenges or at least troubles the clarity of vision and decisiveness of control necessary to sustain this version of the therapeutic process. As Dana Polan has suggested, "The transition to late capitalism has immense implications for the study of mass culture; it may well be that such capitalism implies new forms of mass culture that older analytic models—like narrative analysis centered on logic, coherence, and stability—can no longer explain."[35]

In this context, the therapeutic problematic is an overdetermined strategy. It can be seen as one manifestation of postmodern logic, perpetuating confessional discourses among an array of positions with no master position to which to refer them or to give them a final, determinate meaning. And yet the contemporary therapeutic ethos proposes itself as a response to the loss of logic, coherence, stability, and order. It offers a mode of engagement in its I-you structure of address, what Benveniste referred to as *discours*.[36] At the same time, it evokes, and may even take the form of, narratives and scenarios within the family, as theorized by Freud. It thus has the appearance of something familiar, even reassuring. We recognize it immediately when we catch it in progress; it recognizes us, television viewers, even before we have turned on the television.

Donna Haraway's feminist postmodern theory provides insights into the question of power at stake in postmodern dispersions of meaning that are useful in articulating the implications of therapeutic discourse on television. In relation to her work, therapeutic discourse can be seen as organizing new forms of power, facilitating what Haraway has called "the informatics of domination." "We are," she contends, "living through a movement from an organic, industrial society to a polymorphous, information system—from all work to all play, a deadly game."[37] Haraway's position is crucial because it stresses the radical reordering of the world, a shift from industrial society—where relations of power were strong, but identifiable—to the new networks of multinational capitalism and postmodernism. We are in the midst of a shift from "comfortable old hierarchical dominations" to "scary new networks" that are Haraway's "informatics of domination."[38] The new subject in this worldwide social relation, tied to science and technology, is the cyborg, a human-machine hybrid that challenges traditional boundaries of identity and subjectivity.

> No objects, spaces, or bodies are sacred in themselves; any component can be interfaced with any other if the proper standard, the proper code, can be constructed for processing signals in a common language. Exchange in this world transcends the universal translation effected by capitalist markets that Marx analyzed so well. The privileged pathology affecting all kinds of components in this universe is stress—communications breakdown. The cyborg is not subject to Foucault's biopolitics; the cyborg simulates politics, a much more potent kind of field.[39]

Therapeutic discourse serves these new forms of power. In the informatics of domination, information and communication are significant components of control. Only silence, like turning off the television, is anathema to the new networks of communication, hence the prominence given to stress as communications breakdown. The therapeutic ethos is an incitement to talk, to talk constantly, of oneself to others. It regenerates communication. On television, the therapeutic ethos draws one quite literally into networks of domination, or at least into the dominant networks of postmodern entertainment.

At the same time, the therapeutic ethos preserves something of the subjectivity associated with the former social and epistemological regime, the white capitalist patriarchy that Haraway opposes to the informatics of domination. For the process of confession is linked in its discursive archaeology to the Western self, with all its integrity and sincerity, maintaining the dichotomies between mind and body, animal and human, public and private, nature and culture, men and women.

All of these dichotomies presumably give way in the face of the new cyborg subject. To the extent that contemporary television therapeutics draw on the psychoanalytic tradition, and situate confession and therapeutic discourse within traditional heterosexual relations and the nuclear family, they extend ongoing, familiar versions of gender and power. But in reformulating therapeutic discourses as an agency of postmodern subjectivity and consumer culture, television also produces new versions of gender, power, and knowledge. These new versions are not so much full-blown cyborgs, in Haraway's sense, as they are subjects empowered with relatively more mobility and contradiction. They are akin to Alf, the alien who knows U.S. mass culture (and the English language) even before he lands on Earth, and who, once he lands, readily moves between different age and gender positions within the family. Yet he lands in a conventional, two-parent, suburban middle-class home; and his mobility and fluidity are largely delimited within these confines.

It is in the context of the dislocations of postmodern culture that the analysis of therapeutic and confessional discourses, in their specific manifestations and deployments, find their value and meaning. Theoretically speaking, the mobilizations of therapeutic discourse on television can be seen as a discourse of transition, the fulcrum point between the humanist-capitalist self and the postmodern cyborg subject. It is important to recognize it in its various forms, and to chart its trajectories in relation to consumer culture, popular and academic ideas about psychiatry and psychology, the family, and gender. In the process, we can identify its power for both the individuals and institutions who purvey it.

Tell Me More

Television as Therapy

"The Shows That'll Make You Feel Better," by Dr. Joyce Brothers; "A Psychiatrist Looks at Prime Time," by John P. Docherty, M.D.; "Prime Time on the Couch: A Psychiatrist Wonders What's Happening to Romantic Love," by Willard Gaylin, M.D.; "Your Therapy Could be Watching *Dallas* or *Dynasty*," by Teresa Kochmar Crout; "Can TV Cause Divorce?," by David Hellerstein; "Dr. Ruth to the Golden Girls: How to Keep That Spice and Sparkle in Your Lives," by Dr. Ruth Westheimer—these are only some of the articles that were published in *TV Guide* over the course of the 1980s.[1] They are all notable for promoting the idea that television functions therapeutically within a familial and interpersonal context. Watching television can help or hinder your relationship with your spouse or children. Television can speak a therapeutic discourse and is equally open to being addressed from a therapeutic perspective. On more than one occasion in the pages of *TV Guide*, Dr. Ruth Westheimer gives advice about their behavior to television's fictional characters, while Dr. Joyce Brothers tells readers which programs to watch in order to set a romantic, humorous, or cheerful mood at home.

These articles coincide with the rise of the therapy or counseling show on television in the 1980s, a hybrid subgenre of reality programs and talk shows.[2] A number of these shows gained national prominence, including two programs featuring Dr. Ruth Westheimer, first *Good Sex! with Dr. Ruth*

Westheimer on cable and then *Ask Dr. Ruth* in syndication.[3] Throughout the *TV Guide* articles and the counseling programs, television is promoted as both therapeutic subject and object from a variety of positions and perspectives. The medium functions as a therapist; it sometimes needs the advice of a therapist; it may promote symptoms among its viewers that will lead them to need therapy from an external source; or, indeed, it may lead viewers to the therapists who have programs on television.

The *TV Guide* articles are significant because they repeatedly associate television and therapeutic discourses in the largest-circulation magazine published in the United States. Even if people who subscribe to *TV Guide* do not actually read the articles, at a minimum the headlines, often featured on the cover (and therefore on display at checkout counters in countless grocery and drug stores), promote the idea that therapeutic issues are relevant to any consideration of the process of watching and understanding television. *TV Guide* is a magazine that basically helps people watch television. It includes a detailed weekly schedule of what shows will air when (often including plot summaries), rates movies that are appearing on cable and broadcast stations, provides information on what is happening at various networks and stations, previews forthcoming programs and specials, profiles television personalities, and more generally addresses current issues in television programming (the article titles cited above fall into this latter category).

With this array of information, viewers who read *TV Guide* participate in current institutional and critical discourses regarding television. In this light, it is important that the magazine has regularly promoted recognition of therapeutic discourses on television. Popular consciousness of the therapeutic thereby becomes an integral dimension of television viewing. This is not, strictly speaking, limited to *TV Guide*; rather, I am using the magazine as an exemplary instance of popular media that promote particular ways of watching, and understanding, television programs, personalities, and institutions.[4] In *TV Guide* awareness of the therapeutic is evinced in articles that highlight the counseling programs of the 1980s as an emergent genre, but it is also evident in more socio-logically oriented analyses of how television might have an impact on our lives and in therapeutic analyses of fictional television characters.

Taken together, these articles suggest a pervasive and en-compassing view of therapy as a proper, even natural, dis-course to conjoin with television. In other words, the idea that television functions as a therapeutic apparatus, and should be explored in these terms, is an integral part of the every-day discourses and practices of regular television viewers. In this chapter, I examine these articles, with an emphasis on the ways in which the viewer is invited, or positioned, to par-ticipate in television's therapeutic discourses. I then look at one of the more prominent therapy programs of the 1980s, *Good Sex! with Dr. Ruth Westheimer*, as an example of the most literal (and public) generic manifestation of television's therapeutic practice.

TV Guide: Watching Television Therapeutically

The variety and range of articles in *TV Guide* that invoke therapy make it clear that therapeutic and psycho-logical issues pervade the medium. Characters on television are subject to being analyzed; watching television might have beneficial or detrimental effects on your familial or romantic relations; you might learn something by watching television therapy shows, or even more by participating on one; it might even be appropriate to watch television as part of your own therapy. One article details a psychiatrist's use of television as a part of therapy:

Dr. Young, a Dayton, Ohio, psychiatrist, has been pre-scribing television to help patients increase self-aware-ness and develop more effective ways of coping with problems since 1963. What's more, he routinely discusses the behavior of TV characters at therapy sessions, often underscoring his points by using instant replay—a view-ing room complete with TV set, VCR and a collection of selectively recorded tapes occupies a prominent place on the second floor of Young's spacious office.[5]

As the doctor explains, "We can learn a lot about ourselves by watching our TV twin."[6]

The professional imprimatur for all of *TV Guide*'s perspectives on therapy and television derives from the stature of the authors—frequently identified as psychologists, psychiatrists, or M.D.'s—or from references in articles to professional experts and associations, such as the Association for Media Psychology, the American Psychological Association, or the American Psychiatric Association. However silly the positions expressed in the articles might seem at first glance, the reader is given the necessary cues to recognize the position of authority that sanctions them. The article on the psychiatrist who uses television as an integral part of therapy falls into this category.

As the article states, the psychiatrist in question has been using television successfully in therapy with patients for almost thirty years. Yet toward the end of the article a negative note is sounded by some comments on the potential pitfalls of Dr. Young's strategy that seem especially to underscore the frivolous dimensions of the whole idea of using television in a clinical context. "Sometimes," the article reports, "Dr. Young's prescriptions do go awry. Like the time a patient was following Pam and Cliff's mother [Rebecca] on *Dallas*. 'All was progressing well,' recalls Young, 'until Rebecca's untimely death.' And, of course, dozens of male patients needed new prescriptions following the unfortunate demise of Bobby Ewing."[7] (The reader familiar with *Dallas* will no doubt wonder what happened to those patients when the character of Bobby was revived on the series a year later!) Still, as if to assure readers that they should take this seriously, the article ends with an authoritative statement to support the linking of fiction and therapeutic practice. "I don't see any problem with it," says psychiatrist Jerome Logan, referring to Dr. Young's somewhat unorthodox approach. "It's another tool to stimulate thought on the part of the patient and facilitate interaction between patient and therapist. And if a patient is willing to follow through, it speeds up the therapy." Fiction and dramatization are often used to describe and promote understanding of behavior, adds Logan. "We talk about the Peter Pan Syndrome and the Cinderella Complex. And even Freud depended on Oedipus to get his point across."[8]

Overall, *TV Guide*'s perspectives on television and therapy are structured by contradictory arguments and points of view. This is systematic in their approach to the subject. No decisive opinion or point of view regarding the issue is ultimately allowed to hold sway. In relation to television's therapy programs the terms of the debate are relatively obvious: Are the programs helpful and educational or harmful and distorting? Do they promote more openness and understanding about emotional problems or turn real human suffering into television spectacle for the sake of profits? One article explains the dilemma as follows: "Critics worry that the advice given on TV may be hazardous to a viewer's health. . . . And while TV may demystify the counseling session, it may also distort it. The problem that a patient presents, after all, generally disguises a much deeper psychological question, and it is this that a therapist, with skill and sensitivity, seeks to uncover."[9] Yet in the same article the author writes, "TV can provide current information on common problems. It can, while respecting privacy, encourage the discussion of feelings. Whether the present state of the art is helpful or harmful, however, remains a matter of heated debate."[10]

What is less obvious are the ways in which, over time, the magazine publishes articles by experts representing more distinctive positions and points of view that nonetheless implicitly contradict one another. This may occur over the course of weeks, months, or even years. Thus, an article about how watching television can enhance your romantic life may appear at one time, and an article about how television has contributed to the decline of romantic love may be featured at another.[11] Similarly, one article by a Ph.D. psychology professor advises watching one of the couples on *L.A. Law* to develop successful intimacy, while another by a psychiatrist suggests that television has a profound and primarily negative effect on marriages.[12]

Even within articles by experts there are often subtle, and sometimes blatant, contradictions. Psychiatrist David Hellerstein's article "Can TV Cause Divorce?," for example, begins with the strong implication that the effect of television on couples can only be negative, but by the end of the article the author suggests that a number of shows make beneficial contributions to marriage. And the same program may be referred to by experts as exemplifying both the positive and negative impact of television on relationships. In "Can TV Cause Divorce?" Bill Cosby is cited as a potentially negative influence because he creates a character that real-life husbands cannot match. "To a large degree," the author states, "the couples I talked to gauged the success of their marriages by what they saw on TV. In one couple, the wife is a devotee of *The Cosby Show*. She told me, 'I always compare how my husband deals with a situation with what Bill Cosby would do.' When her husband is crabby or nasty, or can't defuse an argument with a warm Cosby-esque joke, she ends up feeling angry, even cheated."[13] Yet, in the same article, *The Cosby Show* is also mentioned as an example of new, positive tactics in the depiction of couples on television, with beneficial influence. Hellerstein explains: "Take *Cosby*, for example. Dr. Huxtable is funny, warm, and strong, as is Clair, his wife. When they fight, they generally end up solving their problems—with style and humor. Granted, *The Cosby Show* is sentimental at times, and it doesn't deal with many of the complex, irresolvable problems that real life often poses—but still, it represents a step forward for television."[14]

Another article, which deals with the dangers and value of television for lonely people, is no less equivocal. First the author argues that viewers develop an unreal sense of community with figures on television that substitutes for actual human relationships. "Some viewers actually go to bed feeling someone out there is connected to them," she complains.[15] Then later in the same article the author proposes that television can be a benefit to lonely people by providing them with a sense of community.

There are at least two ways, however, in which television provides companionship not only to the very lonely, but to the rest of us as well. One of the feelings that plague lonely people borders on self-pity—"I'm all alone in the world. Nobody knows the trouble I've seen." Some television shows address and assuage this sense of being a pariah. . . . To help people feel, "I am not alone in this; others have similar experiences"—whether or not solutions are offered—is a tremendously reassuring aspect of the best of television's talk shows.

Even more important is the sense of community that television can provide. Since lonely people feel they are not part of anything larger than themselves and have no sense of belonging, television can give them a common language and a common set of references at times. . . . Watching serious coverage on television addresses the need to gather at the river; it is the modern version of an ancient ritual.[16]

The author concludes the article by neatly summarizing this equivocation. "Television—a box with a picture tube—neither causes nor cures loneliness, but can be *used* as a pal or as a trap for the lonely."[17] In other words, the article is structured to pose a question, as it does explicitly in its title, "Is TV a Pal—or a Danger—for Lonely People?" It proceeds to answer the question by presenting conflicting and contradictory arguments, and it concludes by indicating that in the final analysis there is no definitive answer to this question.

Through the course of these articles, the psychiatric and psychological perspectives presented emphasize television's therapeutic function. But the precise or final value of this function is indeterminate, or at least not generalizable. This equivocation is typical of American television. The articles explore and give voice to "both sides of the issue," following the traditional American journalistic formula for objectivity. Pro or con, good or bad, right or wrong—on any issue, be sure both of these perspectives are incorporated; to address only one is to editorialize (and thereby potentially alienate readers, advertisers, and broadcasters). Moreover, the very format of *TV Guide* not only follows this rhetorical model of objectivity but is also highly formulaic, including as one of its primary principles the importance of brevity in presentation. Therefore, the nuances of an argument and complexities in an author's position may be lost, emerging instead as blatant forms of contradiction. And clearly the titles of the articles are designed to attract attention, no matter what the specific arguments of the author may be.

Yet it is crucial that within the general contours of proper journalistic objectivity, these articles—and others like them —persistently assert the importance of watching television in the terms of a therapeutic relation. The articles also suggest that television does have social effects and therefore warrants being taken seriously by the likes of psychiatrists and medical doctors. But since the exact nature and degree of these effects are ultimately equivocal, all viewers as individuals have to take the medium seriously by continuing to watch. Indeed, following these articles, watching television is as likely as not to have positive effects. Psychiatrists watch it and write articles in *TV Guide* for people like you and me; and one in Ohio goes so far as to have his patients watch television during their therapy sessions. Even if you find these positions and opinions suspect, you have to watch some television to confirm its status as a serious social apparatus.

Thus the articles not only encourage a particular posture of viewing—the therapeutic relation—but also promote watching in general. In addition, from the therapeutic perspective advanced in these articles, it is mainly television's fiction programs that are considered important, rather than the news and documentary programs that are more typically considered to fulfill the serious social mission of the medium. As a result, the association of therapeutic discourse with television programs and television viewing also functions as a way of making the medium's entertainment programming a matter of serious consideration and a worthwhile object of viewing activity.

At the same time, by promoting a conflict of opinion about the precise value and meaning of the therapeutic transactions at stake in television, the articles encourage readers (and viewers of television) to make their own assessments. The issue of therapy is set in place for the public from a perspective of authority, an authority premised on the very pervasiveness of the issue as a topic of investigation. But, once the issue is set, readers/viewers are implicitly enjoined to make their own judgments about it. Here journalistic objectivity works to support freedom of opinion among that portion of the population that reads *TV Guide* and watches television. The terms of the debate are set through discourses of television and bolstered by reference to professional authority. However, one cannot contest the existence of therapeutic discourse, since that provides the a priori ground for all these articles. By the same token, the freedom to dispute the value of therapeutic discourse promotes a certain skepticism regarding the professional authorities themselves; they do not have the final word. This too serves to facilitate further viewing since you have to watch in order to assess the situation for yourself, to exercise your freedom of opinion.

Readers/viewers are positioned to judge for themselves when and whether they take the discourse of therapy seriously, even while they are trained to see it widely deployed through the medium. To further complicate the situation, the articles specifically dealing with therapy shows note that although various psychological and psychiatric associations recognize "media therapy" as a practice, they include guidelines that discourage specific diagnosis or treatment on the air. The educational value and impetus behind these shows is identified with the fact of televising general discussion about problems that may be common to many people and encouraging (confessional) talk about one's feelings. In other words, the precise value and meaning of therapy programs is indeterminate; and the imprimatur of professional associations really only applies to programs that do not actually do therapy—at least in conventional terms—in the first place. However, a viewer of the programs would also note—as some of the articles do—that television therapists often engage in diagnoses and directive individual advice that is presumably not allowed by the very professional associations that nonetheless endorse a more generic deployment of therapeutic and psychological issues on television.

These articles, and the programs and viewing strategies they describe, further suggest that conventional therapies are losing their force in contemporary culture, especially in a culture dominated by television consciousness. "TV is not what would happen in an office," says Dr. David Viscott, host of the syndicated therapy show *Getting in Touch*. "But you also have to be a realist. Most people watching television have about as much attention as a morning glory. You are competing with all this 't and a' and also the religious stations."[18] What we are offered is a therapeutic relation that is skeptical of too much authority yet attracted to the celebrity aura that accrues to people on television (as therapist or patient), that introduces more voices in a less hierarchical therapeutic transaction yet infuses all relations with the commodity and consumer effects of the television apparatus (at least as it is constituted in the United States).

If we move beyond the counseling program strictly speaking, we find manifestations of therapeutic discourse permeating the medium. Therapy in all its manifestations and permutations is thus situated as a strategy of engagement. It is a way to attract viewers or a posture a viewer may (perhaps even should) assume in relation to a wide range of programs. The therapeutic is hereby recognized as a discursive strategy, establishing relations between television and its viewers in two directions. Indeed, in the terms of the therapeutic relation, the medium does not simply exercise social effects; it is itself the object of diagnoses that come from viewers. Therapeutic discursive strategies are thus represented as having the potential to overcome the technological limits of one-way communication dominated by the box, as viewers are enjoined to treat television and the people who populate it as patients. In *TV Guide* this posture is modeled in articles by Dr. Ruth Westheimer and Dr. Joyce Brothers, two therapists whose careers and celebrity are intimately bound up with television and radio. Dr. Ruth lets us share her professional perspective on Maddie and David in *Moonlighting* as well as her advice on healthy sex lives for television's Golden Girls, while Dr. Joyce suggests programs that will make us feel better if we watch them.

In *TV Guide*'s promotion of therapy as a constitutive component of television viewing, soap operas and game shows are often mentioned as the generic precedent and functional equivalent of television's therapeutic vocation. The previously mentioned article on lonely people and television notes that soap operas are particularly popular among those who are lonely: "They have pseudo-relationships with the people on the soaps that are very much like real-life relationships— you know all the characters' secrets, how their houses are furnished and what's inside their refrigerators." [19] In another article the program *Crisis Counselor* is specifically described in the terms of a soap: "In true *General Hospital* style, every counseling session seems to contain a startling confession." [20] The impulse that leads people to participate in and watch television counseling programs is compared to interest in the kinds of daytime couples shows that will be discussed in the following chapter. "Down deep in that part of the national psyche to which we seldom admit," one *TV Guide* article explains, "that impulse that has fed for 20 years upon shows like *Divorce Court* and *The Love Connection* still craves something more. For the unsatiated, real people and their real soap-opera lives may be the only things left. Not only for viewers, but for those who so desperately want to use television as their personal confessional booth." [21]

In context, these comparisons are meant to be vaguely derisory. Television's therapeutic discourses are implicitly associated with a specific, gendered audience, sharing with the soap operas and game shows of daytime television a predominantly female audience. This is especially the case with counseling and therapy shows, most of which have existed as syndicated, cable, or local programs airing during the daytime or as fringe programming. In the 1980s the Lifetime Channel was one of the main places where one could find different therapy and counseling programs, including *Couples*, with psychiatrist and family therapist Dr. Walter Brackelmanns (discussed in Chapter 2) and Dr. Ruth Westheimer's first tele-

vision show, *Good Sex!*. Lifetime started out as a medical and
health-oriented cable station. During the course of the 1980s
it evolved into a "woman's" cable station, showing a range of
talk shows, counseling shows, and reruns of situation comedies and dramatic series, as well as featuring some original
fiction series,[22] all considered of primary interest to women
viewers (while reserving Sunday for more serious medical-
issues talk shows).

Generic associations notwithstanding, the therapeutic dimensions of television are by no means limited to daytime
programming. In *TV Guide* articles, not only soap operas
and game shows but also prime-time serials, prime-time dramatic series, situation comedies, and made-for-TV movies
are included as grist for the therapeutic and confessional mill.
The therapeutic mode may be most strongly associated with
women's genres and female viewers, but it is also popularly
associated with the medium as a whole, or at least with the
full range of daytime programs and prime-time fiction.[23]

Good Sex! with Dr. Ruth Westheimer

Dr. Ruth Westheimer is a celebrity sexologist who
rose to national prominence in the 1980s. Her television show
on Lifetime was an offshoot of a radio sex-counseling program and was developed for television in the wake of a series
of successful appearances by Westheimer on TV talk shows
including *The Tonight Show with Johnny Carson, Late Night
with David Letterman,* and *Donahue. Good Sex!* combines
elements of the radio call-in show and television talk show
formats. During the course of the show, Dr. Ruth takes phone
calls from around the country, responds to letters on the air,
engages in dramatized therapy sessions, and has a celebrity
guest with whom she talks (usually about romance, family
life, and sex) and who stays with her while she continues
to take phone calls from viewers. The guests are usually
entertainment figures or authors, not other psychologists,
therapists, or sexologists. During segments where Dr. Ruth
responds to phone calls and letters, she shares the set with

co-host Larry Angelo, who helps with introductions and with transitions from one segment to another or between program segments and advertisements, reads letters aloud, and chats with Dr. Ruth.[24]

Each episode begins with a printed verbal title which is also heard on the soundtrack, establishing Dr. Ruth's credentials and the sexual purport of the show. The double coding—verbal title and voice-over reading—assures that the program is addressed not only to people actually watching but also to those who are within earshot of the television. Nightly, as the program opens, the viewer is told:

> The following program was pre-recorded.
>
> It includes explicit sexual references and may not be suitable for all viewers.
>
> The program is hosted by Dr. Ruth Westheimer, noted sex therapist and adjunct associate professor in the sex therapy teaching program at New York Hospital–Cornell Medical Center.

The implication that the program is not appropriate for all viewers—that there is potentially something improper about it—is immediately counterbalanced by the clarification of Dr. Ruth's institutional standing and reputation. However you may feel about explicit sexual references, the ones that you may hear on this show are clearly authorized. But, interestingly, the program concludes with another title that casts this authority in more relative terms. "The opinions expressed in the program represent the opinions of Dr. Ruth Westheimer and may not represent those of other qualified professionals."

In part these disclaimers and qualifications are a function of television's normal standards and practices and of the legal apparatus to which the medium is subject. Subscribers to a cable service carrying the show might be shocked to discover the expression of sexually explicit material that they find unsuitable for themselves and their family. The program might otherwise be liable to lawsuits from unhappy viewers whose problems are exacerbated, rather than solved, by Dr. Ruth's advice. However, the tension between qualified and unqualified promotion of the star-host's credentials is emblematic of the tensions that pervade the show as a whole. This includes, notably, the tension between Dr. Ruth's status as a serious medical authority on the one hand and her status as a popular celebrity in the world of mass media on the other, and the concomitant possibility of confusion as to who speaks with what authority at all on the program, especially regarding the physical, emotional, and psychological problems and issues at stake in the investigation of sexual matters.

Sexual literacy and mature, informed choice are a recurrent concern of the show, and Dr. Ruth is represented as an authoritative educator, eager to discuss and promote information that will help viewers as sexed and sexually active individuals. In this capacity she excels as the therapist, enjoining individuals to speak freely by reassuring them that their questions and concerns are important and intelligent and that they are not alone in their concerns, problems, or lack of knowledge. Issues discussed in this vein include masturbation, oral sex, orgasm, loss of desire, need for affection, virginity, and impotence. The information and advice dispensed to callers is tempered, however, by Dr. Ruth's intermittent avowals that she cannot "do therapy" over the telephone. This cautionary tactic follows the previously noted guidelines of professional organizations regarding media psychology and therapy. It also puts in place a division between formal clinical therapy and the more diffused social therapy practiced by the show. Here, Dr. Ruth's program exemplifies the tension discussed earlier in relation to *TV Guide* articles about whether what we see on television is or is not therapy—or what kind of therapy it in fact is. In practice, the distinctions between individual clinical therapy, generalized therapy, and education become increasingly indeterminate. This is especially true since each individual call may become the occasion for focusing on a particular problem and strategies for its resolution and also for drawing broad generalizations about sexuality and human relations.

Throughout the program, confession on the part of participants—including those who call in or write, the actors in the staged therapy sessions, and the celebrity guests—enables Dr. Ruth repeatedly to rehearse two simultaneous and intertwined discourses. One of these has to do with the techniques of the body, while the other pertains to issues of morality and limits. Certainly, as a celebrity sexologist Dr. Ruth is best known for the former of these. She is the person who has brought frank talk about sex into the media in the name of education. Thus, discussion of masturbation (for men and women), use of words like "penis" and "vagina," and extensive talk about the importance of foreplay, to take only a few examples, are essential, persistent components of the program (and of all of her appearances on television). Yet this candid talk is accompanied by a strong and equally persistent moral framework. Both on the phone and with the celebrity guests, Dr. Ruth herself frequently giggles in the course of her discussions. In this way she suggests that there is something amiss in all this discussion of sex and pleasure, that it is indeed forbidden territory. There is at least the hint that she is being a "bad little girl" by discussing all of this so openly and frankly in public. (In this context, Dr. Ruth's diminutive size—which works hand-in-hand with the "bad little girl" impression—and pronounced German accent guarantee that she is not identified with conventional representations of feminine beauty in mass culture.)

More overtly, Dr. Ruth has certain perspectives and opinions about relationships that are stated over and over again in the course of her programs. These include the following: whatever two mature, healthy adults consent to constitutes acceptable behavior, as long as no one is coerced; you should have sex only in the context of a monogamous, loving relationship; and you should remain a virgin until you find someone you really love, and with whom you expect to sustain a monogamous, loving relationship. Moreover, Dr. Ruth does impose limits, believing, for example, that no activity that might cause physical pain or injury to one of the participants in a sexual relationship should be sanctioned. (Though sadomasochistic activities are rarely discussed, it is very clear that she does not approve of them.) Sexual pleasures and sexual techniques are thus circumscribed and confined in conventional social relationships.[25] For all Dr. Ruth's image as the popular maven of sexual openness, the values that she purveys are relatively conventional.

Dr. Ruth does not shy away from giving specific, directive advice to some individuals who call her, drawing precise conclusions about the nature of one case or another. In these instances her authority holds sway. For example, one woman called in and explained that she was living with her fiancé, who had recently been staying out all night, and she did not know what to do. Dr. Ruth assured her that she was "the luckiest woman in Texas" because this happened before she was married and had children. "You are very fortunate that this is happening now, and not later in your life." This diagnostic interpretation of the caller's situation accompanied instructions to the woman to break up with her fiancé immediately. The woman ended the conversation by thanking Dr. Ruth for her advice. "I knew you'd help me make up my mind." In other words, Dr. Ruth was able to confirm what the woman already suspected she should do.

Dr. Ruth is also eager to promote general understanding of issues related to human sexuality, contributing to a "sexually literate" society. Some questions from callers set the groundwork for this approach with their informational format: What is the definition of masturbation? What is the difference between a transvestite and a transsexual? Other questions provoke directive advice for the individual caller that can in turn be generalized to apply to viewers with similar problems. The program itself strives to confirm that on a routine basis the advice given to individual callers in fact extends to many viewers. This is, for example, the clear purpose behind Larry Angelo's reading at the start of one show a letter from a housewife with three children who writes that she has been able to correct a problem in her sex life thanks to the advice offered to another caller to the show. Still, information and advice, however directive, are not equivalent to therapy, although to the degree that they are diagnostic, they may initiate a therapeutic process.

While Dr. Ruth does not actually practice therapy on the air, the importance and variety of potential channels for therapy are centrally and repeatedly endorsed. Dr. Ruth suggests to many of the callers that they need to talk further, with a social worker, a therapist, a minister, a mother, an aunt, or *somebody*. What is frequently and forcefully underscored is the necessity of talking with someone else, of continuing to talk. A litany of sources to consult accompanies most of the recommendations made to callers. Sometimes the recommendation specifies a marriage counselor, sex therapist, or physician; other times a general list from which a sympathetic ear can be selected is offered instead. In these instances, therapeutic discourse is not the sole possession of Dr. Ruth, or of television. Yet as the originary instigator of confession, television therapy is rhetorically situated as a significant force in the initiation and dissemination of therapy in the everyday life of program viewers. And, crucially, while sex is important as the focus of all this talk, talk itself increasingly becomes its own end.

Dr. Ruth situates herself simultaneously as an authoritative source of information and as a conduit for articulating problems that can finally be dealt with only elsewhere. Indeed to the extent that she cannot officially "do therapy" over the telephone on television, what she does is serve as a relay for personal confessions in a public medium. In any case, her essential function as one who motivates confessions is crucial. And her ability to function in this way hinges on her celebrity personality. Callers frequently initiate (or end) their phone calls by telling her how much they enjoy her program, a statement of fan club adoration that usually elicits appreciative giggles from the program's star.[26] One episode opened with a discussion between Larry Angelo and Dr. Ruth about her forthcoming role in a feature film starring Sigourney Weaver and Gerard Depardieu, foregrounding her additional talents as a dramatic actor/star.

This combination of authorizing roles for Dr. Ruth—as therapist, celebrity, and actor—is reinforced in the dramatized therapy sessions that occur in the course of the show. These staged sessions have Dr. Ruth playing herself (Dr. Ruth Westheimer, sex therapist), while actors assume the roles of patients. The sessions are extremely brief relative to the traditional fifty-minute session, but they are significantly longer than most of the phone calls or letters to which she responds (though overall more time is devoted to phone calls than to the dramatic sequences in each show). In these sessions Dr. Ruth and her patient review the latter's primary problems, and Dr. Ruth recommends a course of action for the patient. This provides an opportunity for the most extreme intervention and directive advice on the part of Dr. Ruth, since she is dealing with the patient face to face. Yet this occurs in a context where the simulational apparatus is fully apparent, as dramatic reenactment.

These scenes provide the most familiar and conventional form of therapy offered on the show, which is immediately identified with fictional simulation and with the dramas we see elsewhere on television. In the process, any clear-cut distinction between professional therapeutic competence and dramatic acting talent is also called into question. The sessions are introduced with a voice-over narration by Larry 'Angelo that briefly explains the situation in each: a couple's sex life has suffered since they had a baby; a woman's fiancé called off the wedding and announced that he is gay; a nineteen-year-old male is unhappy and embarrassed because he is a virgin, though he now has a girlfriend with whom he would like to have sex. Although the show presents only short scenes of therapy, it implies a larger context extending beyond the confines of the program that sanctions aggressive intervention. Dr. Ruth will give patients specific advice or instructions for the next week, clearly indicating that she expects to see the patient again even though the program does not usually show follow-up sessions. In this way the representational practices of the program demonstrate therapy in one-time sessions, even though an ongoing therapeutic relation is implied via narrative conventions (e.g., verbal references to prior or future sessions). This in turn raises questions about whether the program resembles or replicates therapy in the conventional sense or whether we can even continue to conceive of conventional therapy as a reference point of normative understanding.

The associations between Dr. Ruth as a therapist and the domain of dramatic fiction extend beyond the dramatized therapy sessions on the show. As mentioned earlier, Dr. Ruth's status as the star of the show is repeatedly underscored by the people who phone in. Over and over again, calls begin with people enthusiastically extolling her talents and talking about how much they like her. In part this is a device to get the conversation going, a way to forestall talking about "the problem." But it also prolongs the call, extending the time the caller and Dr. Ruth-as-celebrity are in contact. During the calls, Dr. Ruth herself may raise models from fiction in her responses to questions posed by callers.

In one instance, a woman explains that she has a lot of one-night stands. She enjoys the sex a lot but realizes this is not good for her self-respect. She concludes by asking Dr. Ruth how normal this behavior is. The doctor responds by saying that this is not normal at all; the caller will never find a relationship this way. Dr. Ruth is glad to hear the woman has moved back home as a way of curbing her activity and is lucky she is getting out "without getting hurt like Mr. Goodbar." The reference here is to Judith Rossner's *Looking for Mr. Goodbar*, a best-selling novel (made into a film by the same name), based on a real event but fictionalized for popular consumption, in which a woman who routinely engages in one-night stands is murdered by a man she picks up for casual sex. Finally, Dr. Ruth has published articles in *TV Guide* addressed to characters on prime-time fiction series, giving advice on sex and relationships.[27] All of these combine to suggest that therapy is intimately linked to popular fictional scenarios. In this case, television and therapy find their common ground in dramatic fiction.

Throughout the show Dr. Ruth maintains a posture of moral authority, a position supported by her dual identification as doctor and celebrity. While she insists that any activity engaged in by two consenting adults is acceptable, she even more frequently harps on the importance of a loving, monogamous relationship as the necessary foundation for good sex. All of this must be displayed and diagnosed through confession. Here the talk is more important than the act, since it is through confessional discourse and therapeutic relations that the program exists to begin with. The sexual act (itself multiple: good sex, orgasm, masturbation, what-have-you) is not necessarily the goal, but rather the alibi, of the discourse that maintains the program on television. And it is the maintenance of the program that sustains Dr. Ruth's own visibility as a star/celebrity and sustains viewers as participants within the therapeutic problematic.

The Program = the Relation

The nature of therapy that emerges through the course of *Good Sex!*, and through the course of *TV Guide* articles that address questions of television and therapeutic discourse, results in an impression of therapy in which the positions of therapist and patient are increasingly relativized. On her show Dr. Ruth is the expert authority as well as the star. As such, she controls the terms of discourse most of the time. And yet her position is decentered in a number of ways. In the first place, and most obviously, her position is affected by the structural and institutional demands of commercial television programming. Whatever she accomplishes is done according to perceived demands for entertainment, and within the circumscribed time limits afforded by the medium. Phone conversations are cut short if they go on too long or if an ad break is coming up. The dramatized therapy session fits into the time between two commercial breaks. In all of these contexts, Dr. Ruth's interventions are controlled and delimited by the medium that carries her. Moreover, in the course of the show there are a variety of indications that she is not the authority, or certainly not the only authority, in place.

Co-host Larry Angelo plays a prominent role as facilitator throughout the program, even though he does not speak to callers directly. He is the one who signals transitions, announces impending commercial breaks, and highlights upcoming segments. In this capacity, he speaks with the authority of the medium itself, rather than with the medical/therapeutic authority of Dr. Ruth. He thereby helps to contain Dr. Ruth herself; and it is hardly accidental that the person who fills this role is male. He also helps promote Dr. Ruth's star persona, a position that is from certain perspectives at odds with her identity and authority as a preeminent sexologist with advanced degrees. By the same token, according to the program's own logic, celebrity, medical authority, and dramatic talent are in fact mutually supporting.

The status of Dr. Ruth as the show's authority is further limited by the fact that she frequently appeals to her celebrity guests as experts in the domain of sex and relationships. She will ask people such as Willard Scott, Robert Klein, and Isaac Asimov questions about not only their careers but also marriage, parenthood, dating, romance, and so forth. Usually, one round of phone calls takes place while the celebrity guests are in the studio, and callers can pose questions to either Dr. Ruth or her guests. With this arrangement, Dr. Ruth initially assumes a position as the preeminent expert in affairs of the body, and simultaneously asserts her association with more generalized media celebrity, outside the domain of medical and psychological authority. The media celebrity guests are in turn situated—however provisionally—as experts in the domain of sex and relationships, especially since people who call in during these segments may address questions to them. When callers fail to include the celebrities in their questions, Dr. Ruth will often appeal directly to her guests to participate in the discussion, inviting them, in effect, to join her as a peer. In this way, the very strategies of the program blur the terms of distinction between psychologist-sexologist on the one hand and people whose reputation is based in the world of popular media culture (film, television, and literature) on the other.

The celebrities who participate may not even concur with Dr. Ruth in the course of handling a phone call. Such was the case on one show when her guests were the comedy team of Al Franken and Tom Davis (best known for their writing and appearances on *Saturday Night Live*). First they discussed their appearances on college campuses and the "Freudian" routines they incorporate in their act, such as theorizing the nasal stage of development (involving nasal expulsive/retentive behaviors) and exploring the problem of male penis shame, which causes men to hide their penises over and over again in dark places. During the subsequent call-in segment of the program, a woman called with the following problem. She was a nineteen-year-old virgin, engaged to a twenty-six-year-old man, with plans to marry in two years. They shared the same birthday, and he wanted to take her to Hawaii to celebrate. She came from a strict Italian family that opposed the trip. Dr. Ruth immediately said, "Don't go." Meanwhile, Franken and Davis together said, "Go. Go. Go Nina. . . . What are you, crazy?" Dr. Ruth repeated, "Absolutely don't go," while Franken and Davis continued, addressing both the caller and Dr. Ruth, "Go on, nineteen. Lie to your parents. She loves the guy. They're *going* to get married." Dr. Ruth concluded by asking the caller why she was waiting two years to get married, and proposed, "Tell your fiancé you want to get married in six months and go to Hawaii then."

There is never an attempt to reconcile one line of advice with the other. Since Franken and Davis are comedians the audience does not necessarily have to take them seriously; and their on-camera manner is less sober than that of Dr. Ruth. Nonetheless, as guests on her program, they are granted a degree of authority. This is supported by the opening of the sequence, in which Dr. Ruth appeals to them as experts, who can draw on their personal experiences on tour to comment on contemporary values, sex, and relationships among the college student population at large. At the same time, as men giving advice on sex—however apparently tongue-in-cheek—to a young single woman, their narrational position is not necessarily "disinterested."

To call in to Dr. Ruth is not just to seek help, but to become an educator and an authority for others.[28] Viewers who participate by calling in may be credited with the power to provoke educational and therapeutic effects. This recognition can come from both Dr. Ruth and other callers. Dr. Ruth herself frequently comments on the questions posed by her callers. She congratulates them on asking good questions or indicates that the problem they experience is shared by countless others. And in the course of a program, viewers who call in may refer to earlier calls and the value of the questions and comments that have been voiced by others. The callers are also associated with the celebrity status that comes from having appeared on television and from consorting with other celebrities.

This is tempered by the anonymity that callers can maintain, though most callers provide a first name and the city from which they are calling.[29] The information is sufficient to single out the caller as an individual with momentary star/authority status and yet protect the caller from receiving crank phone calls after speaking with Dr. Ruth and her guests. In all my viewing of *Good Sex!*, I encountered only a few occasions when callers failed to provide at least their first name. Thus, the confessional and therapeutic value of the program—and its value in generating star image and celebrity value—involves a circulation of discourse among a group of people rather than an exchange between two people fixed in the positions of therapist and patient.

Occasionally Dr. Ruth is unable to address the problems of a caller, failing as both educator and therapist; and at times she explicitly indicates her inability to help. When the problem described seems to require medical intervention, Dr. Ruth will instruct the caller to see a physician and cut the call short. (Such advice is given, for example, if the caller mentions experiencing pain during intercourse, or describes the common symptoms of a sexually transmitted disease.) There are also cases where the severity and specificity of the problem warrant a degree of intervention (including diagnosis and therapy) that Dr. Ruth is unable to deal with in the brief time allowed by the program. For example, one woman caller was extremely upset because her daughter had just told her that she was gay and that the daughter's best friend and roommate was in fact her lover. Dr. Ruth tried to tell the woman not to cut off the relationship with her daughter. "We do not know the aetiology of homosexuality. Some live the lifestyle all their life. For some—maybe not with your daughter—it's a phase." When the distraught mother interjected, "But she needs a *man*," Dr. Ruth immediately noted, "I can't do justice to this. There's not enough time. I would have to have you here, and hold your hand. Go and talk to a therapist. Not a friend. You do not need sympathy, you need help." Despite this insistence, the call went on for quite a while, although the mother, obviously rattled, was not reassured by any of Dr. Ruth's advice. Here, although Dr. Ruth immediately indicated that she could not help, the call ended up being the longest one she took all day. For the mother the phone call provided an important context for expressing her distress: "It's just such a *terrible* shock."

In some cases viewers may recognize lapses or mistakes in the exchanges between Dr. Ruth and her callers and feel that the therapist's responses are inadequate. In these instances, viewers who recognize the lapses are in a position of superiority over Dr. Ruth, since they are able to evaluate the caller-patient in different, and presumably more appropriate, terms. At times this takes the form of a breakdown in communication in the conversational exchange.[30] In these cases, the flow of information between caller and Dr. Ruth is out of phase. During a call from Barbara in Allentown, Dr. Ruth provides a series of recommendations to the woman, only to learn that the caller has already done what she suggests. The call begins with Barbara explaining that she and her husband have had sexual problems for over a year. They have two children. When her husband gets home from work, he wants sex but performs without any emotion. Dr. Ruth immediately suggests they see a sex therapist. Barbara explains that they went to see one that very morning, provoking a big fight in front of the children. After further questioning, Dr. Ruth recommends they see a man rather than a woman sex therapist. "But he chose a woman," Barbara explains. Dr. Ruth is forced to change her tactics at this point, since the directive advice has already been followed or has been considered and led to alternative results, tacitly rejected before the fact. In either case, her directive interventions here are not "working." Instead, Dr. Ruth says Barbara is lucky that her husband was willing to go to a sex therapist to begin with, and that she *must* give it another try and not let the problem slide.

Sometimes Dr. Ruth will just get things wrong. She may not hear the caller clearly or might misunderstand responses to her questions.[31] Even in the course of the dramatized therapy sessions, she can make a mistake. In the session with the nineteen-year-old male virgin, she at one point referred to his girlfriend by the wrong name. At other times, Dr. Ruth may try to rush through or brush off a call when the tone of voice and comments of the caller make it clear that she is not providing the degree of assistance and advice the caller thinks necessary. In this sense her support and advice are contingent on callers appropriately signaling their gratitude and satisfaction. One male caller was concerned that his wife was "preoccupied" with sex toys. Dr. Ruth suggests that he talk with a counselor. She says that if the wife uses the sex toys and experiences good lovemaking with him as a result, that is fine. "But I hear that there's something that is really bothersome to you," she adds. "Talk to somebody before it gets worse." The man tries to continue the conversation, but she cuts him off, explaining that she has to go, and thanks him for calling. In this case, the really bothersome something is never actually defined; nor is the caller given the opportunity to explain the nature of the problem.

In some cases, Dr. Ruth herself *is* able to probe and get callers to define the gist of their concerns more precisely. In other cases, callers themselves gradually reveal dimensions of the problem that redefine Dr. Ruth's (and the viewer's) understanding of what is at stake. One male caller explained that he had recently moved to the United States. Back in his native Britain, he had sex with his wife almost daily, but here in the States he finds that he is nervous and feels he "can't satisfy her." Dr. Ruth provides a reasonable response to this problem, suggesting that the move might have made him nervous, but cautioning him that if things do not improve in a few more weeks, he should consult a sex therapist. The caller then explains that what is really bothering him is that he found his supervisor's handkerchief in the closet and thinks his wife is having an affair. He goes on to express his anger toward his supervisor, declaring "I feel like shooting him in the groin or something." The sudden shift in tone, and unexpected redefinition of the nature of the problem, throws Dr. Ruth. Rather than pursuing this new perspective on the man's situation, she fairly quickly gets him off the phone: "No, no, no. Just do go and see a professional and see what the story is. Thanks a lot for calling."

All of these various interactions between Dr. Ruth and callers combine to relativize the ways in which audiences might understand the therapeutic transaction. It becomes a process where individual viewers can find many different terms of appeal and places of access. This understanding of therapy as a narrational strategy is aided and abetted by articles such as those found in *TV Guide* that encourage viewers to recognize the generality of therapeutic discourses in television in the first place and also suggest that the value and structure of these discourses are not fixed once and for all. One can participate in a counseling show like *Good Sex!* in literal terms—by calling in for example—or by finding a place in the confessional interchange. This place can be one of symbolic identification with someone posing questions or with the response; it can involve a recognition of expert authority or of the failures thereof. The apparatus itself provides the terms for the therapeutic relationship that becomes the appeal of the medium, the appeal to watch, in the first place. It is not even necessary to grant television and its counselors authority in order to participate. If someone watches long enough to judge them in the first place, that person is already a participant in the therapeutic transaction—listening to others' confessions and the therapists' responses in order to evaluate whether or not to take them seriously.

Identification per se is not necessarily required. Counseling programs obviously cater to voyeuristic pleasures—hearing and watching others speak about problems and confusions in the domain of sex and interpersonal relationships. The therapeutic relation structuring the discourse authorizes this voyeurism, for the therapeutic relation requires the presence of an interlocutor in the first place. And while this "first place" is initially given over to the therapist-star—in this case study, Dr. Ruth—the program goes on to relativize that position and mobilize the television viewer as an essential participant. The apparatus itself thereby claims the therapeutic relation as its own.

And it is therapy as a strategic discourse, as a relational

transaction, rather than as a fixed hierarchical relation, that counts. For it provides a structure within which one can always appeal for help from elsewhere even while one listens to others' confessions. At the same time, it provides the comfort of authority, however relativized or provisional. Indeed part of the comfort is that as long as one recognizes the therapeutic as the discourse in dominance, one can choose to believe oneself as an authority among all the competing confessional voices. It is within this discursive context that the public is willing—and is invited—to participate. The therapeutic transaction provides the grounds for understanding the appeal that counseling programs hold for viewers and also the readiness with which individuals are willing to confess personal problems to the mass television audience. But counseling programs are not alone in this regard; in the next chapter, I examine daytime couples programs that share this relationship with their viewers and participants.

Engendering Couples

The Subject of Daytime Television

The Relationship Monster[1]

The formation and maintenance of personal relations through therapeutic modes of discourse pervades contemporary mass culture, with television at the center. For television is certainly the most pervasive popular medium in the United States, occupying a position of hegemonic centrality in the habits of everyday life. It is also the most overdetermined cultural apparatus, negotiating a complex range of economic, institutional, social, and cultural interests.

Recent television programming includes a variety of nonfiction genres and formats in which the couple as a body is produced, probed, and provoked through mediated strategies of confessional and therapeutic discourse. A close analysis of these programs enables a more thorough understanding of the complexities and contradictions of therapeutic discourse in contemporary television culture. It also provides a context for recognizing how variable viewing positions are authorized and circumscribed; these programs include distanced, derisory, and superior attitudes as acceptable forms of spectatorship, along with the more conventionally recognized and imputed positions of involvement, identification, pleasure, and sympathy. The possibilities for a politics of oppositional viewing are thereby considerably complicated, if not necessarily obviated, by a therapeutic discourse that anticipates variable ways of watching television.

The analysis that follows contributes to an understanding of the function of the popular media in what might be called the pedagogy of everyday life. From this perspective, it is crucial to account for television's particular modes of meaning and subject production, while recognizing that this productivity occurs in a broader context of social-cultural practices and activities. In other words, the field of possibilities offered by television intersects with, and is crosscut by, other domains of individual experience and practice in variable and unpredictable ways. The central focus of the analysis is "the couple" as a common ideological unit of social identity within daytime, nonfiction television. This couple, resolutely heterosexual, is produced as both the subject and the object of social-cultural currency. In these terms, the couple is dramatized as a split body situated in networks of communication, networks understood as at once institutional identities and webs of signification. This emphasis on the staging of the couple as a split body is subtended by theoretical perspectives on television and its ongoing modes of ideological productivity. For example, the very networks of communication that situate the couple as a social identity simultaneously address viewers as interlocutors—as discursive subjects of communication—and not simply as subjects of consumption.

On *The All New Dating Game* "attractive singles"[2] pick a dating partner from a pool of three contestants, and are sent on a date arranged by the program. On *Love Connection* couples who have gone out together—one chosen by the other from a preselected videotape pool—discuss their date with host Chuck Woolery. *The New Newlywed Game* and *Perfect Match* are game shows for married couples, who are asked questions about one another and their relationship and win points when one spouse's response matches the other's. *Couples* is a counseling show offering thirty-minute versions of consultation sessions of "real people" with psychiatrist and family therapist Dr. Walter Brackelmanns. *Divorce Court* uses actors in dramatized reenactments of divorce trials based on real cases. All of these programs are syndicated or air on cable stations across the United States. They have shown on different channels in different markets at different times of day, usually positioned in fringe time, around network programming. They do not comfortably or easily share a genre. The game show predominates, but the list also includes the counseling show (an emergent genre[3]) and the reality courtroom drama (a genre hybrid). What they have in common is that each program stages the couple as a social body, a unit in division, comprised of two individuals—two bodies—submitted to networks of exchange and communication.

This body is put into play, and under analysis, variably mediated through the family, community, medicine/psychiatry, law, economics, and the television apparatus itself. Taken together, these programs trace a narrative trajectory, marking various stages in the life of the couple as a social body. The story is in one sense absolutely predictable and familiar: a couple meets, dates, weds, and divorces. Yet the very repetition of this narrative fixed on these nodal states of being indicates that the couple is neither a natural nor a stable identity. Rather, the couple is constructed as a social identity through an elaborate apparatus of discursive mediations distributed through time, in a sequence of formation, maintenance, and dissolution that is never finalized. However apparently frivolous or trivial, these programs produce the couple as a body and a site of social currency.

The very familiarity of the couple produced through these shows can be related to the uncanny effects of television's modes of production and distribution. Some of these shows— *The All New Dating Game*, *The New Newlywed Game*, and *Divorce Court*—are revivals of programs that are strongly identified with the 1960s, the decade of sexual liberation following the introduction of the birth control pill, just before the rise of feminism, gay liberation, the increase in no-fault divorce (concomitant with the growing divorce rate), and other social trends that would seem to contravene a fascination with the traditional rituals of courtship and marriage. These programs returned to us in the 1980s bolstered by the appearance of new shows demonstrating similar strategies and concerns. Yet this resurgence is not a simple reassertion of conservative values, for the programs return, inevitably, with a difference. *The All New Dating Game* still has its chaperones to accompany the couples on dates. But all dates are exciting holidays: no more dinners or nights on the town, only vacations, cruises, and long weekends at resort hotels. *Divorce Court* no longer announces that its purpose is "to help stem the rising tide of divorces."[4] Collectively, these programs can be seen as attempts to (re)instate the heterosexual couple as a stable social referent even as they endlessly rehearse the couple as a body constituted in unstable mobility. On the one hand they evoke a nostalgic desire; on the other hand, and at the same time, they provoke a recognition of the impossibility of the (nostalgic) media fantasies—and of the historic media programs—that are their point of departure.[5]

Heterosexual pairs are the a priori condition of narrativization for these programs, the necessary precondition for playing their games and telling their stories on commercial television.[6] The pair becomes a couple through a process of discursive elaboration; the couple is not a natural body, but a fully social being, the product of confession and analysis—of a therapeutic procedure. The couple is naturalized in social relations as the linchpin between public and private identity. As the foundation of the traditional nuclear family, the couple is a site of legalized sexual and economic relations, subject to the dictates of secular and religious law.[7] Thus the couple is never strictly a personal affair, even when it is bolstered by a mythical and mystical ideology of love defined in terms of ineffable individuality. The couple is also a fluid and variable body, a moment of affiliation that is not necessarily permanent. Indeed, the very existence of these shows repeatedly demonstrates that—and how—the pair becomes a couple through participation in certain discursive practices and how the couple reverts to a pair in the absence of communication.

According to these shows the very recognition and self-identification of the couple requires a willingness to submit to specific testing procedures and to participate in a confessional mode of discourse. The participants in this process are enjoined to speak freely and to exercise free choice, but only within the contours of discursive control established by each show. With the exception of *Divorce Court*, with its dramatized reconstructions of actual court cases, one chooses to go on these programs in the first place, a choice encouraged by appeals to participate that are aired during the shows:

> If you want to try out for *The New Newlywed Game*, and are married less than two years, and you're going to be in the Los Angeles area, call us . . .

> If you'd like to talk about a problem in your relationship, and you live in or plan to visit southern California, send your name and telephone number to *Couples*. We might be able to help you. And in sharing your difficulties, you might help other viewers in a similar situation.

On the dating shows, you are free to select the person you want to go out with, within the choice pool of three people preselected by the producers. And within the various shows, you are encouraged to speak openly and to respond to questions as quickly and honestly as possible, whether it has to do with inventing a wild, adventurous scenario to thrill a jungle girl on a date on *The All New Dating Game*, how you enjoyed dinner with your companion on *Love Connection*, which of your friends your wife would like to see in an underwear commercial on *The New Newlywed Game*, or expressing your emotions to your partner on *Couples*.

Once upon a Time . . .

The body of the couple in a narrative sequence produced through the course of these programs is in many ways a familiar construction. The initial formation of the couple is exciting, glamorous, and fun, and involves a particular emphasis on first impressions.[8] After the first date, however, the relationship is sustained only through a process of work; frivolous and impulsive exchanges are replaced by more forthright and difficult communications, and whimsical fantasy construction gives way to the banality of everyday life. Along these same lines, the game of attractions that precedes the formation of the couple is for beautiful bodies—a restricted field of the conventional consumer images of good looks. Once constituted as a body, the couple admits the idiosyncratic variety of ordinary physiques. At least this is the impression one gets if one follows *The All New Dating Game*, *Love Connection*, *The New Newlywed Game*, *Perfect Match*, and *Couples* as a protonarrative sequence. *Divorce Court* initiates the logical reversal of this process, with its use of actors rather than ordinary people. The program involves the dissolution of the couple, the redefinition of the pair as two individuals, as the codes of attractiveness that impinge on singles begins to reemerge. In this context, it is not surprising that the original version of *The Dating Game* is widely known for having featured a number of contestants who subsequently became extremely popular actors, including Tom Selleck.

On *The All New Dating Game* the public appeal for contestants is literally addressed to "attractive singles." The program self-consciously styles itself in terms of frivolity and superficiality, as the first impression is broken down into discrete stages of contact. The contestant who chooses a date is initially barred from seeing the choice pool, identified to her only as Bachelors Number One, Two, and Three; similarly the bachelor contestants cannot see the woman who may choose them for a date.[9] The chooser must rely on the contestants' voices and their responses to her questions, which are obviously pre-scripted and designed to elicit the minimal possible substantive information about the individuals in the bachelor pool. Typical of the questions are "I'm a deejay at an L.A. rock station. Pretend you're a deejay, and in your best deejay voice rattle off song titles that will describe our first date together," or "I find intellectuals very sexy. In your sexiest voice, convince me you're an intellectual."

With questions on this order, the program presents the pairing-off process in terms of make-believe, a self-conscious simulation in regress, where everyone is asked to pretend over and over again as the basis for purportedly assessing potential congeniality and appeal—all, in turn, for the entertainment of the mass television audience. The bachelors have to be ready to spontaneously assume any conceivable mood, attitude, identity, or accent. From time to time the chooser will actually show up with little hats, masks, or other costume paraphernalia that the three bachelors will be asked to wear as part of this masquerade, even though the chooser cannot actually see them in their disguises. In such instances the emphasis is clearly placed on amusing the audience—both in the studio and at home.

To select a date in this way suggests that we must, and do, make choices, but that they are inevitably—even structurally—made on the basis of something other than logic and rationality. The importance of appearance as a part of this process is played out in a number of ways. First of all, the show makes a verbal appeal to "attractive singles," stressing an image of its contestants as participating in a particular range of beauty and good looks. Second, the narrative of the competition plays out the mystery of who won the date for the participants in order to foreground their respective first impressions of one another. After the chooser has made her selection, the three bachelors are brought out and introduced to the chooser one by one, starting with those who were not selected for the culminating date. During this sequence of introductions, viewers watch the participants' reactions—the looks of relief, disappointment, and even apprehension. Indeed the whole sequence is designed to focus attention on these responses. Are the losers disappointed, or thrilled, once they see who their date would have been? Does the chooser end up regretting that she picked Bachelor Number Two over Bachelor Number One? Television viewers who have followed the whole selection process with full awareness of what all the participants look like are in a position to anticipate these responses and to play their own impressions off against the reactions of the participants. How one looks—both at others and to others—thus plays a crucial role in the overall structure of anticipation and narrative engagement generated by the show. The participants initially rely on verbal rather than visual cues. But the confirmation of their impressions, and the climax of the show, has everything to do with looking good, which also, of course, contributes to the visual spectacle of the program for viewers.

The couple is hereby constituted, having been produced through the mediated stages of first impressions and simulated exchange required by the show. This whole process is reconfirmed by the intercession of the host, who consolidates the identity of the pair as a couple with a concluding comment: "Perfect! This is what you call instant chemistry. I love it!," or "Aren't they a cute couple? They're so cool and lovable. I love 'em," or, more ominously, "Those two don't seem too sure about one another." The host speaks as an authority whose regular contact with newly formed couples confers on her particular sensitivity and insight, proclaiming her first impression of the couple as a definitive expert judgment. The reward for participating in this process is always a vacation. One may be sent to a wide range of places, including Ensenada, Tahiti, New York City, Bangkok, Jamaica, Anchorage, or the Bahamas, to name a few. Thus the initiation of the couple in terms of frivolity, fun, and out-of-the-ordinary experience is extended in the very prize that caps the process and confirms the formation of the pair as a couple.

The rules of the game shift when a pair is already defined, however provisionally, as a couple. On *Love Connection* the selection process and the first date precede the program itself. The focus of each episode is the retrospective reconstruction of the date, through discussion with host Chuck Woolery. But, having already happened, the date itself is far less exotic than the anticipatory fantasy projected by *The All New Dating Game*. Thrown squarely into the everyday world, the couples who have already gone out have usually been to dinner, the beach, a bar, dancing, the zoo, or a concert. Moreover, *Love Connection* does not require "attractive singles," but only singles, as prospective participants. Having already gone out as a prerequisite to appearing on the show,[10] the couple is returned to the banality of the imperfect, everyday world. This world includes a wider range of physical bodies, in terms of age and conventional standards of beauty and fitness, than the typical representations on *The All New Dating Game*.

First impressions do count here, as Chuck Woolery often inquires what the couple thought when they first saw one another. But they are hardly definitive or final, since they have already been supplanted by contact that goes beyond an initial moment of encounter. Dates often start well and end in hostility, or vice versa. Sometimes the individuals like each other well enough but do not want to *date* again, asserting a difference between the heterosexual pair and the couple. "The couple" is not just anyone, or rather any two. These programs offer a continual series of examples to model the couple as any two who choose to go out and to define their relationship through confessional discourse, mediated through program structures, host's remarks, and audience opinion.

Between *The All New Dating Game* and *Love Connection* there is a significant shift in the use of competition as a strategy of narrative engagement. On *The All New Dating Game* the process of selection—from a pool of three potential bachelor choices—structures the show as a whole, reaching a denouement with the revelation of the chooser's decision. Within this context, overt competition is emphasized with the regular posing of questions that force the members of the choice pool to comment on one another: "I just won a Linda Evans look-alike contest. Bachelor Number Three, look at Number Two and tell me what look-alike contest he could win," or "I'm overdue for a vacation, but I'm picky about who I go out with. Number Two, look at Number One and tell me what a Scandinavian would say if I went to Scandinavia with him. And sound like a Scandinavian." At the end of the question and answer period, there are dissolves between the chooser and each member of the choice pool, specifically delineating the potential couples that could result from the process, constructing a formal paradigm with a restricted range of substitutions. Only after a commercial break do we learn who is chosen, initiating the formation of the winning couple.

Love Connection operates according to a different logic, incorporating studio audience opinion to produce anticipatory suspense as a strategy of viewer engagement. For each program segment, the chooser is introduced and then clips from the three videotapes that were the chooser's initial selection pool are shown. But as regular viewers know, a choice has already been made, and a date has already occurred. However, before the introduction of the object-choice, the studio audience votes for the person they feel would have been the most appropriate choice. This vote is later invoked for consideration when the chooser is deciding whether or not to go out again, and with whom.[11] The audience vote essentially functions as a "straw poll" to infuse the program itself with a sense of suspense: Who did the audience vote for? Was it the same person initially chosen by the chooser-subject? Was the initial date good or bad? Will the audience vote give the chooser another choice? Will it prove to be better or worse? At the same time, it introduces a simulated community voice into the process of couple formation. The studio audience stands in as a measure of public opinion and common sense for both the chooser-subject and the television viewer.[12]

It is not incidental that this voice is introduced when a provisional couple has been identified—that is, after the two persons have already gone out once. Rather it demonstrates a shift in the terms for identifying the couple, from two individual bodies who operate independently as a pair to a newly consolidated body-in-division that must function socially in relation to a larger community. The studio vote, however indeterminate and nonfinal, represents the consolidation of the couple as a social body. Crucially, social regulation is not represented as prescriptive authority but as the balance of, and willingness to acknowledge, an array of voices: the interested individuals who comprise the couple and the disinterested communal goodwill of the randomly assembled studio audience. The audience vote provides potential advice and options to the participants in the process, but the daters are not constrained to heed this advice. The structure of the show marks the stages at which it is "useful" to rethink the process of dating and the formation of any specific couple as a unit of social identification.

The myth that sustains the dating shows as fantasy is marriage. The programs themselves culminate in the date, whether a romantic holiday or just another night on the town. The contestants are identified as social to the extent that they readily represent themselves as participants within this process. One does not have to win, but only to put oneself in circulation. Indeed, on *The All New Dating Game* "alumni" shows feature members of previous choice pools who were not selected for a date the first time around but are given a second chance; former rejects are thus extended the possibility of becoming chosen objects. The more one is willing to situate oneself in this circuit, speaking the language of the desiring other, the greater are one's chances of being identified in a couple.

Marriage as a possible goal is implicated by the dating programs with the periodic appearance of couples who met through the show and are now married. But it is also an alibi to confirm the need for coupling through mediated discourse in the first place. As a mythic projected end it naturalizes the need to submit to the questions and confessional procedures offered by the dating programs as a guarantee of sociality. Many of the participants on *Love Connection* are identified as formerly married, sometimes more than once, underscoring the relativity of marriage as a narrative telos. Marriage is not necessarily the end of the story—the "happily ever after" of fairy tales—but may be a shift in terrain, initiating a new kind of testing through confession. The married couple is a body with relative fixity within the law, ultimately no more permanent than the dating couple.

In the context of game shows, *The New Newlywed Game* and *Perfect Match* validate the married couple through dual confessions, as couples are asked questions of a personal nature and awarded points when they give matching answers. The couple with the most points at the end of the game is rewarded with a prize. For the contestants, matching confessions are the measure of the prizewinning couple in literal and metaphoric terms. At the same time, the questions are designed and timed to provoke divisiveness within the couples who have come to compete on the program. For the couple is separated, and each spouse must answer the questions individually as the basis for subsequent comparison (rather than, for example, being asked to consult and present a single unified response). Couples are positioned to insult their in-laws and friends, to say demeaning things about one other, or to reveal their attraction to someone other than their spouse:

> When it comes to romance last night, which food will your husband say came closest to how he behaves: hot cakes, cold cuts, or leftovers?

> How will your husband say you would complete this sentence: My husband thinks he's a *real man*. So he probably thinks I'd never tell about the time I caught him doing [*what?*]. But I will.

> How will your wife say you will complete this sentence: If I could redistribute my wife's weight, I would take from her [*blank*] and fill in her [*what?*].

Couples often fight over mismatched answers no matter how silly or banal the topic, even if it has to do, for example, with the kinds of food they buy, a favorite piece of furniture, or the directional orientation of their living room. But they will kiss enthusiastically to reward one another for matching answers, even when they reveal something embarrassing: the fact that one of them is an habitual nose-picker, for example, or that the first time they made love was in a bedroom closet in the home of one of their parents. On *Perfect Match* contestants are supplied with pillows for the express purpose of beating one another when they give "wrong" (i.e., unmatched) answers.

The married couple is represented as a body in division on a sliding scale of relative consonance and dissonance. These games require confession as part of the process for judging and understanding the couple as a social unit. But simply participating in the show guarantees one's identity as a couple. You do not have to match all your answers or win; you only have to confess. In the process of the game these shows enact scenarios of marital discord as well as marital bliss, agreement and disagreement over big and little issues, as the "natural" structuring parameters of the life of a couple. The reasons for engaging in social life as a body-in-division and the desires motivating such engagement remain uninterrogated. They are, precisely, beside the point, naturalized by the tacit assumption that everyone is interested not only in participating but also in having access to what goes on behind others' closed doors. As a group the shows themselves are mutually supporting in sustaining this logic.

Just Gaming

Through the course of these shows the couple as a body is produced, examined, challenged, and probed all in good fun. These are, after all, game shows. And the programs deploy an array of visual and narrative strategies to insist that this is all just play, based in the flimsy illusionistic electronic signals of television, with no substance beyond their simulated surfaces. At one time the set of *The New Newlywed Game* featured silhouette figures of couples facing one another across tables in various poses. At the start of each program the live couples seated in front of this stylized decor were also posed, and lit in silhouette, so that they would blend into the decorative backdrop and its shadowy couples.[13] For a moment, at least, there was no visible difference between the couples present to play the game and the decor in which they sat. On *The All New Dating Game* transitions from program segments to commercials involve transforming the image of the chooser or the couple into an abstract digital image of squares of color that seem to dematerialize before the television viewer's eyes. Here, shifting between program segments and ad breaks mutates the human subjects of the dating process into abstract patterns of video signal.

Love Connection offers an extreme version of this impulse to announce its own technologically mediated fictionality. The date is defined from the outset as a process staged for, and to be aired on, television. Participants often acknowledge their status as figures in a ritual performed for public show. In one case, a couple attended a party, and the friends of the chooser—who knew this was a *Love Connection* alliance— kept asking her date "if it was love yet." In another, a participant who was also an object-choice described taking his date to the drug store where he worked in order to show her off, because his co-workers had insisted that no attractive woman would ever pick him from a choice pool.

This recognition of the mediated, playful nature of participation is reproduced and extended in the very presentational strategies of *Love Connection*. The distinctions between appearing on video tape, on video monitor, and on stage generate a series of relative levels of presence/absence within the confines of the program based on the master opposition between being on television and being on a television screen on television. Only one of the videotape pool of object-choices gets to appear "live" on a video monitor, though that person's presence backstage is acknowledged. The subsequent discussion of the date is a conversation involving three people— Chuck Woolery, the chooser, and the selected date—in which the first two sit together on stage and converse with the third, who appears in medium close-up on a video screen behind them. Then, only if and when the daters agree to a second date, the backstage date—until now only seen on a screen— is invited to join Chuck and the chooser-subject on stage. In this way, procedures of social modeling and regulation of the couple are represented through a complex, internally generated structure of mediation of levels of reality and representation, differentiated on the basis of how one is positioned within this schema of relative presence and absence within the world of video technology. Of course, the whole program is taped for television airing at a later date.

These strategies represent a marketing tactic, the use of modern video technology to give the television image a sense of pizzazz and contemporaneity. They also clearly demonstrate the simulacral order of postmodernism, a process of extended duplication and reduplication of signs with minimal difference described by Jean Baudrillard as the mode of signification characteristic of contemporary society: "Reality no longer has the time to take on the appearance of reality. It no longer even surpasses fiction; it captures every dream even before it takes on the appearance of a dream. Schizophrenic vertigo of these serial signs, for which no counterfeit, no sublimation is possible, immanent in their repetition—who could say what the reality is that these signs simulate?"[14] Yet even if this is no longer the world of representation—if there is no longer any referent beyond the appearance of the sign that declares the absence of any reference beyond itself within the order of simulations—this is, as Donna Haraway has noted, a world characterized by networks of information, power, discourse, transmission, and domination. In other words, Haraway suggests that the order of simulation does not finally dissolve networks of power and domination (as Baudrillard would have it).[15] Instead, power becomes increasingly difficult to recognize because it is multiply decentered, always expressed in terms of systemic dispersal and regress.

The stakes in all of these television games are enstated in the conjoining of the injunction to confess as the very means of self-recognition as a couple with the setting in place of circuits of consumerism. The simultaneous circulation of commodities and of couples as bodies of communication delineates networks of exchange that become mutually interdependent in the course of their repeated—usually daily—deployments. *Perfect Match* makes the question of stakes quite literal, as each couple begins the game with the same number of points and decides how much to wager on each question. Thus the economy of the couple's confessional discourse is bound up with an economy of competitive consumption. But this is virtually the case in all of these shows.

Throughout these programs, the body of the couple is produced as a subject and object of consuming interest. It competes for the rewards of winning the game—a financed date, new bedroom furniture, or a camper for family vacations. Consumer culture thus impinges on the very recognition of the couple as the social unit most likely to avail itself of the widest range of consumer products. The couple as a body-in-division is in turn sold to the audience along with the products advertised during the course of these shows. The viewers' time in front of the television is sold to advertisers in the competitive market of commercial television. The couple as a confessional body is thus inscribed in multiple, simultaneous circuits of exchange whose perpetuation through repetition secures the functioning of consumer culture. Viewers consume confession, which becomes the agency of their own insertion into these circuits of exchange.

The very identity of the couple as a social body requires willing participation in a process of confession that draws all participants—viewers, participating couples, hosts, networks, sponsors—into an overdetermined network of relations. The effectivity of these programs is activated in the movements through, and convergences among, these circuits of exchange. At the same time, complicating the question of who is speaking in whose interest, confession as a discourse of truth undergoes a fundamental reconstrual. It is useful, in this context, to recall Michel Foucault's discussion of confession as a particular mode of discourse: "The confession is a ritual of discourse in which the speaking subject is also the subject of the statement; it is also a ritual that unfolds within a power relationship, for one does not confess without the presence (or virtual presence) of a partner who is not simply the interlocutor but the authority who requires the confession, prescribes and appreciates it, and intervenes in order to judge, punish, forgive, console, and reconcile."[16] What happens when the procedures of confession are relayed through the public, commercial, and highly mediated structures of the television game show? According to the logic of television's therapeutic discourse, confession is rewritten as a dialogic and multivocal process, even before an interlocutor is identified. For the confessional couple speaks with two voices, from two bodies. The position of interlocutor is also multiplied and dispersed in space and time since the role officially held by the program host/authority is shared by members of the studio and home audiences.

In the terms of the rules of these programs as game shows, how to speak is an acute problem, fraught with difficulty and danger. One might say too much or perhaps not enough. As a constituent member of a couple, one cannot judge for *oneself* because in every case another voice has to be taken into account—the voice of the other who will complete the identity of the couple as a body-in-division. One must confess all, but the final truth of the couple as a body requires that it speak with two voices. On *The All New Dating Game* the concern from the perspective of the choice pool is to say just enough to be attractive to the chooser (as a contender for the position of second voice), and no more than that: the game is to produce the confession that will be perceived as consonant and desirable to the person who chooses. Even on *Love Connection*, where the real decisions as to whether or not to go out again are pretty much settled in advance, how to speak becomes an issue. To reveal too much may prove embarrassing, although revelations of this sort are often provoked by the host's questions about, for example, the extent and quality of "romantic" activity. To attack the other half of the couple as undesirable or unattractive may, however, cast you in the role of villain. When couples on the program have had difficult or uncomfortable dates, and one of them starts criticizing the other on the show, the studio audience often intervenes as a vocal peanut gallery, booing or cheering specific remarks by the participants. This is an example of how disinterested public opinion, represented by the studio audience, judges the couple and their dialogic confession as a spectacle for the television viewer. On *The New Newlywed Game* and *Perfect Match* any answer may provoke dissension, as one spouse questions the sanity, memory, or propriety of the other for giving a particular response.

The body of the couple, produced and tested through the division of confession, is thus a body in anxiety-provoking communication with itself. The discourse one must engage in to secure one's identity as a couple is concomitantly, and necessarily, a source of stress, insofar as stress is understood as a breakdown in communicative networks.[17] In the game shows discussed thus far, this may be exacerbated by the interventions of the hosts as the primary interlocutors who activate, even provoke, the double voice of the couple. This is particularly striking in *The New Newlywed Game*, where the slightest disagreements can motivate host Bob Eubanks to challenge one spouse in relation to the other. "Who's the boss?" or "Who's right?," he frequently asks. More often than not, each spouse identifies him- or herself, so that two voices respond simultaneously, "I am." Here the divided body of the couple speaking in contradiction as a spectacle for the viewer is fully exposed.

I Confess

The couple as a body experiencing a breakdown in communications is taken up by, and fully developed in, *Couples* and *Divorce Court*. These programs exist in a continuity with the game shows insofar as they probe and define the couple as a confessional body. However, the avowed focus of attention in these programs is the couple as a confessing body under stress. In most cases, the problems that lead couples to seek counseling or a divorce in the first place are represented as a breakdown in communications between the two individuals who together comprise the couple. Yet this retrospective diagnosis itself depends on the perpetuation of confessional communication. In other words, the process of the cure or the dissolution of the couple—as the case may be—is the same as the process of its formation and testing. To the extent that the couple no longer confesses with ease, the injunction to confess must be enforced through the agencies of the medical and legal establishment: through the institution of psychiatry and mental health care in the case of *Couples* and through the legal system in the case of *Divorce Court*. The host of *Couples* is Dr. Walter Brackelmanns, who is routinely introduced as a psychiatrist and family therapist; Judge William Keene is the star of *Divorce Court*, and his credentials as a real judge in the California court system are announced in every episode.

Couples at once enacts and thematizes communications as the key to relationships. Dr. Brackelmanns's sessions with his clients have three distinct segments, as he speaks with each spouse individually and then with the couple together. In the process he repeatedly insists that the members of the couple have to talk to one another and express their feelings, a process that he facilitates. The point of all couples is to speak together; and in successful (enduring) couples, each partner will take his or her own feelings and those of the other seriously without confusing one for the other. The good couple is defined as a body in harmonious and sympathetic division. As a version of the counseling show, the program is more "serious" than the couples game shows. In keeping with this, Dr. Brackelmanns more readily and expressly generalizes situations for his viewers, stressing the educational point of watching the program. At the end of each session Dr. Brackelmanns sums up the lessons one might learn about sustaining successful relationships, for both the participants and the viewers, based on watching his show.[18]

One powerful point: if a member of a family is detached and angry, he is usually in emotional pain and doesn't know what to do. Be sensitive and caring, and the walls will come down.

There is an important principle of communication here. If your mate tells you about their feelings, *this must be respected*. If you use those feelings against someone, you're not trustworthy.

In your relationship, don't be demanding. It evokes negative feelings and hardens your mate to his or her position. Don't take responsibility for the feelings of the person you love. You can't change or fix them. If you try, it won't work, and it will prevent you from remaining a caring, supportive listener.

Dr. Brackelmanns is a therapist who aggressively intervenes in the course of counseling, repeating the same messages over and over again. We are responsible for ourselves but have to communicate with—to confess to—the other in the couple.

You don't throw away a relationship of six years. And you don't throw away a love relationship. You try to make it work. I don't know any other way. And you've got to take a chance. That's what's *tough* about good relationships: we stick our psychological necks right out there and somebody can chop it off! On the other hand, you

can then have a close, warm, caring, intimate, meaningful relationship with another human being. And it's
worth it.

He promotes the values and the risks of being part of a couple,
insisting his clients take the gamble necessary to sustain a
relationship as a couple. This centrally includes a labor of
loving communication and divided confession. In the course
of sessions he will order the participants to tell one another
how they feel, that they love one another, to hug, kiss, or hold
hands. The participants are rewarded for confessing feelings,
but they are chastised or cut short if they try to make accusations, analyze or describe "the facts," or account for their
feelings by reference to the context of the situation. "Don't
tell him what he did," the doctor typically replies. "He knows
what he did. Tell him how you feel." One *has* to confess one's
feelings and then hope that one's mate will be sensitive and
sympathetic in response.

This emphasis on confession as public emotional display is
reinforced in the very structure of the sessions as they are presented on television. The sessions are edited to fit into a thirty-
minute programming slot (minus commercial interruptions)
and feature the moments of emotional revelation by the participants and the directive injunctions offered by Dr. Brackelmanns at the expense of detailed case histories. Viewers are
given just enough contextualizing narrative information to
make sense of the particular case, but little more background
than that. It is usually quite obvious that Dr. Brackelmanns
spends more time with the clients than is aired during any
program episode. The logic of elision becomes clear, for example, when Dr. Brackelmanns, talking with a couple, refers
to something discussed previously (during the individual consultations) that was not seen earlier in the episode. Thus, he
might assert, "We already heard about your difficult childhood," when no such discussion was presented to the viewing
audience; Dr. Brackelmanns's brief reference provides the
first indication for the viewer that one of the participants had
a troubled youth.

The result for the purposes of the program is that the coherence and continuity of the stories of the individuals are less important than the recognition of the couple as a body willing to participate in the emotional, confessional confrontations provoked by Dr. Brackelmanns. Dual voiced confessional discourse, focused on feelings, constitutes the therapeutic process designed to secure the couple according to Dr. Brackelmanns. The therapeutic process is recognized via confession in inverse proportion to the production of narrative context and personal history. Everyone must speak to another, and listen to the other speak in turn, as part of this process. But what is said is channeled in terms of personal disclosures of emotional states.

Individual narrative and history, lost in the edited therapy sessions of *Couples*, find a more prominent place in the life of a couple on the brink of dissolution. In the chronological narrative of the couple, *Divorce Court* is the final appeal to the couple as a dialogical confessing body, as each member speaks in the interest of finally dissolving (or, in rare cases, conserving) the married couple. The legal contract that binds the couple and defines their obligations, unacknowledged until this point, fully emerges in the process of divorce, retrospectively defining the contractual nature of the couple as a social body. The judge who presides over the divorce court decides who is at fault—which of the spouses has behaved in a manner transgressing the terms of a legal contract that were not specified at the outset—and how the property will be divided, whether spousal support is indicated, and, when pertinent, which spouse will have custody of the children. Fault and material rewards are directly linked, for the spouse who proves to be the guilty party suffers for abrogating the marriage contract by being awarded the smaller share of the couple's assets. Who is at fault is decided through a judicial proceeding that evaluates a confessional form of testimony, as spouses and their witnesses attempt to convince the court of the truth of their charges. The courtroom drama is cast in the terms of confessional melodrama, with each member of the couple telling one side of the story, recounting the details of alleged abuse, adultery, and alienated affections that have led the couple to the courtroom. The decisions reached by the presiding judge often hinge on whose version of events he finds more credible.

The process of divorce represented on *Divorce Court* as a dialogic confession does not necessarily or always culminate in the dissolution of the couple. Rather, the presiding judge is the only one with the power and authority to dissolve the married couple. Indeed he may even function like the family therapist on *Couples*, suggesting that there is hope that a marriage may be saved, overseeing a reconciliation in court, or declaring a ninety-day delay until the divorce decree is final to encourage the possibility of reconciliation. The couple, formed through stages of mediated confession, cannot simply dissolve itself but must continue to participate in the very processes and structures that informed its creation in the first place, at least in the terms of television's representations.

The signs of staging deployed in the couples game shows are equally apparent in these reality dramas. The multiple mediations of fictionality on *Divorce Court* are as elaborate as the relative degrees of presence/absence produced on *Love Connection*. The television audience is carefully instructed in how to watch the show, with a printed verbal title, read by a voice-over narrator, explaining that the cases are *real*, based on divorce cases from across the country, but that the judgments are based on a combination of state laws and thus might not specifically apply in all cases. In other words, the program says, "This is real and not real, actual law but not actual law." This interplay is extended when the program also regularly explains that actors play the roles of spouses, while real lawyers argue the cases, based on a script. Meanwhile the judge—a real judge—makes his decisions independently, and purportedly none of the participants in the drama (actors and lawyers acting) knows his decision prior to the taping. All of this information is provided in titles or voice-overs incorporated into the opening and closing of the show. Thus the actors' responses are presented as being real and spontaneous within the confines of their characters, even though the actors are merely playing the part of litigants in a divorce proceeding. This is in turn emphasized in the dramatic structure of the program. For as the judge pronounces his judgment, the two prime litigants (actors) are shown in split screen. Given all the knowledge provided for the viewer about what is "fictional" versus what is "real" in the program, this presentation foregrounds the moment of legal decision as a moment of self-conscious dramatic performance, as viewers are encouraged to evaluate how well the actors in the case perform their reactions to the judge's ruling.

To further extend the fiction of reality, and the reality of the fiction, the judge's decision—supposedly unknown even by the producers until the moment when it is read during the process of taping—inevitably includes rather playful puns and analogies based on the details of the case, consciously styled in the terms of a witty script. For example, when one case focused on a wife's obsessive relationship with a pet dog, Judge Keene suggested that it "certainly adds a new dimension to the concept of man's best friend." In a case where a father was purposefully involving his children in accidents to collect insurance money, an outburst by the father compelled the judge to threaten him with contempt and a jail sentence. When the man kept yelling, the judge invoked the familiar expression of Clint Eastwood's *Dirty Harry* character, "*Go ahead*. Do it [keep up the complaining]—and *make my day*!"[19] All of this is in turn framed by a professional host/ master of ceremonies, who stands between the courtroom drama and the television viewer. He introduces the cases, in voice-over, and explains the different stages in the testimony. In the process he at once naturalizes and calls attention to commercial breaks, explaining them in relation to the natural breaks in the judicial proceedings: "As Mr. Smith leaves the stand, we will take a short break," or "While Mrs. Adams consults with her attorney . . ."

On both *Divorce Court* and *Couples* the force of the injunction to confess is particularly strict. Dr. Brackelmanns and Judge Keene carry an added professional authority in enforcing the process. Insofar as the couples in these contexts are in a state of stress-as-communication-breakdown, the need for this institutional/professional authority is not in itself surprising. But it would be a mistake to take this authority as absolute. Participating in *Couples* is specifically cast in terms of a dual educational mission. Dr. Brackelmanns can help the couple that cannot help itself. But the couple, in turn, is incorporated as part of the educational expertise offered by the program as a whole. In other words, even being a *patient* on the show is a way of associating oneself with authority and with the celebrity and glamour associated with television appearances. This is made explicit in the program's appeals for potential clients.

Confidentially Speaking

With the reconstrual of confession as a dialogic procedure of discourse—dividing positions of confessor and interlocutor—along with the repetitive, self-conscious strategies of mediation and simulation, television's staging of the couple through the course of these programs asserts the importance of confessional and therapeutic processes in which positions of authority and hierarchy are relativized, especially when it comes to specifying the place of the spectator. For these programs offer multiple and simultaneous potential positions of identification, carefully sustaining a balance between engagement and disinvolvement, proximity and distance. The very thematics of the programs implicate voyeurism, as viewers are offered elaborately mediated revelations of a personal nature. Viewers are held at a safe distance by the devices of fictionality even as they hear confessions of an intimate, even potentially sordid, nature.

At the same time, the deployment of confessional discourses within a therapeutic mode, and the possibilities of multiple identification thereby mobilized, authorizes the very act of listening to strangers discuss their personal lives. The presence of viewers, along with that of the program hosts, is, after all, necessary to the confessional transaction, justified by the position of interlocutor, "for one does not," again remembering Foucault's explanation, "confess without the presence (or virtual presence) of a partner who is not simply the interlocutor but the authority who requires the confession."[20] In this context, viewers may assume the position of the therapist-authority to whom the confession is addressed. This may in turn imply sympathetic authority, but equally can involve smug superiority. A range of attitudes is conveyed by the behavior of the hosts/authorities within the programs who support and promote confession but also respond to the confessions variably—with concern, interest, surprise, and even ridicule.

As the model for this authority, the hosts of the couples-oriented game shows exhibit all of these responses at one time or another; and even the authority figures who oversee relations in *Couples* and *Divorce Court* occasionally rebuke participants. No one remains a benevolent, detached interlocutor. At the same time, the viewer can assume the position of one instructed: one has to listen if one hopes to understand the various permutations and combinations of the couple as a social body. Here the audience is presumably more directly subjected to the program's dominating hegemony and the consuming strategies of social regulation expressed therein. In between these two extremes, viewers may identify—provisionally and unpredictably—with the participants (contestants) in the process, recognizing themselves and their own problems in the course of others' confessions.

These programs do not construct a single ideal or stable subjectivity or mode of reception, for they produce couples and address viewers in terms of circulation and division. A viewer may find moments of recognition and misrecognition, engagement and disengagement, within the multiple discourses deployed by these programs considered individually or as a group. These programs thereby contribute to the production of a subjectivity that is contradictory and decentered. This process is not per se specific to these programs, but rather a confirmation of how they operate in a medium whose popular appeal (i.e., its ability to draw and hold large numbers of viewers) can be traced in its inscription of heterogeneous terms of address and in its recognition of the mass audience as a heterogeneous mass.

Yet this recognition, linked directly to marketing, has important implications. For the very logic of these programs, in producing confession and subjectivity as they do, engages ambivalence as a central strategy of therapeutic engagement that captures viewers in the first place. According to the structure of these games and trials, participants must speak and are rewarded for participating via confession. This process is aided and abetted by program hosts who incite participation but also make fun of those who willfully participate in a playful and derisive manner. This reached one extreme when comedian Paul Rodriguez took over as host of *The New Newlywed Game*.

This ambivalence extends to what the participants actually talk about. Typically, the hosts' derision comes on the heels of their incitement to disclose the details of personal and sexual relations. The interplay of disclosure/confession/therapy as what is at once expected and yet unacceptable repeatedly plays itself out in verbal and dramatic terms. Thus, in some of these shows intimate sexual relations are constantly referenced, but only in indirect forms, such as "making whoopee" or "getting romantic." (A similar strategy is evident in *Good Sex! with Dr. Ruth Westheimer*, where frank talk about sex is encouraged in order to evaluate and regulate sexual behaviors, and *not* because anything goes.) On *Divorce Court* participants may report the extramarital sexual affairs of their spouses. But wholly unexpected revelations that erupt in the course of the courtroom proceedings require elaborate shifts in staging. In such instances, the scene itself shifts from the public spectacle in the courtroom to the privacy of the judge's chambers, once again suggesting that even when it comes to serious judicial proceedings, not just anything can be spoken in public. Transitions of this order are not frequent, but they are familiar to the regular viewer. The private melodrama of unforeseen revelation moves us, quite literally, to another scene.

The particular fascination of the programs—and their specificity in relation to the larger process of subject construction—lies in their play on the borders of romantic fantasy and middle-class decorum and propriety. By playing with hegemonic social identity, they invoke fantasy scenarios in terms that are themselves fundamentally ambivalent. They activate aspirations of fulfillment in conventional terms—marriage, family, the acquisition of consumer goods, middle-class life-styles—at the same time that they hint at the anxiety, even the impossibility, of its achievement. Singularly and collectively, these programs threaten to undermine the conventional gender roles and middle-class values that they simultaneously uphold as terms of reference.

In terms of romantic fantasy, these programs invoke and rework contemporary cultural myths of true love, love at first sight, and marital bliss that are already in place. While they flirt with the possibility of a "happily every after," they also dramatize the limits of these myths in practice. In the process they draw on the "eternal battle" between the sexes. The couple—man and woman, male and female, husband and wife—is shown to work together by being pitted one against the other. The body-in-division of the couple is confirmed in disunity because it is also always, in these shows, comprised of two sexes. Heterosexuality is presupposed as the necessary foundation for constructing the contented couple at the same time that it furnishes the very terms of instability—man and woman.

To sustain the gender roles that allow the myths to function, in the difference between the sexes that supports the magic of true love, is precisely to generate the stress and anxiety that will undo them in the long run. According to the dramatic narrative enacted by these programs considered together, the struggle for true love and perfect union is constant but essentially undecidable. The programs are unable finally to confirm or deny the truth of the myths of love and romance, even as they are mobilized as key terms of reference. The pleasure of viewing the shows lies, in part, in the possibility of investing in the myths of true love while simultaneously recognizing their long-term impossibility.

Moreover, the ambivalence of romantic fantasies is dramatized through a confessional mode of discourse that itself threatens to transgress the limits of proper middle-class decorum. For the injunction to tell all can lead to saying too much—the revelation of intimate habits and private affairs. We are not properly expected to discuss sex, or our feelings about close friends and relatives, in public or in front of strangers, much less in front of the impersonal mass of the television audience. Yet this is precisely what these programs promote. There is an undeniable fascination and pleasure to be derived from witnessing this overstepping of the bounds of middle-class propriety. The immediate subjects of this process—the couples who agree to participate—are models of transgression at the same time that they implicate themselves as potential objects of derision, because they do not represent themselves as proper, conventionally self-restrained middle-class subjects. This is at least the case in principle, if not in frequent practice, since all of these shows are taped in advance—and many are heavily pre-scripted—and can be edited or, in extreme cases, not even aired. Participants talk in general about personal affairs; but more often than not, what they actually end up saying is not all that astounding. In addition, the question of voice, not only in terms of who speaks but also under what constraints, must be considered.

Given the constraints of pretaping, the range of speech allowed on these shows, especially the apparent mistakes, is worth examining. Mistakes of this sort are most frequent and obvious on *The New Newlywed Game*, where the couple is at its most stable point in the narrative circuit of its existence. In one case, wives were asked with which friend of their husband they would most like to take a bath. The intention was clearly to raise the image of the (newlywed) wife's sexual interest in another man; questions of this order, posed to both men and women, are routine on the show. In response, one woman gave the name of a female friend, raising the eyebrows of the program host and, subsequently, the ire of her husband, specifically because she named a woman rather than a man. (His effort to match her response had, more "properly," named a male friend.) She had simply named a good friend, someone with whom she would feel comfortable bathing. Of course the issue of the appropriateness of the response revolves around sexual preferences for married couples and the intimation here of lesbian desire.

However, this inkling of an alternative to heterosexuality in the middle of daytime commercial television cannot simply be considered transgressive in any immediate sense. For it can also be taken as titillating in at least two senses, both of which function at the expense of women. In the first place, it enacts a scenario of the stupid woman, who does not even understand the question to begin with and is publicly chastised by her husband for her misunderstanding. Second, certain forms of female-female sex are conventionally included in male-oriented pornography.[21] Moreover, this sort of transgressive potential, emerging out of a misunderstanding, is expressed in a show that is relentlessly heterosexual, daily featuring recently married couples, including many women who come on the show visibly pregnant. Any intimation of sexual transgression is thus allowed only when it is already circumscribed (which does not a priori determine the way it will be taken by individual audience members).

The very existence of all of these couples programs signals a blurring of the distinction between personal and social, private and public, individual and mass. But this blurring of conventionally distinct domains may be taken in several ways. On the one hand, the subjects who confess break the bounds of a conventional middle-class morality that prescribes what can be spoken, by whom, in what contexts. On the other hand, these shows delineate the ways in which public and private experience are equally permeated by institutional and impersonal strategies of power—including the community, law, and psychiatry—while requiring the involvement and complicity of subjects who will speak for themselves in their capacity as free, private individuals. Here, the difference between the private and the public is effaced in the interests of the consuming social body. These programs project the couple as the site where private and public interests commingle, and they invite individual viewers to share in this image of social subjectivity as a consuming therapeutic spectacle. The relation between the individual subjects and the institutional imperatives remains unstable.

These programs consolidate the couple as the social body whose circulation as simulation secures the repetition and displacement of consuming interests and passions, where the social is always personal and vice versa. This body is constructed as unstable and decentered; it is always already in division and under stress. At the same time, these shows engage viewers in terms of confessional and therapeutic modes of discourse, encouraging participation in a process whereby one's personal affairs have currency in the public sphere. They even suggest that personal identity within the social can best be secured by participating in the discursive networks they repeatedly deploy. The couple shows function as social regulation to the extent that they channel "free speech" in the terms of a therapeutic problematic with the power to diagnose social identity. In this context the inclusion—even the promotion—of transgressive speech serves as a strategy of containment, confining it within the networks of confessional discourse and consumerism at the center of these programs. But the production of meaning and of subjectivity is constantly renegotiated, a process exacerbated by the daily renarrativizations of these shows. The very strategies of discourse that work to secure and regulate subjectivity are the means for expressing and recognizing social transgression.

These programs signal the anxiety of hegemony, including voices that threaten the logic and interests of bourgeois social control and cannot always finally be contained. Thus it is by no means clear that social control wins out all of the time, for all viewers, or that everyone will even identify social control in the same terms. This suggests that sometimes complicity with the hegemonic forces of consumer culture can provide the means whereby individuals discover their own (counterhegemonic) power and that the expression of transgression can be readily consumed by hegemonic interests. This means that we must constantly engage in a process of critical reading, without mistaking singular intellectual conclusions or consuming passions for the final word: confessional discourse is dispersed through an unstable series of therapeutic transactions whose effects are not necessarily predictable in advance. Moreover, these modes of therapeutic and confessional discourses, conjoining the family and consumer culture, are not restricted to one place within the institution of television. It is to some of the other places they appear, especially cable, that I turn in the next two chapters.

Watching the Girls
Go Buy

Shop-at-Home Television

There's something oddly intriguing, and at times even hypnotic, about home-shopping shows. Yet, home shopping is tacky, ghastly, vulgar, and boring. Those are easy judgments to make. The real question is why people tune in—including, apparently, some viewers who never buy anything.—Mark N. Vamos, Business Week

When Programming Is Sales

It is a truism of television theory and analysis that television viewers are commodified in the process of watching TV. Viewing habits, measured by the ratings industry, map patterns of consumption that are bought by stations and networks in order to be sold, in turn, to ad agencies representing commercial sponsors. An essential corollary of this perspective is that programs are the lures that attract viewers in the first place. Different forms of programming hold different numbers and kinds of audiences in place—within the field of reception—so that they might receive the commercial messages dispersed through the course of broadcasting. Viewers are thereby positioned as consumer-commodities. As individuals who may consume the products and services promoted during the programs they watch, viewers are the currency of exchange value among sponsors, ad agencies, networks, and stations. Within this schema, the viewer can be a cipher within the mass audience or can be particularized and valorized in terms of age, class, gender, race, or geography as specific shows, genres, and programming dayparts are correlated with specific cross-sections of the medium's mass audience. In an ideal industry scenario, target audiences could be attracted and held through entire dayparts, allowing for the systematic and continuous matching of consumers and commercial sponsors. In practice, the conjunctions of audience, program, sponsor, and time of day prove to be relatively diverse and approach, rather than achieve, ideal results, at least in the terms of this model.

This perspective on American television has been central to the understanding of its historical and institutional specificity. Programming flow, multivocal strategies of address, and the pleasures afforded by particular programs, genres, and dayparts have emerged as aspects of television's textual economy that demand attention as the medium mobilizes multiple spectatorial positions.[1] The viewer is situated in the position of being a relay between individual episodes and a series as a whole; between an episode and the part of the day in which it is aired; among different genres and modes of programming; between program segments and advertisements; and among stations, producers, networks, ratings services, agencies, and sponsors. While the system is supported by extended consumption—of all programming and products— the individual program remains the anchor that sustains the logic of the system. This is, at least, the impression conveyed by the emphasis on ratings expressed in terms of individual programs, as well as through the bulk of promotions for television both on television and in the popular press.

However, the appearance of the phenomenon of home shopping stations and programs challenges this widespread and commonly held understanding of the pleasures and attractions of television programming. For in shop-at-home programming, the programming *is* sales—a continuous flow of products offered directly to the viewer, one at a time, for purchase. In other words, the programming provided by television shopping services is not differentiated from the commercial appeals of the advertisement. On the contrary, the programming on shopping channels is a continuous segmented sales pitch. Therefore the distinctions maintained by commercial television—however tenuously—between programs and advertisements, between consuming television in the home and consuming the products it advertises in the marketplace, or between a position of potential consumption and actually buying something in a store are collapsed. All a viewer has to do is call the 800 number posted on the television screen, offer a credit card number or send a check, and wait for the item ordered to arrive.

Television's force as an apparatus and agency of consumer culture is fully and explicitly enacted by television shopping services that sell things directly to their audience twenty-four hours a day. Station income—profits or losses—is not determined by the mass audience of prospective, potential viewers but by the number of items actually sold in the course of the day. Indeed the very idea of "station income" is subject to aggressive redefinition, no longer comparable to a standard broadcast operation or even the conventional cable service supported through monthly subscription fees and/or conventional advertising. Some cable-only shopping channels actually pay local operators a small fee to carry their signal, reversing the typical financial flow between franchise operators and cable networks.

A closer look at the phenomenon of shop-at-home broadcasting helps to clarify how television can exist, and even prosper, in the absence of conventional programming. This inquiry into the Home Shopping Network (HSN) has the potential to call many basic assumptions about the television apparatus into question. At the same time, it contributes to an understanding of the minimal requirements of programmatic representation within the contemporary formation of television as an apparatus of consumer culture. Pleasure seems to persist in the absence of conventional entertainment and information programs, as television shopping extends and exacerbates the ideological keystones of commercial television, even while it challenges all familiar theories of the television apparatus derived therefrom. In this light, it is striking that the Home Shopping Network appeals to its viewer-shoppers as members of a community, indeed a family, of consumers connected through exchanges of confessions and testimonials between program hosts and call-in purchasers, constructing a therapeutic discourse of consumption.

In the process of selling its products, HSN provides appropriate terms and guidelines for its own use by the viewer, with a particular emphasis on the female as the ideal consumer and on domestic space as the ideal site of consumption. Indeed, since both a television and a telephone are necessary to shop with HSN, the home is very nearly the only location from which one can shop. The very networks of exchange set in place by the home shopping transaction include not only the viewer and the television but also the telephone and consumer credit industries. Capital and telecommunications are thus conjoined, with the shop-at-home television viewer as the linchpin in a system of financial, informational, and ultimately symbolic circulations. The viewer-shopper becomes a subject within powerful and abstracted circuits of communication.

The Home Shopping Club: A Television of Attractions

Television sales programming catapulted to prominence in the 1980s, garnering the attention not only of viewers and broadcasters but also of the financial and journalistic community. In the second half of the 1980s, the television shopping industry was profiled in a wide range of mass market magazines and in the trade press, including regular coverage in *Broadcasting* and feature articles in *Business Week*, *Esquire*, *Film Comment*, *Forbes*, *New York*, and *TV Guide*. The Home Shopping Network received particular attention as the first and most prominent of the television shopping channels.[2] As an indication of the success of the Home Shopping Network, the June 1987 issue of *Channels* ranked HSN as the number one achiever of the year in its annual survey of media industries.[3] And HSN is not alone in the field of television merchandising; it has had to compete with a growing and changing number of rival networks including Sky Merchant, the QVC Network (Quality Value Channel), and the Financial News Network's TelShop, among others. The success of HSN is also measured by its massive market expansion and a consonant increase in revenues in the course of the late 1980s in particular and by its ability to endure as a mainstay of cable television, notwithstanding its financial vicissitudes.

Based in Clearwater, Florida, HSN was started in 1977 as a radio sales program. In 1982 it began selling products on the local cable system, and it expanded to a national scale in July 1985. Since then, HSN has purchased twelve broadcasting stations to assure nationwide major-market coverage and to include markets not covered by cable.[4] HSN provides twenty-four-hour-a-day programming in the form of television marketing via two services, HSN I and HSN II. These services are programmed respectively on the twelve broadcast stations owned and operated by the network and on cable systems across the country. HSN also sells its service to other stations to be aired in particular dayparts, especially in the late-night and early-morning fringe. As an owner of so many stations, and an originator and seller of programming, however unorthodox, HSN might legitimately be considered the fifth "commercial network" in the United States, behind ABC, CBS, NBC, and the Fox Broadcasting System.[5]

HSN provides its shop-at-home services under the name of the Home Shopping Club (HSC)—the corporate "network" identity thus distinguished from its programming—which individuals can join with the purchase of any product. The club offers items for purchase one at a time, and the items can be bought only while they are displayed on the television screen.[6] Usually, between five and fifteen items are displayed each hour, though during special "bargathon" close-out sessions, merchandise comes on and goes off far more quickly. Conversely, on occasions when guests appear with the host— for example, athletes paired with the selling of sports memorabilia—products often move on and off screen at a slower pace. Items appear in a random and unpredictable order, though sales hosts usually hint at the kinds of things they will be presenting in the next few hours. Special segments feature only clothing or jewelry for one to five hours at a time. The day is subdivided into program segments according to the individual sales hosts, who introduce and describe each item and talk with call-in purchasers.

The program uses a limited and highly regularized repertoire of images, with particular emphasis on the close-up product shot. Each item is shown in a series of tight shots that may go on for several minutes at a time. All products are shown with a column on the left side of the screen indicating the "retail" price and the HSC discount, as well as the toll-free number to call for purchase. Occasionally additional text appears in the upper right-hand corner of the screen or as a crawl along the bottom edge or under the identifying label at the top of the screen. This text provides additional information about the product being presented (e.g., 15 rubies, 1.25 carats) or urges the viewer to use "Tootie," the computerized sales system, for making a purchase.

For smaller items, the program can avail itself of specific production equipment to show off merchandise from multiple perspectives and jazz up the image. Early on, the point of a knitting needle, protruding into the frame, jiggling a pendant or a gold chain, was used to create light reflections. While the knitting needle has not been totally abandoned, the network has gradually acquired specific, and more sophisticated, equipment for displaying merchandise, such as tabletop rotating platforms, mirrored stands, and refraction and star filters (which are usually reserved for jewelry). A model's hand is often included to help define scale and demonstrate a particular item in use; thus the hand might be seen turning the dials on a radio, wearing a ring, or unzipping the different compartments of a piece of hand luggage. Clothing, which is frequently sold over the air, is the principal exception to the close-up mode. It is usually displayed on a live model in long shots, intercut with extended closer views to show off garment detailing such as cuffs, buttons, embroidery, or seams.

Over the course of an hour, the pervasive close-up perspective may be broken with cutaways to the program sales host framed in a medium shot with an American flag in the background, screen left, or to the salesroom as a whole, where a roomful of operators seated at computer terminals might wave in unison. Occasionally the television viewer will see the HSC logo slide, or even the "studio" space—a draped table in front of several lights and two small video cameras. But the overwhelming emphasis remains on the close-up product shot, first with the descriptive voice-over of the host, later with the testimonials of buyers. Often a series of products will be shown in close-up one after the other without any visual interruption of the repetitious, catalogue-style visual representation.

The details of these visual strategies are important for a number of reasons. Because the programming is the same all day long—a succession of objects for sale—there is little variety available in terms of visual style. Moreover, the formal tactics of product presentation on the Home Shopping Club are far removed from the strategies of representation more commonly associated with television advertising. Indeed, commercial advertising on the networks is usually considered to be the arena of greatest audio/visual experimentation and play on television,[7] while the appeals of the Home Shopping Club are made with a highly restricted audio/visual repertoire. In the HSC context of continual selling, the signs of formal visual difference are extremely minimal; but they are crucial, as, for example, the shot scale stays the same but a star filter is introduced. There is a clear effort to play with the image, evidenced by the use of diffusion and diffraction filters, different color backgrounds, and the like. From time to time this even assumes the level of highly self-conscious playfulness. On one occasion, the program hosts introduced the image of a mouse as an ad hoc mascot and periodically included brief cutaways of the mouse image while products were being sold.

Clearly, some degree of visual variety is considered necessary, differentiating the television sales show from the conventional catalogue or news/weather teletext. At the same time, the program's strategies of visual presentation are hardly subtle. On the contrary, the close-up view and repetitive repertoire of shots highlight the intervention of the techniques employed. The use of, among other things, knitting needles and a woman's hand to create movement and light reflections for jewelry also emphasizes the bargain-basement production values while making them fully visible to the audience.

The means of production are not hidden from the viewers in any systematic way. Indeed, callers may comment on the production equipment, especially when it is first introduced. Thus, when the program first started using refraction filters, callers would talk about the nice visual effect created by the new lens. In addition, with these minimal visual differences across the relentless repetition of close-up product presentation, the importance of sound, and sound-image relations, is heightened. In terms of production values and formal practices, HSC's strategies for presenting merchandise combine to define the minimal terms of visualization and variety considered appropriately "televisual."[8] The program's strategies of visual presentation also have implications in terms of connoisseurship and gender, which will be elaborated below.

The unceasing flow of items presented in this way conveys the impression of a plenitude of goods and immense variety. However, the regular viewer quickly learns that certain kinds of products tend to dominate Home Shopping Club sales. These include jewelry, collectibles, clothing, and small electric appliances. The prevalent kinds of jewelry are gold chains in various weights and sizes; cubic zirconia products—especially rings—in all imaginable shapes, colors, and sizes; and an array of fine gemstone jewelry products, also with an emphasis on rings. The range of collectibles includes Capodimonte, a brand of decorative Italian porcelain; clown figurines; different brands of designer and collector's dolls; lead crystal animals; and music boxes. The small appliances range from air ionizers and cordless telephones to electronic insect repellers, AM/FM radios, and radar detectors. In the category of clothing, outfits for women, often including larger women's sizes, are the most frequent offerings. The club also sells lamps, luggage, small leather goods, thermos bottles, tools, stereos, end tables, display cases, and similar products. But the greatest emphasis and variety is found in the smaller, luxury items.

From the perspective of bourgeois distinction, most of the merchandise offered by HSC could be categorized as the conspicuously consumed trinkets of working- and lower-middle-class lifestyles and taste cultures within American consumer society.[9] In this vein, many of the products, especially the jewelry and collectibles, are imitations or cheaper versions of the fine china and crystal figurines or jewelry one might find in upscale department stores or in specialty shops like Tiffany's. In surface texture, and at first glance, the HSC products offer an image of wealth. But they lack the manufacturer and designer imprimatur that would constitute "value" in the same way as the upscale products that are their model. The program encourages viewers to invest in its products in the name of long-term value and images of wealth that the objects do not necessarily carry in the mainstream bourgeois marketplace, which is the hegemonic definer of material and monetary value in American culture.

Through the products it sells, HSC constructs an image of a taste culture that correlates with an audience comprised of working-class viewer-shoppers. Yet this affiliation of the audience with a particular taste culture does not necessarily determine the economic class identity of the program's actual viewers. On the contrary, the strategies of selling and consuming developed on HSC variously reconfirm and undermine the initial impression of working-class identity. The initial assessment of the audience in terms of the products sold on HSC, as working-class subjects, is primarily meaningful to those who position themselves apart from that group identity and identify instead with "proper" bourgeois taste. For, to the extent that working-class taste culture implies the absence of regular bourgeois discrimination in matters of taste it is largely a term of derision. In other words, one viewer's worthless bauble or cheap, ugly, tasteless porcelain figurine is another viewer's favorite ring or cherished centerpiece. One can only label HSC's products and primary audience as participants in *working-class* taste culture if one more readily situates one's own taste somewhere else (e.g., with proper bourgeois taste culture, avant-garde style, a subculture, or an ethnic identity).

The association of the Home Shopping Club with working-class tastes and habits has not escaped popular commentators. Symptomatically, many descriptions of the program assume a tone of condescending superiority toward those who so avidly purchase the kinds of products it sells.[10] This includes implicit criticism of the audience for its overcloseness to the general image of consumption purveyed by the program and the way in which viewers get caught up in the frenzy of accumulation. From this perspective, the typical, implicitly working-class viewer of HSC suffers from a double lack of discernment: she or he is unable to recognize that the products are not really valuable and is equally unable to establish any distance from the hucksterism and the intensity of the appeals to buy that are at the heart of the program. "Unless you have bionic will power, you can easily find yourself making an unnecessary purchase just because it seems like a 'steal of a deal' (to quote Krista Fordham from HSN) or simply because, like Mount Everest, it's there. After a few impulse buys, addiction begins to take hold."[11]

In these terms, the program and its viewers are readily understood in terms of conventional, denigratory paradigms of feminized masses who readily succumb to the appeals of the media and mass culture.[12] The following highly edited version of one reviewer's perspective on the typical home shopper is representative, if extreme, in this regard.

Who is the typical *Home Shopping Club* shopper? They are those people in restaurants who can't tell if the coffee they're drinking is real or if it's Folger's freeze-dried crystals. They seek to get ahead in the world by studying diesel mechanics, dental hygiene, or welding. They try to draw "Sparky." They buy life insurance from Lorne Greene, Roger Staubach, and Glenn Ford. They are injured in auto accidents and select a personal injury attorney who has an "800" number and who will not charge them anything until they receive a settlement. They enjoy half-time shows. They wear powder blue tuxedos to get married. . . . They call "976" numbers for prerecorded psychic advice from The Tarot of Madame Ruth or Jeanne Dixon. . . . They are called opportunity seekers, in the parlance of direct mail hucksters, and are sent an unending stream of sweepstakes newsletters, easy money wallet inserts, lottery hints, and shopping surveys. . . . They have a W. C. Fields figurine on top of their free-standing veneer liquor cabinet. They have free-standing veneer liquor cabinets. . . . They have "Enquiring" minds. They purchase glamour-length press-on fake fingernails. They made stars out of Dick Van Patten, Slim Whitman, and Ed McMahon. Robert Schuller and Leo Buscaglia tell it like it is. Their personal statements consist of stationery and clothing bearing the logos of teddy bears, cats, rainbows, flowers, unicorns, or a professional sports team. You know the type. Not people like us.[13]

Yet this and similar assessments of HSC and its working-class audience fail to account for the ways in which the program so readily enables, even encourages, the kind of assessment expressed in the cited example. For in a crucial sense, HSC inscribes audiences in relation to bourgeois and working-class taste cultures simultaneously, projecting a certain audience taste culture and its critique simultaneously.

Moreover, all HSC viewers are also addressed and presented as knowledgeable and informed shoppers in general. In conversations between program hosts and shoppers there is a constant dialogue about the quality and value of the products being sold; and viewers always seem to know the "retail price" of any object. In this regard the program projects its viewers as experts who fully understand the larger world of consumerism and the merchandise that circulates within it. Thus, if the program offers the image of a working-class taste culture, the subjects who populate this culture are constructed as discerning, active, and educated consumers. In this sense the program makes working-class taste culture visible and available to its audiences in order to celebrate it, perhaps more readily and directly than most other forms of television programming.

At the same time, as suggested above, the programming plays to the vanity of those who recognize their ostensible superiority to this culture. This further begins to account for viewers who may watch without actually buying anything. For, at an extreme, one can envision the Home Shopping Club viewer as a cross-class voyeur, engaged by the pleasures of consumerist slumming. In promoting these positions as potential viewing stances—celebrating working-class taste culture, promoting the image of educated consumers, and providing an image of working-class taste culture and its participants as inferior "others"—the program itself is complicit in devaluing the very taste culture it also constructs. The whole question of class inscription is thus crucial, but also far more complicated than emerges at first glance, especially in terms of how the network itself and its hosts construct a class position through the accumulation of products resulting in an overarching lifestyle image.

Tensions in the program's representation of the class status and taste culture of its viewer-shoppers is extended in the contradictory ideas of value promoted in the sales strategies of the Home Shopping Club. Ideas of value are constructed in relation to the price of any item, both in absolute terms and in the relative context of a larger national marketplace. Value also unstably circulates in relation to the quality of the products that they sell, in particular the tension between fake and real. Jane Desmond describes how this can function in relation to gemstones and their cubic zirconia doubles:

> Occasionally, lesser-quality versions of real gemstones are offered. And here the patter must tread a narrow line. It must extoll the superiority of the real, without denigrating the limitations which make up most of the inventory. To make the fakes more attractive, nature's mistakes (real rubies are often cloudy) are pitted against the wonders of the imitative (C-Z rubies glow like a fire from within). With the "real" items the word bargain is never used. Price, we are told, is not the important thing here,

but rather "timeless elegance" (i.e., true class). "Nothing's quite so elegant as a diamond ring on your lady's finger." [14]

Desmond understands the display of tension, in this case and others, as a crack in the more consistent illusion of upward mobility promoted by HSC. I would argue that this tension, along with tensions in the class and taste identity of viewers and in ideas of value, are prominently displayed and available for viewers as an essential condition of the popular success of the network. In this sense, cracks in the veneer are the very surface HSC offers to the public, so that all members of the HSC audience can, in one way or another, situate themselves as "in the know."

Value is also constructed as a function of the uncertain and unstable availability of club merchandise. Because they are presented on television, products implicitly belong to the viewing public at large, whose members all have an equal opportunity to participate in club bargains. In this sense, nothing is an exclusive or exceptional value for viewers in general. At the same time, access is restricted to those lucky individuals who are able to get in on the deal by watching at the right time, phoning quickly, and getting through to an operator. The program imposes time constraints, limiting the amount of time an item will be on screen and thus available for purchase. Furthermore, the unpredictability of offerings, unknown quantities, and the difficulty of simply getting through on the busy phone lines contribute to the rarefication of each item, considered on its own. [15] While regular viewers and shoppers know that many club products are offered repeatedly over the course of a week or month, the programming itself is structured in such a way as to intensify the pressure to buy. One can never be sure if this particular ring or doll will be sold out in the next five minutes or if it will be offered for sale half a dozen times in the next few weeks; and in any case, one cannot be sure of being home and watching when it comes back again. If one Capodimonte piece sells out, another—perhaps this time a soup tureen instead of a platter—is sure to appear in the near future.

HSC often inserts an LED counter in the lower right corner of the frame, adding up the total sales for a given item. Another frequently used LED counter is a timer inset in the upper right corner of the frame, showing the time remaining to get in on the current deal. These counters offer a representational measure of the product's power to activate the consuming habits of the HSN audience. In doing so they embody the relation between commodities and desire in relation to an arbitrary idea of time, as they presumably count the increasing power of the product to attract investment in proportion to a diminishing period of availability. The abstraction of temporal determination is enacted when the time is removed from the screen as it approaches zero, while the product continues to sell for longer than originally asserted, but without the benefits of a representation of a standard of measurement. The counters also represent the anxiety of consumption, for a rising number of purchases indicates product popularity and concomitant active phone lines that make it harder to get through. The counters stimulate desire and attach it to a specific product, and at the same time they visibly convey the difficulty of gaining access to the very object thus imbued with the power to attract consumers. This is exacerbated when the process of selling—introducing products and taking them away to replace them with others—goes on twenty-four hours a day.

Yet with all the pressures generated on this basis, the sheer volume of items offered by the Home Shopping Club twenty-four hours a day is very nearly overwhelming, with one "rare" bargain following another. As an ongoing service, the club assures the viewer that there is always something available to buy, even as its sales strategies exacerbate the anxieties of consumption, as the presentation of each item carries the capacity to provoke concerns about whether or not a viewer will be able to get in on each new bargain.

With its bargain-basement production values, random order of sales, and limited purchase time, the Home Shopping Club begins to define the constraining contours of the mode of consumption appropriate to its own success. The strategies for presenting products encourages continual, semiattentive viewing to ensure that one gets the best products the club has to offer. Since viewers can never know for certain when a particular item will be offered for sale, they are challenged to watch as much as possible if they are interested in buying. The phone calls from viewers provide substantiating evidence—by means of a continuous auditory representation of random typical buyers—that the club's most avid shoppers are equally avid viewers who are fully tuned in to the patterns of reception and watching that will encourage their own consuming habits. The phone-in buyers who talk to the sales hosts routinely mention that they turned on the club as soon as they got home from work; that they have been waiting and watching—for days, weeks, or months—for a particular item to (re)appear; or, quite simply, that they now do all their shopping with the club.

With its particular strategies of visual and temporal representation to sell its products, the Home Shopping Network establishes its own internal flow as a function of product space and commodity time. The prevailing shot scale is geared to the size of the items being sold, while temporal duration is influenced by a combination of inventory stock and the number of calls a particular item attracts. These strategies are in many ways similar to those theorized by Tom Gunning in relation to early silent film.[16] For Gunning, early cinema is characterized by a fundamental discontinuity, absence of diegesis, and an emphasis on spectacle in and for itself. This is a "cinema of attractions," characterized by exhibitionism, embodied in the recurring direct looks into the camera by actors. It is a cinema that displays visibility and aggressively solicits the attention of the spectator. Indeed, the cinema of attractions, as Gunning defines it,

> directly solicits spectator attention, inciting visual curiosity, and supplying pleasure through an exciting spectacle—a unique event, whether fictional or documentary, that is of interest in itself. The attraction to be displayed may also be of a cinematic nature, such as the early close-up . . . , or trick films in which cinematic manipula-

tion (slow motion, reverse motion, substitution, multiple exposure) provides the film's novelty.[17]

On HSC, the attractions are the products presented to the viewer for sale, combined with the devices of display discussed earlier in the chapter. One by one, each product presents itself to be viewed by the television audience. Narrative and diegesis are replaced by the spectacle of commodity space-time. This is extended in the movement of products on and off screen: now you see it, now you don't. In the process the relation between the attraction as an aspect of contemporary life—here represented in everyday products and the qualities of televisuality in and of themselves—is immediately tied up with consumer culture. The succession of attractions is presented in order to "shock" viewers into buying what they see on television. Narrative, to the degree that it exists, comes in obliquely, in the voice-over phone calls that viewer-purchasers carry on with program hosts.

Pedagogy in the Television Marketplace

The nature of the merchandise offered and its mode of presentation set forth a version of connoisseurship, contributing to upwardly mobile class aspirations in which all viewers can participate equally—as long as they have access to a television and a telephone.[18] Each item offered for sale is described in detail by the sales host, encouraging an awareness of minimal—at times one might even say irrelevant—traits as signs of superior quality and absolute difference. These descriptions elevate all information to the level of distinction, no matter how common. A viewer can hear that a remarkably ordinary AM/FM radio is UL listed (as are most small electronic appliances sold in the United States). "This means that the Underwriters Laboratories has approved this radio; it has been tested and received the approval of the Underwriters Laboratories," a host intones. Hosts will repeatedly point out the "black onyx eye accents" on a 2 ½-inch lead crystal turtle or wax eloquent over the "Tiffany setting" of a particular cubic zirconia pendant. The close-up scale allows the viewer to discern the differences and variations clearly while the host provides the expert perspective via the vocabulary of discernment. The viewer is invited to participate in an HSC-defined discourse of connoisseurship and expertise. Viewers can see (and learn how to look for) the difference between dolls with painted eyelashes and "real" ones; between marquise, pear, teardrop, and emerald cut cubic zirconia jewels; between gold chains in the diamond cut and those in the box, the serpentine, and the herringbone—or now the snail (to adopt the preferred HSN terminology)—cut.

This scrupulous attention to distinctive detail contributes to repeated consumption and extended accumulation by promoting difference and completeness as two complementary categories of concern for educated consumers. For with a newly acquired understanding of refined detail, viewers may come to recognize the value of having one of each kind of gold chain, different gemstones in the same ring design, or the same gemstone in a range of different cuts. Viewers are also encouraged to assemble full sets because collections are valuable in and of themselves. A viewer may already have the three-carat cubic zirconia ring, appropriate for everyday wear; but the five-carat version is just the thing for an elegant evening on the town. And if you have just ordered the cubic zirconia sapphire earrings for your daughter, wouldn't it be nice to get her the matching pendant? This Capodimonte candlestick, with eleven petals, in the white, with pink accents, will perfectly complement the Capodimonte basket with the three flowers ordered last month. And now HSC is offering a curio cabinet, ideal for displaying the clowns, or perhaps the lead crystal animals, you have been accumulating through the club.

The emphasis on distinguishing minutiae as a reason to possess a particular item works hand in hand with appeals to the collector's mentality, to the pleasure and value of accumulation for its own sake. Connoisseurship is constructed as a strategy of discrimination among products to isolate what is unique to one, at the same time that it encourages collections by the amassing of lots of objects whose distinctiveness lies in small details. Moreover, this emphasis associates the mode of consumption promoted by Home Shopping Club with femininity. The Home Shopping Club thus participates in the history of the detail in art, literature, philosophy, and theory traced by Naomi Schor.[19] Schor argues that while today "the detail enjoys a rare prominence," historically the detail has been viewed with suspicion and hostility.

> To focus on the detail and more particularly on the *detail as negativity* is to become aware, as I discovered, of its participation in a larger semantic network, bounded on the one side by the *ornamental*, with its traditional connotations of effeminacy and decadence, and on the other, by the *everyday*, whose "prosiness" is rooted in the domestic sphere of social life presided over by women. In other words, to focus on the pace and function of the detail since the mid-eighteenth century is to become aware that the normative aesthetics elaborated and disseminated by the Academy and its members is not sexually neutral; it is an axiology carrying into the field of representation the sexual hierarchies of the phallocentric cultural order. The detail does not occupy a conceptual space beyond the laws of sexual difference; the detail is gendered and doubly gendered as feminine.[20]

Schor goes on to argue that modern aesthetics has reclaimed the detail in a process of desublimation, witnessing "a remarkable transvaluation of the detail accompanied by its no less significant degendering."[21]

In the context of the Home Shopping Club, however, there is a peculiar imbrication of idealist and realist aesthetics in which the detail is celebrated precisely in terms of its ornamentality and its everydayness conjoined in consumerist discourse. This postmodern reconfiguration turns the detail back toward the domain of the conventionally "feminine." This is literally figured in the hands that so frequently show up on screen, in close-up, along with the product, with long red gleaming nails. The close-up that reveals the product being sold *in detail* also figures the details of a woman's ornamented body. Metaphor and metonymy are hereby collapsed in the use of details to represent and sell products through the club. The conjunction of femininity, details, and consumerism in these images also recalls the associations of femininity and mass consumer culture.[22] Indeed, in this vein, it is worth noting that Schor includes in her study of the detail a discussion of Duane Hanson, whose sculpted subjects would seem to be the perfect exemplars of the working-class home shopping audience.

These strategies validate consumption in terms beneficial to HSN, and they are extended and personalized in the patter of program hosts and the conversations they hold with call-in shoppers. The hosts, male and female, are usually relatively young (mid-twenties to mid-thirties), though a few of them are somewhat older. They are uniformly enthusiastic, if not downright exuberant, in their promotion of club merchandise. They share a common Home Shopping Club idiolect for describing the items they sell. The slight grammatical awkwardness in their mode of speech works hand in hand with the vocabulary of discernment, as if to say, "When the educated consumer deals with special values, language becomes more studied and technical. We are experts in this area and address you (viewers) as partners in the field of shopping." For example, viewers rarely hear of fourteen-carat gold chains but rather of jewelry "in the fourteen-carat gold." Sales hosts can establish their individuality by adopting catch phrases or themes to incorporate into the standard repertoire of salesmanship. This may involve discussing their families, showing photographs of their children on the air, or answering the phone with a set phrase.

During his programs, host Hans Burt used to include discussions of dinner, inquiring what a given caller ate, or mentioning what his wife served that evening. This individuating line of inquiry was familiar to his viewers, so much so that a phone-in shopper might ask, "Aren't you going to ask me what I had for dinner?," if he failed to pose the question himself. He even made a joke of this, when selling electronic flea collars, asking one customer what her dog had for dinner that evening. Host Krista Fordham would regularly discuss her daughter and occasionally show her daughter's picture for ten or fifteen seconds, interrupting the close-up shot of the items being sold. Hosts' vacation schedules are also part of the ongoing exchange of information with viewers, so that phone-in customers inquire about forthcoming holiday plans or welcome back a favorite host. In this way the club fosters a sense of familiarity between sales hosts and their audience, mimicking the perceived value of personal service promoted by finer department stores. This familiarity is extended when certain hosts attract repeat calls from specific viewers who come to function as shopper-fans. At times, hosts come to recognize callers by their voices or by the way they initiate a phone call. Thus a caller may begin by saying "Hi handsome," and the host will respond, "Oh, Ann. Hello." In such cases program hosts may even remember that the caller previously purchased the item on display and is therefore calling with a shopper's testimonial to confirm the value of the item.[23]

All callers identify themselves by first name and location, and are asked questions from an established litany: What made you decide to buy this item? For whom are you shopping? How long have you shopped with the club? What else have you bought today? Have you enjoyed your club merchandise? The formal patterns of talk that inform these calls are similar to the visual patterns engaged in presenting items for sale. In this sense the calls provide something of an audio model of connoisseurship and accumulation; they are distinctive and personalized only within highly repetitive and formulaic boundaries. One call after another expresses the same thing: enthusiasm for a product, often accompanied by a desire for the host to give an affirming ritual toot on the bicycle horn, and so on. This is in part due to the host's questions that orient the responses from shoppers. But callers frequently launch into a lengthy spiel on the beauty of a particular ring, or praise a great bargain on a brass lamp, with little prompting. In such instances viewer-shoppers participate in the ritual of shopping through Home Shopping Club. Those who are willing to speak on the air readily assume the position of shopping enthusiasts and experts in terms appropriate to the culture of HSC.

The phone calls from viewer-shoppers combine with the descriptive promotions of the hosts to construct verbally the process of consumer culture. Indeed, one of the essential functions of the calls is to directly implicate the club's viewer-shoppers in the process of (re)generating sales. In the course of these conversations, people from all over the country elaborate on why they buy, what they buy, and how they buy. Each call extends and refines the knowledge of the audience as a whole by providing models for consuming habits, and for habitual consumption, from within the confines of one's own home.

Hosts specifically appeal to callers as regional experts who can testify to the quality of club merchandise and are familiar with the consumer market in general. Customers are routinely asked if they have priced a given item in their area, and how much the item would sell for in a retail store. Inevitably, club members insist that even the retail price proposed by HSC is too low, assuring that the discount price is even more of a bargain than it seemed at first. In the process, callers become sales hosts, if only provisionally, encouraging others to participate in the process of shopping with the club.

For example, when the club was selling electronic flea collars, a large number of calls came from repeat buyers. In many cases, they were now purchasing the collars for the pets of relatives and friends. One woman explained that she was planning to use them herself, putting one around each leg to fend off pests when she was outdoors. A few minutes and several phone calls later, another customer referred back to this call, saying that she thought this was a great suggestion and that she was buying two of the flea collars for her sister who had recently moved to Florida and was complaining about the bugs there. The phone calls are thus a key component of the larger process whereby HSN represents the greater culture of shop-at-home consumption, extending well beyond the confines of the TV screen.

The repetition and circulation of shoppers' perspectives validate all purchases and valorize all products while personalizing the Home Shopping Club transaction. The mass buying public, impersonally charted by the on-screen LED counter, is redefined according to its individual members and their personal interchanges with the hosts. Buyers often mention prior conversations with a host that took place weeks, or even months, earlier, just as hosts may recall shoppers they have spoken with previously. And callers regularly confess to spending large amounts of money on club merchandise. Usually this is conveyed as a customer eagerly describes other dolls, jewelry, music boxes, or Capodimonte arrangements already ordered—or lists a range of items purchased that very day.

In one instance, a woman called in with a testimonial for a ring that she already owned—a small sapphire surrounded by even smaller diamonds, costing several hundred dollars. She went on to discuss her buying habits, noting that she had "worn out" all of her credit cards, her phrase for spending up to the assigned credit limit, shopping with the club. However, her husband had seen the ring on the screen and told her about it so that she could call in and share her satisfaction with other viewers and potential buyers. She was also wondering if the host was going to be offering the same ring in the amethyst. For she had ordered it the previous week, unfortunately on one of the "worn out" credit cards, so the order did not go through. Her husband had discovered another credit card since then, and she was still hoping to get the ring in the amethyst. Throughout the call the host responded with support and enthusiasm. "What a nice husband! I'm so glad you enjoy shopping with the club!"

At times like these, the comments by the hosts are subject to being read ironically. Certainly the remarks by the host in this particular case seem somewhat incommensurate with the narrative recounted by the caller, and the encouragement somewhat hollow. Indeed, in the most general sense, the relentless good cheer, loud volume, and arch-enthusiasm of the hosts open the way to variable interpretation. In the hosts' very tone, one may detect a hint of derision or insincerity in almost all of what they say. This is in fact one of the main ways in which the programming can be said not only to construct a forthright image of a certain working-class taste culture but simultaneously to criticize it. On rare occasions, this undertone of derision and insincerity erupts overtly in the comments or reactions of the hosts, establishing a critical distance between the hosts on the one hand and the products they promote and the people who buy them on the other.

For example, in midsummer one of the hosts was selling a music box with an animal design. When the production staff finally figured out how to get it to play in a demonstration, the tune was a Christmas song. This provoked an outburst of hysterical laughter on the part of the host, which lasted for over five minutes, extending into the presentation of the next item for sale. She was so taken aback by the Christmas jingle in a generic-designed music box being sold in July that she could not control herself. When a woman shopper called in with a testimonial about the music box that she had previously purchased, the host's laughter persisted throughout the call and seemed particularly derisive, insofar as it suggested that the music box was a ridiculous item and could not be taken seriously. Yet such overt demonstrations challenging the value and charm of club merchandise on the part of sales hosts are rare. And any suggestion of substantial critical distance and negative valuation of the products is left to be read in the far more ambiguous displays of excessive affect that are more typical of the hosts.

Consuming Confessions

Home Shopping Club viewers are encouraged not only to buy but also to talk about the strategies and tastes that inform their shop-at-home habits. Disclosure begins with the initial purchase, as first-time buyers are subject to substantial marketing research questions by the phone sales operator. After making a purchase, shoppers are then invited to go on the air. The shoppers' confessionals create an impression of avid—even voracious—consumption that is celebrated with the ritual toot of a bicycle horn offered at the end of each phone call. These are so popular that viewers will request extra toots for their children, spouses, and pets.

The best viewer-shoppers are full-fledged fans who vocally express their enthusiasm for, and understanding of, the accumulative possibilities afforded through club membership, in both literal and figurative terms.

The volume of consumption expressed by many of the callers raises questions about the relationship between class identity, actual income, and taste cultures in American society, especially as it is represented on television. On the one hand, there is clearly the possibility that all kinds of people who cannot afford to do so are being provoked to spend lots of money.[24] Here the availability of consumer credit functions in collusion with the program itself, luring viewers with appeals to the value of accumulation for its own sake. On the other hand, it is unreasonable to assume that all, or even the majority, of those who shop with the club spend significantly or dangerously beyond their means or that their relative degree of consumer credit is necessarily worse than that of shoppers with more conventional bourgeois taste who accumulate credit debt at Bloomingdale's, Bonwit Teller, or Marshall Field's. Thus viewers who actively participate in this taste culture may in fact have sufficient disposable income to buy the things they like. From this perspective, the representation of extensive buying and accumulation on the program, including the phone calls, may function as a pleasurable fantasy of accumulative possibility more than a material reality for the majority of home shoppers. This possibility is supported by the fact that the Home Shopping Club is one of the rare places on television where working-class taste culture is so consistently and forthrightly depicted.

The Home Shopping Club clearly proposes an incitement to consumption and accumulation; and it does so in a particularly intense and blatant way. This is supported by appeals to the viewer as a therapeutic subject, a position constructed through the mobilization of shopper confessions as a key component of programming. All viewer-shoppers besides being virtual subjects of consumption also participate in the therapeutic process constructed via the injunction to confess to the sales host and viewing public about their purchases. Indeed, all viewers participate in the therapeutic process, even if they do not buy a thing, as implicit confessor figures who hear the confessions of others.

At the same time, those who confess on the air are also situated as authorities within the culture of consumption, experts who testify to the beauty and value of the products displayed on the air. Indeed, the position of confessing subject— with its tacit working-class identity—is attractive because it simultaneously sanctions all purchases, establishes a personal relation with the sales hosts (a celebrity within the world of HSN), and confers authority on those who speak as knowledgeable subjects. Furthermore, the process of confessing in this way results in a crossing of the lines between personal and public roles. The confession is at once always a public and a personal affair. The confessional discourses thus mobilized suggest that the accumulative possibilities proposed by the Home Shopping Club, whether as fantasy or material reality, fulfill a therapeutic function in consumer culture.

The therapeutic value is confirmed in the phone calls from confessional viewers and shoppers. For the testimonials and endorsements of repeat buyers indicate a community of highly satisfied customers. Over and over again HSC viewers hear of consummated desires. The air ionizer has made people sleep better, be more relaxed, and be less susceptible to colds. People have received endless, and envious, compliments on a ring; and no one can tell the difference between the cubic zirconia diamond and the "real thing." Viewer-shoppers become so well versed with the club's codes and routines that hosts barely have to ask questions to provoke perfect responses from callers. One man, buying a porcelain bridal doll, explains with almost no prompting that he is getting it for his wife who has been wanting a bridal doll, that this one is just beautiful, and that his wife has been collecting dolls "ever since you've been offering them on the club."

Moreover, with its unending stock of costume jewelry, collectibles, and decorative *objets*, the club represents its target viewer-consumers as prevailingly working-class women. While fishing rods, hand drills, and attaché cases are included in the club inventory, they do not begin to compete with the female-oriented consumer products in sheer volume or variety. This fact is confirmed by phone calls, which are overwhelmingly from women buyers.

HSC buyers are situated in specific social contexts, as the sales hosts reinforce conventional ideas about how products may be used within familiar networks of family and social relations. One way this is achieved is through the identification of potential recipients for different items in the form of helpful hints. A briefcase is proposed as the ideal gift for a husband or for a son or nephew going off to college in the fall. A glass and brass trinket box is described as a nice item for an aunt or a teacher. Predictably, these pitches increase at identified gift-giving seasons: Christmas, Mother's Day, graduation, etc. Callers are regularly asked for whom they have purchased an item as well as why they decided to buy the particular item and whether they have priced it elsewhere.

Shopping is thus construed as an activity that *naturally* has social implications, indeed is firmly based in social and familial relations. In turn, confessional viewers readily reconfirm the social relations of the shopping transaction. All of this combines in an overall impression that women do most of the buying in the household because they are the active center of social-familial networks of exchange, constantly looking out for the appropriate things to give to the right people within the family circle—a circle whose definition seems largely shaped by consumption via HSC.

The club represents the exemplary viewer-consumers that have made it successful as members of a larger community of desire that everyone can join. Anyone can share equally in the taste culture, the bargains, and perhaps the consumer debt that the club promotes. Viewer-shoppers are applauded for acting to fulfill their desires through a process of accumulation that will never be complete because there is always another Capodimonte piece, music box, or household gadget to be purchased. There is always another occasion that warrants a gift for a spouse, relative, friend, or even oneself. With their personal phone calls and cheery enthusiasm, the sales hosts are incorporated into the domestic and social circles that are the context for the ever-expanding consuming possibilities offered by HSC. Individual purchases are constantly (re)defined in terms of extended networks of familial relations. Even if a caller buys something for herself, it is going to contribute to the beauty or comfort of the home, or the purchase is possible because of the generosity of a husband who granted the use of yet another credit card. Moreover, once something is purchased, a daughter, uncle, or out-of-town friend who sees it will surely want to own one too. This encourages viewers to continue to watch and wait for items to reappear on the Home Shopping Club, so they can be ordered again.

With consumption literally based in the home, the female consumer—situated in these familial and social networks—becomes the focus for regenerating consuming desires. HSC offers a therapeutic discourse that circulates in relation to the family, home, and consumerism. The Home Shopping Club's strategies for representing patterns of consumption and its modes of address aid and abet this process. The pleasures of consumption and accumulation for their own sakes combine with the possibility of recognizing that, and how, consuming habits connect viewer-shoppers to a larger community of desire, national in scope but brought together by the club. The viewer-shopper is not isolated in the home. On the contrary, shopping from the home with the club may be more personal and community-oriented than an afternoon at the local shopping mall. For here the viewer shares the experience with a host, who may even remember the last time she called, and with other shoppers who are part of the common culture of shop-at-home consumption.

The Home Shopping Club and its parent, the Home Shopping Network, represent the pleasures of buying in the very process of selling their merchandise. Their program constantly reconfirms the value of staying home and watching television—HSC in particular—as the best way to secure familial and communal relations; it also validates the position of women as the center of these relations. Thus the history of twentieth-century consumer culture is positively reinforced for a contemporary generation of participants. With these emphases, conventional forms of entertainment and information programming are not necessary as the alibi or lure that situates all viewers as virtual subjects of consumption. In the world according to HSC, the television apparatus affords direct participation in the pleasures of personal and economic exchange to consolidate the family as the subject of an improved standard of living, while more conventional television programming offers these pleasures only in more vicarious forms.

A Traffic in Souls

Televangelism and *The 700 Club*

And Now On CBN . . .

And now on CBN, an up-close look at the events
shaping our lives on *The 700 Club*: . . . There are
more homeless people today than at any time
since the depression. . . . If you have children
at home, you'll want them to watch. We'll be
meeting a woman who's put a new twist in fairy
tales. . . . Wall Street has opened 1987 with a
bang. How high can the stock market go? . . .
Howard Finkel's submission to peer pressure led
to a lifestyle destined for death. . . . On today's
special edition of *The 700 Club* we'll be discussing
AIDS, whether or not kids should face manda-
tory AIDS education in school; and we will meet
someone dying of AIDS, and open phone lines for
questions to the Surgeon General. . . . The question before us today is: Can the American military
survive without South Africa's precious metals?
Sanctions may backfire against the U.S. . . . Is the
church pushing away many who desperately need
to hear God's message of love and forgiveness?
Find out on today's special program, "A Time for
Action."[1]

The 700 Club is a religious television program produced by the CBN Family Channel, formerly the Christian Broadcasting Network.[2] It is aired daily on the Family Channel, broadcast on independent stations across the United States, and distributed internationally. Adopting a news magazine format, it includes reports on current events, lifestyle features, human interest stories, and celebrity and expert guests, along with prayer, healing rituals, religious teaching, appeals to conversion, and fund-raising. With this combination, *The 700 Club* (along with its parent cable network) represents one version of a model media system from the perspective of the Christian Right.[3] Fully integrated in the discursive and institutional practices of contemporary American television, it aims to provide an overarching, morally correct perspective on the world in concert with the evangelical call to save souls.

Ideally *The 700 Club* is intended for everyone, or anyone who happens to watch the show, whether the person purposefully tuned in to participate in the born-again Christian fundamentalism it celebrates or chanced upon it while changing channels. This virtual inclusivity is inscribed in the program with its wide variety of features, among which are celebrity interviews, advice on money and time management, stories on relevant social issues (such as the homeless, AIDS, and drug abuse), and features on the fashion industry. But this generality of topics—familiar in its reduplication of mass culture issues—is regularly and quickly reoriented to serve the interrelated religious, political, social, and cultural requirements of CBN as a fundamentalist Christian institution. The program thus sets in place a shifting balance in its terms of address, moving between a version (or the appearance) of the broad marketplace of ideas that is typical of American television as a whole and the more consciously and narrowly focused concerns of conservative Protestant fundamentalism.[4]

Ultimately the possibility for enacting a transformation on this order is supported—even structured—by the repeated deployment of confessional strategies of discourse, in the dramatized stories of individual salvation that offer a personalized model of a larger and more abstract religious injunction. Confessional discourse is promoted as a religious ritual, a narrational strategy, and a therapeutic procedure, all of which are intertwined and interdependent spheres in the world according to *The 700 Club*. Therefore an analysis of the program's particular constructions of confession, which include regulated mediations and negotiated hierarchies, provides one way into the mechanisms of financial, symbolic, and imaginary investments that sustain the CBN. With this emphasis we can trace the interrelations and interdependencies of fantasy, therapy, consumerism, television, and fundamentalism that organize the program. Moreover, through the conjunctions and disjunctions of these discourses, the status of *The 700 Club* as an instance of contemporary American television—as an extended reduplication and an alternative version thereof—may become clear.[5] Before looking more closely at the program itself, and its intertwining of fundamentalism with strategies of commercial television, meeting in the therapeutic discourse of confession, it will be useful to situate the program in the larger institutional context of televangelism and the CBN organization. For although *The 700 Club* is distinctive, its strategies are exemplary of the vicissitudes of American televangelism in general since the 1960s.

In the course of the 1980s, televangelism came to represent a highly visible and controversial aspect of religious broadcasting in the United States. The growth of cable and independent stations since the 1960s, concomitant relaxation in Federal Communications Commission regulations, and the prominence of the religious Right in the political arena since the late 1970s contributed to public familiarity with such media ministers as Jim Bakker, Jerry Falwell, Oral Roberts, Pat Robertson, and Jimmy Swaggart.[6] While fundamentalism, evangelicalism, and religious broadcasting have their own histories, television's "evangelical upsurge" generated widespread attention in popular and academic religious, political, and media circles.[7] The most visible religious programs that emerged on American television in this context did not represent mainstream Protestant religious practice; instead they featured evangelical Protestantism with a fundamentalist or Pentecostal emphasis. In this sense, the conservative religious doctrine purveyed by the programs embraces a popular, conservative religious subculture.

In part the success of televangelism in the United States can be attributed to the ability of a particular group of religious broadcasters to exploit television as an apparatus of mainstream popular culture in order to give visibility and voice to a popular religious subculture. At the same time, this group of broadcasters also succeeded in affiliating their subcultural religious doctrine with resurgent conservative social and political agendas in mainstream American politics in the 1980s. In the process, through the articulations with conservative politics and television (along with other aspects of American consumer culture), fundamentalism itself was able to take on the appearance of a dominant cultural practice. Yet even with this newfound prominence, televangelism continues to be strongly based in fundamentalist/evangelical/Pentecostal religious practices that remain subcultural (rather than dominant or mainstream) religious formations.

Many of the most prominent televangelists are not only media personalities but also preside over extensive religious corporate empires that include social, educational, cultural, and political activities on a national and global scale.[8] Jerry Falwell, minister of the Liberty Baptist Church in Lynchburg, Virginia, and host of *The Old Time Gospel Hour*, is the founder of Moral Majority and also runs Liberty Baptist College. Jim Bakker, former chairman and president of the PTL (Praise the Lord/People That Love) Television Network, produced *The PTL Club* (popularly known as *The Jim and Tammy Show*), ran a cable network, and developed Heritage USA, a Christian theme park and resort hotel in South Carolina. When he resigned in March 1987, in the wake of family problems, financial scandal, and an alleged takeover attempt, Jerry Falwell assumed interim chairmanship of the PTL board of directors at Bakker's request. The PTL has since been effectively disbanded. Oral Roberts, host of his own television show, is head of a university that bears his name, and has built a major hospital and medical research center. Thus for most of the prominent televangelists, some version of fundamentalist religious belief provides the organizing focus and starting point for a wide range of activities requiring continual fund-raising to sustain the scope of their outreach.

All of these institutions, along with the TV programs that have made these televangelists media stars, are privately financed, largely by contributions from the television audience. A constant flow of donations and influx of new supporting members are required to maintain and expand these programs, both on and off television. Efforts to increase viewership, and to increase donations from established viewers, are the central means of economic support. Of course this is true in principle for all of American television, even if the specific circuits of exchange may vary. In the case of commercial stations, advertising rates, and thus potential profits, are calculated in relation to audience numbers and demographics; cable stations rely on audience subscriptions to determine profits and losses; and public television stations combine corporate sponsorship with limited advertising and direct appeals to viewers for contributions with periodic telethons or TV auctions. In the case of paid-time religious broadcasting, viewer donations are the primary source of income.[9] In all cases, the principle of competition for viewers who will pay for programming—directly or indirectly—is the same. This competition also involves identifying or defining particular subgroups within the viewing public as a whole as the target audience for particular kinds of programming.

As a religious media empire, CBN and the Family Channel have been exemplary of developments in religious broadcasting since the 1960s and represent one of the largest televangelical organizations operating in the United States and abroad. However, *The 700 Club*, the primary religious program produced and aired by the network, is not the stereotypical preacher show. Structured by the conventions of the news magazine show, it offers itself as a program with a broad-based potential appeal. Its verbal and visual strategies are designed to be familiar to all regular television viewers. Indeed, if one were to rely on its introductory teasers announcing the featured stories of the current episode, one might be hard pressed to distinguish *The 700 Club* from such programs as *Good Morning America*, *Hour Magazine*, *PM Magazine*, or *Donahue*. And these associations are hardly accidental, but are rather an integral strategy of the program's evangelical mission.

Televangelism and the CBN Organization

The Christian Broadcasting Network, presided over by Marion G. "Pat" Robertson, is an exemplary organization within the context of corporate televangelism. CBN is perhaps most widely identified with its cable station, the CBN Family Channel, which provides twenty-four-hour-a-day programming on many cable systems in the United States. It is distributed free of charge to cable operators on the satellites that are sources for some of the most popular cable services, including Home Box Office, Cinemax, MTV, and C-Span. But CBN more generally sponsors a range of educational, media, and welfare initiatives. Along with *The 700 Club*, CBN produces a number of original television programs. *The 700 Club* is distributed worldwide, including in Canada, El Salvador, Japan, Nigeria, and the Philippines. CBN's global operations include Middle East Television, a station run by CBN in southern Lebanon since 1982, along with international radio broadcasts, ministry centers, and videotape distribution. CBN University is a graduate school in Virginia Beach, Virginia, the home base of CBN operations, offering degrees in biblical studies, business, communications, education, journalism, law, and public policy. CBN is the publisher and promoter of *The Book*, a popularized and modernized version of the Bible designed to encourage mass readership. Operation Blessing is an umbrella organization for CBN charity projects, started in 1978. It provides support for shelters, soup kitchens, and similar charitable institutions; sponsored a literacy program; and participated in such activities as the 1986 wheat convoys from the Midwest to farmers in southern states suffering from drought. CBN also runs a twenty-four-hour prayer-counselor phone service providing support, advice, and consolation to people with problems.

In addition to ongoing social and educational projects, CBN regularly launches specific campaigns in line with its national and global religious mission. Such programs allow the organization to respond to specific perceived social and political agendas over time. And insofar as they require new infusions of funding, they also fit into the consumerist imperative to renew marketing strategies. For example, to mark the twenty-fifth anniversary of CBN in 1986, CBN initiated Operation Good Shepherd, a national public relations campaign to promote wider general religious participation. Through this project, CBN offered media packages to churches and religious groups across the country to encourage active attendance and involvement. The media kits included designs for billboards, radio spots, and newspaper advertising that the local organizations could readily adapt for use in their own communities. While Operation Good Shepherd required extensive financial support—and provided the occasion for intensified fund-raising by CBN—it can be seen as a response to critics who often charge the televangelists with displacing local churches and community involvement with impersonal media ministries.[10] All of these programs and social services are widely promoted on *The 700 Club* as part of the issues actually addressed on the show, as well as in the form of advertisements. *The 700 Club* viewer is thus familiar with the full range of activities undertaken by CBN at large.

The 700 Club is the centerpiece of CBN activities. Self-styled as an alternative to mainstream American commercial television, *The 700 Club* and the cable network that carries it reproduce the strategies and formats of the institution it critiques. Drawing on the fantasies of plenitude and fulfillment that effectively structure consumer culture, the program offers itself and its parent corporation, CBN, as the agency of salvation, with a traffic in souls rather than consumer products. In the process, *The 700 Club* addresses a constituted conservative religious subculture of viewers (a subculture it shares with other fundamentalist or evangelical religious television programs) but also aims to attract all of its potential viewers—all television viewers in general—to join this subculture. The challenge it thus establishes for itself is to effect a transformation on the part of the television audience from partial or potential religious belief (or even nonbelief) to a full commitment to the version of Christianity espoused by Pat Robertson, head of CBN, and his *700 Club* co-hosts. In the most general sense, the very regularity and familiarity of the program contributes to this goal, as the hosts effectively create the impression that they speak for, and to, millions of people who share their perspectives and beliefs.

As a daily program with a news magazine format, *The 700 Club* readily accommodates the publicity and fund-raising requirements of CBN. Whole weeks at a time can be devoted to fund-raising when desirable, and on a day-to-day basis feature stories and commercial breaks highlight CBN projects and appeal to viewers for contributions.[11] For example, in the fall of 1986, Operation Good Shepherd was introduced in the course of two weeks of special event programming on *The 700 Club*. During the first week, "Seven Days Ablaze," Pat Robertson and his co-hosts celebrated the twenty-fifth anniversary of CBN with a call for national and international religious revival, including regular segments on revival movements in history and the contemporary importance of praise and prayer.

Throughout the week, viewers were urged to participate in this spiritual awakening by becoming CBN prayer partners, pledging fifteen minutes of prayer a day at a fixed time. Prayer, like broadcast programming, is here fit into established and regular daily time slots, to assure full twenty-four-hour coverage. Banks of busy telephone operators were prominently featured, with volunteers constantly on the lines. Program co-hosts Ben Kinchlow and Danuta Soderman reported on the stream of incoming calls: "A woman from Ohio is going to pray every day from 7:00 to 7:15"; "Here's a call from Houston, Texas, praying from 8:00 to 8:15." Along with prayer pledges, prayer requests, involving every sort of spiritual, physical, and material need, were also received by phone and mail. The magnitude of the need for prayer was continually dramatized by the constant phone activity and by the piles of mail heaped on the table and floor of the studio where Pat, Ben, and Danuta met with guests and sat to lead the studio and home audiences in prayer.

The second week formally initiated fund-raising efforts for Operation Good Shepherd, building on the established pattern and momentum of phone-in pledges from the previous week, as viewers were urged to give $100.00 to support the new project. (Of course, all the phone calls from the previous week also provided CBN with names and addresses to add to their computerized mailing lists, another important source for targeting potential donors.) Over the course of the week, Pat reviewed the various projects supported by CBN and lectured on the biblical context for, and the pragmatic implications of, the new CBN initiative. Thus, in a very pointed way, spiritual and financial investment were conjoined as two necessary and related contributions to the larger goal of national and international religious revival: we need you to pray and we need your money. In this case, the consistent telethon format over the course of the two weeks stressed the continuity in spiritual and financial fellowship.

More often, appeals for donations and for spiritual participation are subsumed in the course of regular *700 Club* programming. Thus, for example, in a series of stories dealing with the problem of the homeless, a pretaped segment told the story of a destitute man in Tampa, Florida, who was fed and clothed by a Christian soup mission whose assistance eventually led to his personal salvation. This story was intercut with a report on the Christian ministry that runs the soup kitchen in question—which is supported in part by CBN's Operation Blessing—and discussion of how the audience could contribute to such efforts. Here, the ministry work of CBN, individual salvation, worldwide salvation, and financial support are brought together in the context of an in-depth examination of a current social issue (the homeless) that requires concern and attention and in relation to the personal story of one man's transformation from poverty and despair to material and spiritual security.

In drawing together these concerns, *The 700 Club* engages topics and rhetorical strategies that are familiar to all viewers in the sense that they are already found in American media culture more generally. Not only the homeless but also South Africa, AIDS, stress, drugs, peer pressure, and the World Series are among the consuming interests of the American media. *The 700 Club* offers itself as one voice among many others to further viewer knowledge and awareness of the world through information and entertainment programming. The fact that almost all of these issues are developed, one way or another, in terms of a conservative political perspective and fundamentalist Christian faith normalizes the program's status within television. It demonstrates that fundamentalism does not require giving up concern with ongoing events and issues in the world, while drawing on the form and substance of regular commercial television programming (both broadcast and cable.) It simultaneously supports the very idea of pluralism in television, as the program offers itself as one free voice among many in a democratic medium, precisely through emphasizing the particularity of the voice of CBN and *The 700 Club* within the pluralistic media chorus.[12]

Family Programming

In the context of contemporary American television, the Family Channel promotes itself as an alternative to mainstream American media systems, fulfilling the moral and ethical requirements of a religiously committed audience. Publicity material distributed by CBN explicitly defines the philosophy of the network in these terms: "Sometimes, turning on your television can be depressing. Many of today's programs are saturated with violence, sexual immorality, and greed—attitudes that begin to slowly wear on your sense of well-being. The CBN Cable Network is an alternative to those programs: It's a network committed solely to family programming."[13] CBN identifies the network with morality, wholesomeness, the family, and enduring values, presumably in distinction to the rest of commercial television. Both in its programming and in its publicity (primarily direct mail), CBN heavily promotes itself in terms of its difference from the networks and other commercial stations. For on its cable network, wholesome family values are not restricted to designated dayparts, as is the case in network programming and nomenclature, but subsume the whole programming schedule. Indeed, this emphasis is signaled by the change in the network name, from CBN to the Family Channel, emphasizing the broad-based appeal the network might have for everyone concerned with the family. (This name change also follows on the heels of the televangelical scandals of the mid-1980s; and it seems as well to exploit demographic trends in the United States that identify the marketing appeal and importance of rising birth rates, especially among the professional middle class, and the so-called new nesting instinct that keeps these middle-class families at home.) However, an examination of CBN programming makes it clear that differences between the CBN network and commercial television in general are both variable and relative.

Programming on the Family Channel is not restricted to religious shows. During the week *The 700 Club* is shown a number of times each day. Early-morning programming is devoted to religious shows and children's programs created by CBN and other religious groups (*Superbook*, *Flying House*, and *Davey and Goliath*), and the rest of the schedule features syndicated reruns of television series representing a wide range of genres (including, over the past few years, *Hazel*, *Father Knows Best*, *The Flying Nun*, *The Big Valley*, *Remington Steele*, *Dobie Gillis*, and *Burns and Allen*) and movies.[14] Weekend programming is similarly filled with syndicated reruns and movies, including a large number of westerns, with a range of religious programs concentrated in the morning and late-night hours. (Most of these are not produced by the CBN organization, but feature other televangelists such as John Ankerberg, Kenneth Copeland, James Robison, and Jimmy Swaggart.) The Family Channel also sponsors a number of family-oriented, first-run, off-network programs. In 1990, these included two situation comedies: *Brother Jake*, about a multiracial (and multireligious) foster home, and *Maniac Mansion*, starring Joe Flaherty, perhaps best known for his work on *SCTV*.

With the Family Channel's schedule dominated by syndicated reruns, the difference between CBN and other independent stations seems minimal. There is a larger concentration of programs from the 1950s and 1960s on CBN than is found on most other stations. This creates a program flow that might be characterized, on balance, as wholesome and nostalgic, expressing CBN's moral difference from the rest of television in terms of temporal distance. Rhetorical literalism hereby props up alterity, as old-fashioned family values and morality are represented on the CBN network in programs from the "good old days." But this equation is both partial and unstable. For CBN is not the only network that shows programs from the 1950s and 1960s, and the CBN schedule includes programs of far more recent vintage. More importantly, the CBN programming strategy reproduces and extends that of television as a whole, with its regular exhibition of old and new shows, repeats and premieres, as simultaneous choices within the overall programming schedule.[15] Especially in the context of cable (which gives viewers a wide range of commercial, network, independent, public, and pay services), the Family Channel does not immediately stand out as exceptional.

For example, albeit an extreme one, at one point, at 7:00 P.M. on weekdays, CBN was showing *Hardcastle and McCormick* while *Airwolf* was on USA, *Marcus Welby, M.D.* was on Lifetime, and WTBS showed *Sanford and Son* and *The Honeymooners*. At the same time, other stations were broadcasting a variety of current and rerun shows, including *M*A*S*H*, *Barney Miller*, *Entertainment Tonight*, *Wheel of Fortune*, and *The People's Court*. The CBN selection in this case was neither the oldest nor the most traditional program available for viewing, and it was hardly the least violent among the viewing options.[16] At another extreme, Nickelodeon—a cable service that programs primarily for children—has an evening lineup of popular programming from the 1960s that it aggressively promotes in terms of hip nostalgia, appealing widely to an audience of adults who grew up on these shows, as well as to their children, and contemporary college students. Thus the CBN Family

Channel provides wholesome, alternative entertainment that is fully in fee to mass consumer culture as produced and represented by television itself and its history. Even with the preponderance of relatively older programs (which, from an economic standpoint, may be the only way the network can afford to offer regular, twenty-four-hour programming), CBN fully participates in commercial television culture, in which the old and the new are systemically integrated as simultaneous and mutually supporting categories.[17] (Indeed, many television scholars and nostalgia buffs see the CBN Family Channel as a valuable cultural resource.)

Yet this retrospective impulse, however partial and unstable, does provide an anchoring point for the network's efforts to represent an alternative set of choices within contemporary television culture. The very concentration of shows from the 1950s and 1960s stands as a sign of a preferable era, when the traditional nuclear family was the unquestioned social norm and American's role as a dominant world power was unchallenged. Within the confines of commercial consumer culture, the presentation of television's historical, nostalgic texts supports a retrospective social and cultural myth, which in turn helps to define CBN's contemporary function: the CBN Family Channel perpetuates and reinvigorates the (purported) values of the era that produced these shows.

That these values can be and are active in the present, and how they are active, is precisely the purview of *The 700 Club*, as familial and interpersonal relations, consumer lifestyles, and current events are examined in relation to fundamentalism. The tensions and contradictions that situate televangelism and the CBN Family Channel are equally apparent, perhaps even more concentrated, in *The 700 Club*. At stake here is the program's status as an alternative, a difference that is both variable in nature and relative in degree.

The Religious Calling

In some ways *The 700 Club* is absolutely predictable and homogeneous: whatever issues it raises, whatever stories it tells, it will always end up expressing the archconservative social and political values associated with the religious Right and justifying the fundamentalist interpretation of the Bible as the absolute truth of God's word. The program is virulently anticommunist and aggressively profamily, and it endorses the political and social policies affiliated with these positions. In news perspectives, Pat Robertson warns of the consequences of economic sanctions against South Africa; supports home-work policies as a way of enabling, even encouraging, women to stay at home while they earn a living (ignoring the low wages and lack of benefits that are characteristic of home-work); and uses a news story on a CIA defector to express his support of American covert action operations around the world.

The show's hosts and guests repeatedly diagnose social and cultural ills, announcing that mainstream secular society is godless, materialistic, and humanistic; that its culture is pervaded by greed, violence, and pessimism; and that we all live in a media world that fosters negativism, secular humanism, and despair. The proof of this pervasive degeneracy and decay is found in alcoholism, drug abuse, the divorce rate, child abuse, homosexuality, teen suicide, and so on. Only God and the Bible can solve problems. It is necessary to pray for forgiveness and accept Jesus as a personal savior in order to be born again. Only then will problems cease, as individuals are healed through the force of God's love. Jesus is the answer to all problems—spiritual, emotional, material, and physical, if one devotes one's life to him. Indeed, prayer solves very nearly every problem an individual might encounter: "Prayer is answered. Relationships restored. The hungry are fed. The naked clothed. The homeless given shelter. The lost are saved. The sick are healed. The lonely are loved . . ."[18]

These are the pervasive ideas and perspectives expressed on *The 700 Club*. To describe the program in these terms is to summarize its dominant, fundamentalist religious discourse and to explain how it speaks to the already-converted. For viewers who share the religious convictions and/or the conservative political ideology of *The 700 Club*, the show validates their beliefs. Even in these terms the audience is, already, potentially divided (a division that is by no means absolute) between fundamentalists who follow Pat Robertson's ministry but do not necessarily subscribe to his political agenda (or all aspects thereof), and political-social conservatives who do not necessarily participate fully in the version of religion practiced by the program (which, for example, includes electronic faith healing). At the same time, *The 700 Club* presents many of its stories as issues of current, general, social and political interest. In this it strategically acknowledges and addresses an even broader potential viewing audience. This is not a narrow fundamentalism that ignores the world around it. Rather, public leaders, best-selling authors, sports stars, rock musicians, health experts, financial advisers, and marriage counselors are among the guests regularly included on the program.

The news magazine format itself provides a context for inscribing multiple and divided terms of audience address in the interest of conquering all potential viewers in the name of fundamentalism. *The 700 Club* often highlights a particular topic or issue, which is then developed through a series of program segments—a news report, an interview with an expert, and a profile of an individual implicated in the issue at hand. (The issue may be youth gangs, the problem of the homeless, or AIDS.) The profile usually deals with an exemplary ordinary citizen who has dealt with the problem at hand and found a solution in religion, someone who has been born again. This often leads directly into the evangelical focus of the show, as Pat Robertson or one of his co-hosts directly addresses the television audience and urges viewers to pray with him, accepting Christ as their personal savior. This appeal is initially specified in terms of the issue of the day and then generalized to include anyone who wants to pray. The prayer is in turn followed by an invitation to call CBN's 800 number to ask for the free pamphlet "What Now?" This is, of course, also a way of adding to the computerized mailing lists CBN uses for fund-raising. "You call and tell them, 'I just prayed with Pat, and I want to know what to do next.'"

This development is typical (although it is not followed on every episode of the show), and allows the program to balance general appeal with its prescribed religious imperatives. While all issues and topics serve, at one point or another, as Christian moral lessons, they are nonetheless presented in terms of their broader interest and implications. In the process, the issues are also elaborated in a variety of generic formats: the impersonal news perspective is recast in the terms of an informal discussion with an expert and/or an individual melodrama. This contributes to the potential appeal of the program, as individual members of the audience may be engaged by the generic formulation with which they are most comfortable—news and/or melodrama, the expert interview and/or the personal confession.

In orchestrating these different forms, the program may also introduce variable and conflicting points of view, in spite of the hegemonic religious conservatism that determines its production. And this does not usually occur because the guests introduce dissonant points of view. On the contrary, the experts and celebrities who appear on the program are very nearly uniform in representing and endorsing a conservative evangelical perspective. Rather, in the course of offering multiple generic versions of the same event, the program itself, as a source of narration, and its hosts are often forced to assume a variety of positions in relation to the material; and this can lead to a sense of disjunction and disunity. In such cases, the program's use of varying generic forms of narration produces a simulated pluralism that functions as a patina over an essential univocal position on issues.

For example, this was especially evident in an episode devoted to the issue of AIDS. The program began with a news story on the surgeon general's report on AIDS and the controversy it aroused in the Reagan administration over the question of sex education in schools. The news story included extensive discussion of criticism that had been leveled at the report by conservatives, while merely noting that it had been by and large endorsed by liberals. In particular the news story harped on the fact that one specific sentence in the report— "The best way to avoid AIDS is a mutually faithful monogamous relationship"—had been subject to criticism because it did not include "heterosexuality" as a modifier. The reporter also noted that several groups were concerned with the recommendation that condoms be used during sex to prevent the spread of AIDS, since condoms are not 100 percent reliable. The news story even included a quote from *The Advocate*, identified as "a national gay magazine," to support this criticism. (Of course, *The Advocate* is not a regular source of authoritative citation on *The 700 Club*.)

The news report was followed by a live studio interview with Surgeon General C. Everett Koop. Danuta Soderman led the interview; then she opened phone lines for viewers to call in questions and was joined by co-host Ben Kinchlow. Throughout this segment of the show, first Danuta, and then Ben, took up the voice of conservative criticism defined in the news story, as they posed questions implicitly critical of the surgeon general for being too liberal and soft on the issue of AIDS. Ben suggested that "mutually faithful monogamous relationship" should have been specified as a *heterosexual* and *marital* relation.

Danuta was even more aggressive in her criticism. At one point she challenged Koop for not recommending that people with the AIDS virus be tracked through sexual partners, like people with venereal diseases. She even suggested that perhaps people with AIDS should be quarantined to protect the rest of the population. Koop replied that it was impossible to quarantine 3 million people in the first place and that there were all sorts of people who would like to see others quarantined for one reason or another. Danuta responded emphatically, "We're not talking about politics here. We're talking life and death!" Thus through the course of the news report and the interviews, *The 700 Club* conveyed the impression that the proper Christian attitude to assume in relation to the AIDS issue is hard-line, conservative, and aggressively judgmental.

Later the show featured the story of a (born-again) man who is dying of AIDS. In a pretaped profile, viewers were told that Mark Perry learned he had AIDS three years after quitting "that lifestyle" (i.e., homosexuality) and six months after his marriage to Shireen. A live satellite interview with the Perrys followed the taped sequence. In the course of the discussion the Perrys stressed the support and understanding they had received from their friends, colleagues, and church group. Both Ben and Danuta exhibited sympathy and concern for the couple and posed questions that would lead the Perrys to speak of their faith and of the compassion they had been shown by the religious community. In particular Danuta asked, "We so often hear of people who have AIDS being rejected and spurned by society. Why is your case different?" Shireen answered that their friends walk in the steps of the Lord, and thus show compassion and love. The interview also included the pastor of the Perry's church, who emphasized the church's need to be informed, indeed to take the lead in ministering to AIDS victims and the gay community. Here Ben and Danuta, as representatives for CBN and the program, promote a different Christian perspective from the one heard only moments earlier in the show. Now, it seems, the proper Christian attitude is one of charity, forgiveness, and compassion.

Through the course of a single program, the voice assumed by Ben and Danuta in relation to the issue of AIDS changes from judgmental extremism to sympathetic concern. At one moment they advocate the harshest possible repressive measures; at another they promote Christian love and support for those suffering from AIDS. This shift can be accounted for in a number of ways. It indicates a division between an impersonal social perspective that allies AIDS with the homosexual lifestyle vilified by fundamentalism (even as the disease is recognized to have implications for the population at large) and a personalized empathy that can be extended to individual victims of the disease, *especially* if they have already been born again. This could also be seen as an indication of how well the evangelical community supports its own members, no matter what they may have done in the past. Thus, the humane concern and divine forgiveness expressed during the interview with the Perrys is not necessarily generalizable to the community of everyone suffering from AIDS, especially those whose sexual preferences or habits are at odds with the tenets of fundamentalism (including homosexuals, the sexually promiscuous, and drug users).

Yet the transformation in tone, particularly on the part of

Ben and Danuta, remains striking. Early on, Danuta quite vehemently promotes quarantine as a viable way of handling the problem of AIDS. Later, when talking to Mark Perry, she sympathetically discusses problems of individuals with AIDS who are rejected by society, as if she had not already implicated herself in that group through her quarantine argument with Koop. This occurs in the continuity of a live-on-tape program; both interviews, with Koop and with Mark Perry, are presented as taking place live, in the same present tense of the program. Ben and Danuta even go so far as to ask questions of Mark Perry that suggest he should be dissatisfied with God, because his religion has not done enough to help him. Ben, for example, asks him if he was counting on a miraculous healing and is disappointed that it has not (yet) come. And one wonders how someone who recommends quarantine measures for AIDS victims can later imply that some people with AIDS experience a cruel and heartless rejection by society, as if she had not already shown herself to be one of those who would reject and spurn individuals suffering from the disease.

Thus even within the context of a unifying fundamentalist grounding, *The 700 Club* does not escape the pluralism of positions, however limited, that characterizes American television in general. Adherence to fundamentalist doctrine and belief in Jesus Christ as a personal savior may be the solution to all problems; but in the face of a complex and contradictory world this does not guarantee that the issues are clear-cut. God's word is absolute, but the secular world is not. It is because of this worldly complexity that a show like *The 700 Club* is necessary in the first place; and the program implicates itself in this complexity in direct proportion to its engagement with the genres and issues of commercial media.

The program situates itself as a link between the divine and the earthly, as the agency translating the one for the other. As the public media leaders of CBN, the program hosts carry the absolute truth, leading the audience in prayer and offering "words of knowledge" from God that speak of miraculous healing. But as television talk show interviewers, the same co-hosts ask leading questions and play devil's advocate to *The*

700 Club guests and each other. In the process they relativize their own positions, if only provisionally, introducing multiple and alternative perspectives, even adopting the roles of naive listeners who need to be instructed.

For example, in the course of one show Ben will authoritatively explain that we must believe in miracles in our lives—miracles that will heal the faithful of chronic disease, reunify broken homes, and cure drug addiction—because it is given as a truth in the Bible, from which he will quote various passages as evidence. In another episode Pat will speak for the power of miracles, and Ben will pose naive, leading questions, implying that he does not quite understand what Pat is saying. Here, the familial talk show format offers a comfortable and familiar position for the viewer, who may identify with either the authoritative speaker or the naive questioner in this dialogue. Yet over the course of a number of episodes, this can relativize the authority of the interlocutors, since it may appear that Ben and Danuta know less than they ought to, especially if they are going to lead prayers and offer words of knowledge. By the same token, the position of naive listener may be recognized precisely as a device to promote discussion. A viewer might respond with skepticism about the whole process or might find confirmation and recognition in the position of the self-styled knowledgeable viewer who understands that this is only role-playing on the part of the hosts.

These variable possibilities are triggered as the program offers moral and religious instruction in the form of a casual, talk show chat. The program thus negotiates and balances a variety of potential perspectives in a way that is not available in the one-way sermon and thereby addresses a range of potential viewers. Even more than the wide range of syndicated programs shown on the Family Channel, the network here reveals its canny understanding of commercial television's strategies of appeal. At a profound and strategic level, *The 700 Club* simultaneously addresses viewers who are fully committed to its religious-moral project and viewers who may initially know little, and care less, about the particular form of fundamentalism purveyed by Pat Robertson.

Consuming Crisis

The system of religious belief developed in the course of the show is self-validating and self-sufficient. Once one is inside the system that holds the Bible up as the literal word of God, all of its arguments make sense. We believe in miracles, or in the law of patriarchy, because God tells us to in the Bible. Quotations from scripture are frequently invoked by Pat, Ben, and their guests to substantiate any point they may be making—about miracles, the power of prayer, domestic relations, sexuality, charity, or communism. Moreover, any behavior, belief, or practice that does not conform to their perspective is ascribed to the work of the devil. When it comes to articulating the religious doctrine head-on, we live in a world of absolutes where good and evil, Jesus and Satan, struggle for control. It is here that the program threatens to become most inaccessible to the viewer who does not already follow the tenets of Protestant fundamentalism. Indeed, to hear that Satan may have one by the throat, that various international conflicts are the prelude to the Tribulation preceding the Rapture, or that a viewer who claimed a word of knowledge through the airwaves has been miraculously cured of cancer or heart disease situates the show, for nonbelievers, as something of a curiosity (on the order of a circus sideshow) and even an object of derision.

There is, however, a certain fascination in this discourse, especially in its insistent repetition and its mediation through the aesthetic and technological conventions of television. One may wonder who, and where, are all the people purportedly healed by the words of knowledge emanating from the television screen, channeled through Pat Robertson and his cohosts. One may be captivated by the melodramatic structure that informs so many of the stories. One may be struck dumb, and yet engaged, by the contradictory pronouncements and points of view that are all finally unified by the absolute truth of biblical quotation. Even watching from a position of superiority or detached bemusement is authorized, because in the course of watching one may suddenly find oneself interested in, or identifying with, one story or another, and thus be unexpectedly engaged as a potential target for the program's message.

Indeed many of the personal, confessional dramas include this as a key moment in their plots: the depressed, alcohol- or drug-addicted, faithless, divorced, lonely subject, casually flipping through television stations with a remote control, happens upon *The 700 Club* and suddenly realizes that precisely his or her problems and situation are being addressed. Thus is the subject saved. As is so often the case with television, one first has to watch, even with disdain, to be a potential subject for conversion. In this way, even at the extremes of its doctrinal hermeticism, *The 700 Club* relies on the familiarity of the medium, its commercial genres and narrational strategies. All of this is crucial to the efficacy and the power of *The 700 Club* to attract an audience in the context of American television culture.

In presenting its various stories, *The 700 Club* promotes a rhetoric of crisis to infuse its issues of the day and its religious perspectives with a sense of urgency. As a strategy of discourse, the invocation of crisis compels discussion, insists that we pay attention, as it defines the field of problems that demand solutions. This serves the demands of programming for *The 700 Club* with its talk show format, since one appropriate response to crisis—in order both to clearly define its contours and to seek a solution—includes generating sufficient talk to fill two or three episodes of the program five days a week. The discourse of crisis also allows the one who speaks it to orient the terms of solution; and any solution is all the more compelling to the degree that it responds to a crisis. Indeed in the face of a crisis situation, solutions are necessary remedies rather than optional plans of action developed in advance.

At the same time, the program's use of crisis thinking is indiscriminate: very nearly everything is a crisis.[19] According to *The 700 Club*, a crisis may be international, national, communal, institutional, familial, or personal in scope; it may refer to human, natural, or supernatural activity; it can apply to a war, a drought, unemployment (statistical and individual), an illness, a gambling problem, or even a person who smokes. *The*

700 Club repeatedly insists that the social, political, cultural, and interpersonal fabric of our lives is permeated by crisis, and developments around the world are understood in terms of multiple, local crises. Indeed one slogan and theme for CBN fund-raising was "Lives in Crisis." Advertising and program promotions continually announced, "Everywhere we turn there are lives in crisis."

Crisis thinking also serves here as a denial of historical perspective, insofar as it isolates a phenomenon as unique and pressing in a way unlike anything else. Finally, the assertion of crisis offers a way to control discourse, via reigning paradigms for understanding and action, creating a problem by virtue of identifying/naming a situation as a crisis in the first place. By definition this insists that there is an urgent problem, as well as a need for immediate intervention. The discourse of crisis thus serves multiple purposes in the CBN domain, supporting the specific televisual needs of *The 700 Club* and inviting the solutions of fundamentalist religious belief at the same time.

As the public platform for CBN, *The 700 Club* signals the organization's attention to, and intervention in, these crises. "The CBN is here to offer a call for help, with hope, love, and compassion."[20] The program proposes that adherence to fundamentalism and prayer is the most effective way to counteract the crises and the moral decay that surround us. But it also insists that individual or general religious belief be channeled through CBN and *The 700 Club*, as the institutional sites that maximize the benefits of belief for individuals and for society as a whole. The evangelical project of saving souls by producing born-again Christians is thus inextricably bound up with the self-reproduction of CBN.

Viewers are constantly urged to use the 800 telephone number, if they have a problem, have just prayed with Pat to accept Jesus as their personal savior, or if they want to help others by becoming a member. "Every member of The 700 Club cares enough to care for others."[21] *The 700 Club* and CBN offer themselves in this way as the agency of crisis resolution. God may be the answer to our problems, but CBN is the organization that can guarantee his intervention, as it acts in his name. "Jesus cares. That's why we care. Please send your most generous gift right now so, together, we can reach out to the many thousands who are ready to receive Him!" [22]

Moreover, whatever one does to support and perpetuate CBN will contribute to personal enrichment as well, in a number of ways. Contributions to CBN create affiliations with the community of Christian fellowship it represents. One identifies oneself as someone who cares "enough to care for others." Even if viewers already embody the Christian ideal, participation in CBN via financial contributions demonstrates an understanding that others may be in need of help—in crisis; at the same time, it promotes a valued way of life on a national and international scale. The more people who come into contact with CBN, the greater the likelihood that the world will be transformed in accordance with the values and lifestyle to which contributors already adhere.

Yet the benefits of contributing are not restricted to this abstract level of good works. In the world according to *The 700 Club*, God is a capitalist in a system that assures profits to those who invest in his religious project. This understanding is substantiated by principles elaborated in the Bible. The practice of tithing—giving (at least) a tenth of one's assets to the church—is regularly promoted on the program as a concrete expression of faith and support. In return, one is rewarded in direct proportion to one's generosity. Donations are described as "seed faith"—planting a monetary seed in religion that will blossom and return to the donor: as you sow, so shall you reap. Contributions are literal investments that will multiply in God's eyes and return in unforeseen, even miraculous, ways. Material gain in and for itself is decried; but material security and comfort in the eyes of God is aggressively promoted.

In this vein, stories about people in dire financial straits who finally profit from selfless contribution are common. During fund-raising telethons, people will call in and donate a portion of their last unemployment check and then call back to announce that the day after they sent their money to CBN, they miraculously found a new job. Certain tales of material security achieve an almost mythological status and are repeated in publications and on the air as evidence of the miraculous powers God will exert *if* you exhibit the proper degree of faith, including regular contributions to CBN. Thus, for example, Pat Robertson recounts the story of a Florida farmer who prayed regularly and supported CBN, and whose orange crop was the only one in his area to survive a major frost.[23]

In promoting endemic crisis, and itself as a response thereto, *The 700 Club* establishes potential appeal by proposing to fulfill needs that it also constructs. The traffic in souls is thus construed in the terms of consumer culture. In making certain problems visible and defining their parameters, it creates a need for solutions. But the solutions it holds out are the logical a priori that determines how problems are posed in the first place, even though the narrativizing process reverses this logical order. As part of the self-reproducing and self-perpetuating logic of consumer culture, the solution offered by *The 700 Club* can never be total or final (at least until the Rapture). Perpetual crisis is the status quo sustaining the program and its institutional base, even for viewers who have already been born again. There are always more crises that beset individuals, their families, their communities, and their countries. There is therefore a continual need to pray, and pray again, for ourselves and for others, and to donate yet another $100.00 to secure the world for God through CBN. "Join us and help us train more counselors and open more phone lines. Call now and reach out to Lives in Crisis."[24]

The Bible and God offer absolute truth and a fixed hierarchy of being that serves as a point of reference for a world that is too variable and that is always already too corrupted and corrupting to be dealt with without the mediations of CBN. CBN represents this fixed hierarchy and absolute truth, a position it maintains quite literally throughout the world, with its international religious initiatives and media programs, including worldwide distribution of *The 700 Club*. The ways in which CBN embraces the world for God are dramatized in programming, especially in stories that address international concerns and issues. For example, Benigno Aquino was once a guest on the show, discussing how his religious faith, including his familiarity with *The 700 Club*, had helped him during his imprisonment by Ferdinand Marcos in the Philippines.

Yet CBN does not express its global vision in multicultural terms. On the contrary, it subsumes the whole world—all countries, all races—within the universalism of evangelical Christianity. International diversity is embraced only to the extent that it conforms to this vision. With its prominent position on television, and within contemporary consumer culture, CBN clearly demonstrates its ability to address a large and diverse constituency for God. Co-host Ben Kinchlow, who appeared on the show in the 1980s, is African American, a fact that is patently visible in his skin color but unremarked in any other way on the program. He does not specifically speak for or to the black constituency of the program, but represents color as a fact of apparent indifference within the larger projects and goals of CBN. Difference, one must assume—especially racial and ethnic difference—is part of the variable earthly world that is rapidly reconstrued according to the steady truths and universal vision offered by God through CBN. The appearance of diversity and variety remains important as a sign of the embracing vision that ultimately denies the differences it finds in the everyday world, the world of CBN and *The 700 Club*.

In the current social conjuncture, television is perhaps the most logical site for enacting the mediations between God's truths and the variability and corruption of everyday life. In diagnosing problems—at an individual, social, and global level—and representing itself as the agency for dealing with them, *The 700 Club* serves a therapeutic function. It holds out a cure as a lure, even as the cure turns out to be interminable. This interminability in turn confirms the necessity of *The 700 Club* within our culture and within television. Moreover, *The 700 Club* and CBN do not simply offer themselves as a product that will solve problems, but more specifically engage in mediated therapeutic processes requiring confession as part of the interminable, strategic repetition.

On *The 700 Club* the force of confession as a discursive strategy is associated with religious rituals and melodramatic narratives. It is thus one of the crucial narrational strategies to draw together the whole range of potential viewers. It also secures the role of CBN and the Family Channel as mediators between the spiritual and material worlds and between the individual faithful and God. Prayers of repentance, initiating one into the fellowship of born-again fundamentalism, are a regular feature of the program. At least once, and often twice, in the course of the show, Pat or his co-hosts will lead viewers in prayer, enjoining them to pray along, acknowledging prior sin and now accepting Jesus as a personal savior. At the end of these prayers, viewers are encouraged to call *The 700 Club*'s toll-free number to announce that they have just prayed with Pat. CBN offers a free pamphlet "What Now?" that will let the newly born-again know how to proceed. On one program, Ben Kinchlow elaborated on why the viewer who had just prayed should call in and confess conversion to CBN prayer counselors:

The Bible says you believe with your heart, but confession is maid to salvation. In other words, when you confess this thing, you establish it in the heavens, and then God Almighty takes your confession and he says, "I concur. I agree. I stand with your confession." And then it begins to happen in your life. And you have to keep doing it every day. Every day you keep saying "Jesus is my savior. Jesus is my lord."

Belief is thus inadequate in the absence of confession, a process that requires an interlocutor. *The 700 Club*, along with CBN, is there to listen, to serve as the one to whom a person confesses. Moreover, confessing only once is also insufficient. One cannot be fixed once and for all within the ideal order of religion but must constantly engage in a process—here, confession—to situate oneself in relationship to it. As a solution, religious salvation is not a state but a process, a movement, a narrative that is always threatened by instability. As a daily program, *The 700 Club* helps to maintain one's proper orientation, holding out the telos of an ideal narrative, as well as informing viewers how best to achieve their goals in the context of everyday, contemporary life.

For *The 700 Club* viewer, the therapeutic process is over-determined by multiple levels of confession and representation within which proper subjectivity is defined. This includes confessing to God, confessing to CBN prayer counselors, the possibility of becoming a prayer counselor to whom others will confess (without oneself having to stop confessing to others), and possibly even becoming the center of a feature story on *The 700 Club*, spurring others to reproduce the same trajectory. At the same time, television viewers are implicitly situated on both sides of the confessional process—they both confess and hear confessions within this trajectory. Indeed, as a viewer one even hears the confessions of the head of the CBN family, Pat Robertson himself, as he leads prayers and enjoins the audience to join him, giving themselves over to God.

Of course, this overdetermination of position—which includes a split position within the confessional relation, the linking of confessional and therapeutic discourse to consumerism, and the conflation of financial and symbolic investments—is precisely the point of continuity between televangelism and *The 700 Club* on the one hand and other forms of commercial television on the other.

That is to say, the televangelical subject—represented in the show, but also implicating the viewer—is comparable to those who seek therapeutic advice on their sex lives from Dr. Ruth Westheimer; to the couples who date, play newlywed games, and divorce on daytime television; and to viewers who shop with the Home Shopping Club. These are all subjects who are set into televisual representation (sound and/or image) in direct proportion to their willingness to participate in a therapeutic transaction through confession, in a context wherein representation is always commodified, one way or another. (Though it is important to remember that there is little in contemporary American culture that escapes commodification. This cannot be, in itself, automatic terms for absolute critique; the issue instead is negotiating one's position within this context.)

The Holy Family

The personal stories of ordinary people regularly featured in the show contribute to this process as paradigmatic cases. Regular features on *The 700 Club*, these stories offer highly mediated models for living in the form of emotionally overdetermined tales of crisis, struggle, and triumph through Jesus Christ. These human interest stories combine interview footage, dramatic reconstruction, and voice-over narration in the structure of a news report. A reporter introduces characters and provides the explanatory transitional information to unify the narrative. Within this context the main characters tell their own stories—of crisis and its resolution, of sin and redemption, or of loss and salvation. Confession is situated within the larger narrative frame, as narration is divided between the voice of the reporter and that of the subjects of the story.

As a rule, the narrative subjects speak to represent exemplary states of being, describing their own behavior or thoughts at fixed moments within the narrative (both high points and low points), while the reporter furnishes background information, motives, and causal-temporal links. This reinforces the position of the narrative subjects as one in which the confessional and melodramatic are inexorably linked, since the speakers represent their own lives as a series of abstract moral, mental, and emotional states. At the same time, the stories demonstrate the importance of confession for individuals as a response to crisis situations; the reporter sets up the narrative terms of personal crisis, and the subject in the story responds with confessional revelations. The mediation of the confessional voice is further heightened by the way in which these pretaped reports are framed by the program's hosts, who explicitly draw general moral and religious lessons from each individual story.

Through these levels of narrative framing, a hierarchy of power and knowledge is delineated, with individual melodramatic subjects who speak for themselves at the bottom. The Cheri Foster story is exemplary in this regard, containing within it many of the issues that are typically raised in stories of this sort, including family problems, child abuse, fatal illness, and divorce. When it aired, Ben Kinchlow introduced the story by explaining that it was about the problem of control, featuring a woman whose response to being molested as a child was to want to assert total control over her own life. In the reporter's introduction we learn that Cheri had a troubled early life. Her mother left the family when Cheri was eight years old. Cheri was subsequently molested by her grandfather, and several years later by a friend of her brother. "When so much happens at such a young age, the most important thing to have is control—control of one's life and control of one's future." In an interview, Cheri summarizes the emotional stakes, directly describing how much she hurt as a child and how she had no hope left in her life.

The reporter then recounts the next important stage in Cheri's life. Having decided that a family offered a normal way to live, Cheri got pregnant and married at the age of sixteen. "Within a year of Yvette's birth, she found out her husband was having an affair. Once again hope was lost. Once again she lost her control." Cheri is again introduced, and she describes her depression at this point in her life, so extreme that she rarely left the house for nearly a year. Then, the story continues, Cheri's daughter developed a rare and fatal disease, for which there is no known cure. "That's when Cheri decided she would do something, it would seem, no one had control over. When she would do it depended solely on how soon Yvette would die." This mystifying and grammatically awkward comment by the reporter sets up the terms of narrative that lead to the first significant confessional revelation in the story, as Cheri explains that she had decided to kill herself after Yvette died. But Yvette did not die. Through a neighbor, she "came to know Jesus Christ," and her disease slowly disappeared. In addition, Yvette began to pray for her mother and for Cheri's new boyfriend. "While Yvette prayed, Cheri's boyfriend Pete worked as a singer in a bar. Often women were attracted to him. And in spite of her live-in relationship with Pete, Cheri got jealous." This voice-over narration is accompanied by dramatic reconstruction, as we see Cheri, Pete, and another woman sitting in a bar. The "other woman" and Pete are talking together, and Cheri gets up and walks off alone. In voice-over, Cheri then discusses her jealousy.

Cheri and Pete began to attend church with their neighbor and spent more time praying and reading the Bible together. "God was drawing them to himself." With their newfound belief, they could no longer continue living together. Pete moved out and "Cheri had to come to grips with the fact that she might never marry him." At this point she had a serious talk with God; and in the story, she recounts her confession in her own words: "I said, 'God, you know what I need. Maybe it isn't Pete. I love him and I want him. That's what I want. But because you might have a different idea for my life, I'll give him back to you right now.'" Wedding photos signal their reconciliation. "But the lessons didn't end there. They went on to include Candace, born a year and a half later. Breathing difficulties, hemorrhaging, and other complications were mercifully healed. But not before Cheri put her faith in God in action." Cheri explains that once again she accepted God's plan—whatever it was—and in prayer acknowledged that God should do what he thought best with Candace. Now, with Candace's full recovery, Cheri and her mother, who also "came to the Lord," both work as volunteer phone counselors for *The 700 Club*. "Understanding what it means to really let God control her life, Cheri is now able to share that liberating truth with others."

Throughout the course of this story, the reporter provides the tragic, narrative highlights to frame and narrationally motivate Cheri's confessional revelations. Time is telescoped to focus only on key events: molestation, marriage, marital failure, the discovery of fatal illness, a live-in boyfriend, the discovery of religion, marriage, another child with medical complications, healing, and work for the CBN organization. What happens in between is ignored, is even considered a distraction from the desired emotional impact of specific events and feelings. Cheri's life is told in terms of a series of crises that are dealt with one by one.

In this context Cheri speaks to describe a specific way of feeling—hurt, despair, and concessions to God, which are also retold confessions. Moreover, in the narrative order, religion helps overcome each local crisis as it arises—Yvette is healed, Pete and Cheri are married, Candace is healed. But none of these events signals the overarching happy end to Cheri's story. Rather, it is Cheri's work for CBN that represents final narrative resolution, fulfilling the promise religious faith has to offer. And this refers not only to Cheri's work as a prayer counselor for CBN but also to the fact that she is now featured in a story on *The 700 Club*.

The story is framed by the departure and return of Cheri's mother. Indeed the mother's abandonment is the first disruption experienced by Cheri, immediately followed by her molestation, as if a causal motive. By contrast, participation in the church and in CBN activities is expressly linked to familial stability, health, and fulfillment. Cheri's mother reappears suddenly at the end of the tale, a fellow follower in the steps of God. Broken families, bar life, illness, and self-reliance are associated with godlessness and personal misery. All of the elements of the story combine to support the project of religion as expressed through CBN. Within this world view, to assert too much individual control over one's own life means that God is missing from the picture. As Ben explains, "God lets your life get out of control to show you that He's in control. When you are totally out of control, you have nowhere to go but to Him."

Cheri's grave sin was the contemplation of suicide, an attempt to control her own life by controlling her own death. This may also contribute to the awkward grammatical construction of the sentence used to introduce her suicide attempt by the reporter in the story. On the one hand, in the interest of narrative suspense, the event cannot be named too quickly. But in the world order of fundamentalism the suicide attempt also stands for an out-of-kilter world, here modeled in language. Cheri learns her lessons by repeatedly conceding control to God, in relation to both Pete and Candace. She thus demonstrates her recognition that God's plans for her family and for herself are more meaningful than her own mortal desires. CBN, religious faith, and the family are thus inextricably conjoined in a narrative that seems to be a condensed version of a daytime soap opera.

The use of melodramatic conventions contributes to the appeal of *The 700 Club*, as a familiar genre is cast in terms of the institutional and philosophical imperatives of CBN. Melodrama is the television genre that has persistently focused on familial and interpersonal relations, and this emphasis is apparent even in *The 700 Club* human interest stories that involve single people. One such story dealt with a college student who, through a religious group on campus, found friendship, fellowship, and meaning in his life after a period of meaningless debauchery that included experimentation with drugs and alcohol. The final image of his newfound fulfillment showed him strolling in a sunny park with a female companion (his girlfriend, we are to assume), following earlier images depicting his isolation and alienation from his environment. While the woman did not figure in the narrative—she was never mentioned by the boy or by the reporter of the story—the final image served to confirm the fulfillment the boy had achieved through Christian fellowship and belief in God, including the couple among the rewards offered by his new lifestyle, as well as his appearance in a featured confessional melodrama on *The 700 Club*.

According to CBN philosophy, religious faith and the family are intimately connected. The family is the earthly social unit that models the heavenly order. This is clearly explained in one of the promotional brochures sent to viewers who call the CBN phone numbers frequently listed on the television screen. The brochure states:

> To begin with, we know that God created man, male and female, in His image. This means that God must have both male and female characteristics. This also shows us that the coming together of a man and woman in marriage brings about a union—a picture, so to speak— that helps us understand the nature of God. God has fatherly characteristics. He gives us good gifts, as an earthly father would do. He also has motherly characteristics. He comforts us as a mother comforts her child. . . . The family, in other words, is there to show people what our heavenly family will be like. It should be a shadow

of things to come. A family is an example to believers and unbelievers alike of the love and acceptance we have from God.[25]

While God may have fatherly and motherly characteristics, on earth these are divided between men and women, each embodying different traits and assuming different responsibilities within the family unit: mutual interdependencies model heavenly relationships. Husbands are enjoined to love their wives, to admire and praise them. "This creates an atmosphere of mutual respect. And what woman can resist a man who truly loves and cherishes her?"[26] The man in turn carries ultimate authority within the family, to which the wife must submit:

> The husband-wife relationship is compared in scripture to the Father-Son relationship, "The head of the woman is the man, and the head of Christ is God." We know that Jesus and God the Father are equal. But the woman, as Christ, willingly submits herself to her husband. Not because she is forced to, but because she chooses to, recognizing this is God's will for her life. She defers to her husband because she loves him. In turn, he lifts her up. The key is love.[27]

Gender roles within the family are thus fixed in a logical hierarchy determined by the Bible. The hierarchical scheme of familial duties is at once absolute and relative, in that everyone has a pregiven position to assume but must in turn submit to the higher authority of God himself. Husbands submit to Jesus, just as wives submit to husbands. Given this interpretation of scripture, it is hardly surprising that the imagery deployed by *The 700 Club* in its melodramatic narratives and in CBN ads is highly charged in terms of traditional gender roles. And yet, together, men and women are "children" to God the father. Based on this logic, the figure of the woman readily serves as an image that stands in for the faithful in general.

In this regard one of the ads used for the Lives in Crisis campaign is particularly suggestive. At a wedding, the bride celebrates, laughing joyously, embracing her husband and various guests. This is intercut with a woman who is sitting alone, watching the bride, nervously fingering her pearls, until she finally gets up and leaves. A voice-over narration, apparently designed to arouse a viewer's worst anxieties, accompanies the scene. "You always feel like you just don't fit in; you never have and you never will. All your life you've been picked on, laughed at, made to feel like nothing. You used to tell yourself it would get better. But it hasn't. What can you do? Is there anyone who cares?" Another voice then takes over and urges viewers to call in and help, as the image track carries a series of shots of CBN phone counselors at work. The visual narrative here literalizes the aphorism "Always a bridesmaid, never a bride" to dramatically exemplify, even to provoke, the fear and misery of loneliness in the culturally overdetermined, and gender-specific, image of the bridesmaid. The narrator constructs an implied past for the lone woman in the scene, a past filled with bitter rejections. This is a "life in crisis" par excellence, one of millions that may be helped by *The 700 Club*'s counseling centers, especially with the financial assistance of the viewers.

The ad is clearly intended to appeal primarily to female viewers. But additionally, the image of the single, rejected woman bears the imprint of more generalized and widespread feelings of alienation and rejection. In a crucial sense she sits in relation to the married couple and their happy family like the (unsaved) viewer of *The 700 Club* in relation to God. Both the woman and the viewer must support and make use of CBN if they are to resolve the crises that confront them and achieve the full benefits available to the faithful. As the program narrativizes and renarrativizes crisis, evincing the need for intervention, and as it repeats the need to call and to support CBN—the necessity of confessing to them and through them—all of its viewers are figured as excluded bridesmaids. This position is finally necessary to assure the perpetuation of CBN and of *The 700 Club*, as expressions of conservative fundamentalist Protestantism in tune with the workings of contemporary therapeutic consumer culture on television.

Mediating Relations

Prime-Time Series

The Lure of a Story

"That was then; this is now." These words are spoken by Cary Maxwell (played by Tony Franciosa) during the denouement of an episode of *Finder of Lost Loves*, an hour-long television drama that aired during the 1984–85 season on ABC. The logic of the statement, here cut loose from its dramatic context, is the result of linguistic tautology, with the pairing and opposing of two sets of shifters, each linked by the intransitivity of being: that/this, then/now, was/is. The logic of the linguistic syntagm is anchored by the paradigms of difference within it, which are at once spatial, conceptual, and temporal: that-then-was/this-now-is. One could not assert with equivalent force that "that was now; this is then" or "that is now; this was then." Therefore the meaningfulness of the statement—its ability to be comprehensible to a viewer-listener—is based on the logic of the code of the English language. Indeed its meaning is at once self-evident and self-contained.[1]

As linguistic tautology, the assertion carries a decidedly weak referentiality. Cut loose from the context of utterance, it proposes itself as an instance of signification, a discourse in search of a speaking subject. Emile Benveniste's analysis of pronouns, verb forms, and shifters has demonstrated the theoretical inseparability of language, discourse, and subjectivity.[2] In relation to this, a statement such as "That was then;

this is now" reveals the amorphous and unspecifiable limits of a subjectivity constructed in language. As a linguistic postulate, it represents a truth of discourse and subjectivity, linking being and meaning in a form that is irrefutable in the terms of the language in which it is formulated. At the same time it implicates a subjectivity that is held by no one, or may be filled by anyone.

That was then; this is now. The juxtaposition of discontinuous phrases signifies disjunction and conjunction at the same time. A relation is proposed but not specified. Rather, it constitutes the lure of a story, an invitation to narrative, which it also summarizes and subsumes. It is at once a code waiting to be elaborated and a conclusion, what one might expect to hear at the end of the story. In this sense it begs to be elaborated and integrated into the particularity of a narrative, a dramatic context. But what story does one tell? "That was then; this is now" expresses the concatenations of *histoire* and *discours* in the sense elaborated by Benveniste.[3] The story it invokes is that of history, fairly tales, psychoanalysis, and subjectivity. Indeed the assertion works to hold all of these possible narratives in balance, providing a meta-narrative key to the fantasy of therapy offered by the program in which it is spoken and, more generally, to the fantasy of therapy offered by television's dramatic fictions.

In television drama, therapy is at once a narrative and a narrational issue. It is something the characters might do, and also a way of engaging viewers to participate via fantasy and identification in the worlds of television fiction. In this chapter I analyze some of these fictions in terms of their therapeutic strategies. I examine three programs in particular— *Finder of Lost Loves*, *The Equalizer*, and *Midnight Caller*— as exemplary instances of prime-time fiction in which the therapeutic problematic is central. For each program, the analysis focuses on a single episode that epitomizes the general and repeated narrative problematic of the series. The episodes were selected because they so clearly express the stakes of therapeutic discourse as a narrative and narrational television strategy. However, it is my contention, based on extensive viewing, that these episodes and, more importantly, the therapeutic strategies they deploy are hardly exceptional for these programs. Moreover, the strategies I discern are by no means limited to these three programs.

Finder of Lost Loves

The fiction of *Finder of Lost Loves* centers on Maxwell, Ltd., an agency whose function is to locate missing persons, in particular ones who have been loved and lost, such as former boyfriends or girlfriends, parents, children, spouses, or other close friends and relatives. As one of the agency's clients is told, "We usually take cases involving people who are looking for people with whom they have a history." The company was established by Cary Maxwell, formerly a pilot, after his wife died (sometime prior to the temporal diegesis of the show) at a tragically young age. As explained in the premier episode, Maxwell decided that while he cannot have the one person he loves most, he can at least devote his life to helping others from suffering a loss similar to his own. Daisy Lloyd is his business associate and his sister-in-law, the younger sister of his deceased wife. Most episodes of the program involve two cases, one handled by Cary and the other by Daisy. Cary and Daisy periodically exchange counsel and support as each leads a client search, unites a client with a sought loved one, and oversees a period of reconciliation, which is usually, predictably, emotionally fraught.

In the episode under consideration here, Cary's case involves friends, two fellow pilots from his past. Thad comes to the agency and asks Cary to join him in helping Mike, who has let his personal and professional life deteriorate since the three of them stopped working together twelve years earlier. Thad has also arranged for them to be joined by Beth, a woman who ran out on Mike on the eve of their marriage at the same time, twelve years before. Thad suggests to Cary that Beth is the cause of Mike's problems; if Mike can get her out of his system, he will be able to get his life back on track. "They don't belong together. They never did," he explains. In the course of their unexpected reunion, Mike and

Beth discover that their feelings for one another are as strong as ever. Yet they each fear that if they get too involved again, they will be hurt as they were in the past, that history will in a crucial sense repeat itself. At the same time Cary learns that Thad actually engineered Mike and Beth's original breakup, forging a "Dear Beth" letter in Mike's name, then telling Mike that Beth ran off with another man.

This revelation disrupts the renewed relationship among the friends. In a fit of anger, Mike flies his crop-dusting plane perilously close to Cary and Thad's car while they are driving down the road. Beth prepares to leave again, explaining to Cary, "I can understand his [Mike's] anger at Thad. But I can't understand why he finds it more important than the love we just found. Will you tell him goodbye?" Cary suggests she should speak to Mike directly, but she refuses. He and Thad go to find Mike in his hangar in order to warn him of Beth's impending departure. Mike and Thad argue until Cary intervenes.[4] Mike accuses Thad of costing him his marriage, but Cary interrupts. "That was then; this is now. She's always loved you Mike. Do you want to do something about that? Or stay in this rut you've dug yourself?"

Throughout this half of the episode, Cary serves as the figure of authority and stability to whom the others repeatedly turn. While Thad initiates the search that brings his lost loves together, Cary's presence is crucial for the transformative/restorative process to occur. Beth suggests to *Cary* that she did not just dump Mike in the past, enabling him to unravel the truth of Thad's duplicity. As the program's constituted authority, he demands an explanation from Thad, insisting on his own power to provoke confession: "This is me. It matters." The recovery of the truth of the past also sheds new light on Thad's possible motives for bringing these people together in the first place. He claims that he wants to help Mike "get over" Beth. At the same time, by assembling this particular group of people for the first time in twelve years, he is very nearly assuring that his role in separating them in the past will come out. In this case Thad is the person who actually *finds* the lost loves, locating both Mike and Beth for the reunion weekend, carrying out part of the work usually done by

Maxwell, Ltd. Yet Cary's presence is necessary, in the terms of the program, as mediator and, more crucially, as the figure who requires confessions and explanations. In his absence, it is unclear that the lost loves would finally be reunited.

"That was then; this is now." In its most immediate context it refers to Thad's intervention in Mike and Beth's relationship. Thad cost Mike his marriage *then*, twelve years ago, but has reunited him with Beth *now*. Here, the distress of the past has been remedied, and the present is seen to offer a terrain of positive potentiality. But this context is quickly generalized, and the possibilities for how we might understand the statement are thereby dispersed. "Do you want to do something about that? Or stay in this rut you've dug yourself?" *Now* Mike is in a rut, suggesting that *then* he was not. Do you want to do something about *that* then, or stay in *this* rut now? Thus the values that can be ascribed to past and present, then and now, are reversed.

Mike's anger is justified but temporally displaced. This leads Beth to leave him now, just as she had twelve years before, or at least to start to leave. Mike has decided that it is more important to blame Thad for his problems than it is to go on with his life, at least in the terms of Cary's interpretation of his behavior. But Cary and Thad are there in the first place because Mike has been blaming Beth and has not been "going on" with his life, at least not in the terms of middle-class family life that the program implicitly invokes as a measure of success. Instead, Mike has abandoned a high-paying, upwardly mobile career with an airline company to run a small, independent crop-dusting business in the country, and he has remained single and socially isolated in the process. Thus "that was then; this is now" subsumes a complex knot of narrative and dramatic repetitions and reversals that cannot be easily disintricated. Yet whatever was then or is now the case, this particular story concludes in a conventional happy ending, as Beth and Mike are reunited romantically, and Thad promises to arrange for Mike to be rehired by the airline company where he once worked.

The parallel story in this episode, overseen by Daisy, involves a minister, Evan, who is looking for an old girlfriend,

Linda. They dated in high school, and she got pregnant; but they were kept apart by their parents, and the child was given up for adoption. Several years later the adoptive parents died in an accident. When the authorities were unable to locate the birth mother, Evan, then in divinity school, gained custody of his daughter Vicki. She is now a teenager, and he feels she would profit from meeting her mother. Daisy finds Linda in San Francisco, where she runs a high-class bordello. Linda tells Daisy that she would prefer not to face Evan or meet her daughter. However, owing to a lapse in the agency's usually discreet search procedures, Evan and Vicki have followed Daisy to San Francisco and learn of Linda's whereabouts. (The agency tries to assure that a sought person is willing to be found before initiating a meeting between the parties involved.) When Evan becomes aware of Linda's profession, he reluctantly consents to her meeting Vicki only when Linda promises to keep it a secret from their daughter. Yet inevitably the truth comes out, and Vicki, distraught by the situation, runs away to join her mother, though she eventually ends up reunited with her father.

Through their confrontations, the program suggests that Evan and Linda still feel strongly about one another, even though Evan is distressed by the divergent paths their lives have followed. As he explains to Daisy, "I repented for my sins by becoming a minister. She's making a living out of hers." What he would like is "to turn back the clock and undo the past." Later Linda tells Daisy that she has tried to replace Evan with "hundreds of men." Her life as a prostitute is represented as the displaced effort to reconstitute her past by finding a replacement for the (illicit) love of her youth. For both Evan and Linda, their present state is readily explained as a direct result of their mutual past. In their parting scene, as Evan prepares to leave with Vicki, the irreconcilability of their present lives is underscored, in spite of their mutual desire to overcome the factors that obviate the possibility of reuniting.[5]

In this episode of *Finder of Lost Loves* the narrative situations and their resolutions are different, but the problematic is the same: that was then; this is now. In one case the trajectory of the past has led to irrevocable conclusions. Instead of a harmonious reunion and a bright future together, the characters must reconcile themselves to their separate fates under the watchful eye of Daisy, who is second only to Cary as a confessional sounding board and mediator between estranged parties. In other words, and crucially, a reencounter does not assure renewed union but is a necessary context for some sort of conciliation. According to the logic of the program, one always lives in the shadows of one's past and yet must work through them, facing them in the light of day, so to speak. Actions have enduring if unpredictable consequences that must be confronted. Then and now, before and after: these are the boundaries within which subjectivity is played out over and over again on *Finder of Lost Loves*, a repeated and variable process where the results are not given in advance.

"That was then; this is now" at first seems to be an incidental comment that pops up in the midst of all of this. But its efficacy and value lie in its virtual repetition, as it contains and subsumes a panoply of relations—similarity and difference, conjunction and disjunction—enacted in dramatic confrontations among characters. It is a structuring motif of the program as a whole and is in fact uttered more than once in the course of *Finder of Lost Loves*. In another episode, Daisy takes the case of a former boyfriend, to help him find a woman he claims he wants to marry. She discusses the case with Cary, who advises against professional involvement when personal feelings are at stake. But Daisy persists, "He's looking for the woman he wants to marry. I think that makes it pretty clear where he's coming from." "Where are you coming from?," Cary asks. "I'm the one who wanted to break up," she replies. "That was then; this is now," Cary responds. And, of course, as she pursues the case, the truth of Cary's words is fully exposed, as the search for and reunion with this other woman becomes the occasion for renewed attachments between Daisy and her former boyfriend, culminating in a marriage proposal.

Far from incidental, the statement offers a terse formulation of the program's hermeneutic and symbolic codes,[6] as episodes repeatedly involve encounters between individuals with figures from their past. "We usually take cases involving people who are looking for people with whom they have a history." According to the logic of the show, the always unresolved past must be revived, renarrativized, and reenacted to secure the terms of one's present emotional and familial (and often, though unforegrounded, professional) situation. This process does not occur through individual effort, but is carried out under the auspices of Maxwell, Ltd. Cary and Daisy hear people discuss their problems; help them to seek out hidden, missing, or lost aspects of their past; and oversee the psycho-dramas that inevitably erupt in the course of the confrontations they instigate.

The familiarity of this trajectory derives from its evocation of the narrative of therapy as constituted through psychoanalytic and psychological discourses.[7] Indeed therapy can be seen as the motive force of the program's narrative logic. For Cary and Daisy are not conventional impersonal detectives with expertise in locating missing persons, although this is an important skill they offer to clients. If they did not operate in the guise of detectives, many clients would not seek their services, since most of their clients do not recognize or admit to the need for a therapeutic experience as such but are looking for detective services of a personal and confidential nature. As detectives in disguise, Cary and Daisy's exceptional talents lie in their therapeutic abilities, as the narrative weight of each episode concentrates on the reunions and negotiated reconciliations they oversee. Each subplot thus offers something on the order of a case history.

The analogy between the program's narratives and the process of therapy informs every stage of its episodic trajectories. Clients are awkward and often embarrassed about coming to Maxwell, Ltd., in the first place, though they are inevitably reassured by the agency's discretion and the sympathetic concern expressed by Cary and Daisy for their situations. Yet even so, a form of resistance figures prominently in these narratives, as the initial rationale for a search frequently turns out to be an alibi or a decoy. In the context of dramatic television this contributes to a sense of suspense for the viewer. Regular viewers quickly learn not to trust any character's expressed reasons for initiating a search and are thus engaged in figuring out *if* any given reason is the correct one—and if not, when and how the more correct motives for the search will come out. At the same time, within the fictional drama, the revelation that a client's initial explanation of a problem was erroneous may provoke Cary's ire and become the grounds for doubting even a second explanation. Both of these function as potential generators of tension and suspense subtending the progress of the narrative of any given episode.

Still, it rarely proves to be the case that clients simply lie. Rather, their understanding of their own motives is often multiple and confused, as in the case of Thad in the episode discussed above. Similarly, they may be too ashamed to tell the whole story (as in cases involving illegitimate children or abandoned spouses) or may fear the case will be rejected if they reveal the whole story to Cary or Daisy in advance. In this way, the construction of the therapeutic problem as a process of discovery and clarification is an integral part of the process of the cure within the course of the narrative and its resolution.

In one episode, a journalist, Robin Sloan, asks Daisy to help her with a story she is researching by locating a reclusive horse breeder, Maggie Singer. It turns out that Maggie had an affair with Robin's father many years earlier, an affair that Robin betrayed to her mother, ruining her parents' marriage and her relationship with both parents. Robin's mother has recently died, and she now realizes that Maggie was the "true love" of her father's life. Thus Robin's initial claim to Daisy— that Maggie touched her life in a profound way—is true, but not quite in the terms in which it is first presented. Robin arranges for her father to meet with Maggie as a way of compensating for previous familial disruption. But it is unclear whether this will facilitate the reenactment of her own childhood trauma of discovering her father with another woman— an adult repetition to reconfirm her childhood betrayal—or if she hopes to reconstitute a new happy and stable family in the wake of her mother's death. In either case, and in every case that Maxwell, Ltd., takes on, the familial problematic is central, as the family romance is played out in multiple variations and in variable stages.[8]

Cary and Daisy repeatedly guide clients from uncertainty based in an unresolved past to a state of present familial conciliation. This may involve full-blown reconciliations, with the re-formation of couples or parent-child ties that were broken in the past. But it can equally involve a resolution of confirmed separation and the recognition that former bonds and alliances are a part of one's past, a past that must now be put to rest and transcended. Whatever results from a particular subplot is situated, in advance and by the very nature of the show, as the proper adult response to the obsessions of one's past. The process that confirms the result, a therapeutic process, is more crucial than the specific terms that constitute narrative resolution, which are variable from case to case. The conventional and unifying happy ending is common but by no means the rule. On the contrary, the program often suggests that true happiness results from investigating and confronting one's past in order to move on and not necessarily from repeating or reengaging it.

The economic and temporal terms of the cure also vary on a case-by-case basis, depending on the means and needs of individual clients. The cost of the services offered by Maxwell, Ltd., is rarely mentioned, except in situations where a potential client has only a limited amount to spend. In such instances Cary usually tells the client not to worry about the expense, though it is clear that all clients pay something. Similarly, the length of the cure is subject to fluctuation, though it is always intensive and delimited. Two days or two weeks may be necessary to resolve a situation. But for the duration of each case, Cary, Daisy, and their clients devote most of their time and attention to working things out. This instability constitutes Cary and Daisy as radical therapists, as the terms of economic and temporal exchange are not rigid or regular. And although the duration of most of their cases is short, it is an intensive experience. But this lack of orthodoxy is compensated by the situating of the program within the regularity of network broadcast prime-time television.

With the exception of preemption for network specials, the

program aired at the same time on the same day each week, according to a conventional model of therapeutic treatment. Within this context commercial breaks might be taken as the regularity of economic support for each session. However, it does not necessarily follow that there is a simple analogy to be made between doctor and patient, Cary/Daisy and their clients, and television and its viewers. Rather, to propose *Finder of Lost Loves* as a model for therapy involves recognition of the complexity and confusion of identifications and of doctor-patient relations at the very core of the program. For it is not simply the case that Cary and Daisy function as amateur analysts to the string of clients who appear at the offices of Maxwell, Ltd.

As mentioned before, Cary Maxwell started the company after his wife died. His cases thus manifest something on the order of a repetition compulsion, reenacting a scenario that will always remain incomplete for him even as his clients are led to successful resolutions. His wife is dead and can never be found; or she can be found only in the displaced figuration that each case represents. It is quite literally his lack that grounds the fulfillment of others, which, as noted above, is not always achieved as a vision of plenitude in the first place. For according to the premise of the show, if his wife were still living, Maxwell, Ltd., would not exist. Presumably, Cary would still be a pilot. The company name achieves its full significance in this context, its limitation being the impossibility of serving its founder in any direct way. It thus bears the name of the founder constituted precisely in relation to a figure of the absent woman in his life.

This absence is compensated in yet another displacement by Daisy, the sister-in-law whose presence redoubles and exacerbates the tension between Cary's unresolved desires to reclaim his own past and their displacement into the cases he successfully pursues for his clients. For Daisy is not only an associate and confidante, but also a stand-in for her sister. Through the course of *Finder of Lost Loves*, the relationship between Cary and Daisy is played out as a continual unconsummated flirtation-romance, frequently standing as a third subplot in episodes. This relationship, perhaps more than any other, advances the problematic repetition and difference in the sphere of familial/interpersonal relations that is at the heart of the program.

Cary's attraction to Daisy hinges on the symbolic force of the absent wife/mother. In the terms of the therapeutic problematic and within the narrative fiction of the program, her presence is a necessity, even though Cary exhibits a compulsive inability to consummate the relationship. Daisy is directly associated with the absent wife through the genetic code of familial relations. But she is *not* her sister. For Cary to consummate the relationship would be to supplant the wife, even if within the code of the biological family, transforming her from an absent presence to a present absence. In other words, it would represent a successful cure in the terms usually applied to Maxwell, Ltd., clients.[9] This would also obviate the function of the agency for its founder as the displacement-supplement for the absent wife (and, we might add, terminate or radically transform the underlying symbolic problematic of the program). Daisy is thus an inadequate substitute; and her presence as such brings into full relief the double and imbricated therapeutic problematic that underwrites the program as a whole. This involves not only the weekly cases, represented by guest stars, but also the characters at the very center of the show: not only Cary but also Daisy, who stays with a love who will always be lost to her.

While *Finder of Lost Loves* was only successful enough to stay on prime-time television for one season, its strategies and preoccupations are symptomatic of a narrative and symbolic problematic that cuts across a wide range of prime-time programming. *Finder of Lost Loves* is not unique; it is exemplary of strategies in American dramatic series in which the formation of couples and families is the product of submitting to confessional and therapeutic practices. Moreover, while certain structural factors—such as a recurring star of a show—contribute to a sense that someone has mastery over this process, a sustained analysis of the program reveals that this mastery is provisional and unstable. There are always mobile and multiple perspectives at work that relativize authority and mastery within the therapeutic problematic.

On the one hand, this opens the possibility of overturning traditional hierarchical positions within the therapeutic relation. On the other hand, and at the same time, it extends the therapeutic process itself to a point where everyone is subject to it, wherein no one can ever have mastery but must always submit—implicitly or explicitly—to someone else. The implications of this in terms of gender and power are developed later in this chapter. At this point it is necessary to turn to some other shows, in particular programs that do not share the genre of romantic melodrama with *Finder of Lost Loves*, to demonstrate the operation of the therapeutic problematic not only as a narrative structure of mastery over others but as a problematic in which a powerful male hero is often centrally implicated. For an important part of my argument is that the therapeutic process is by no means restricted to traditionally female-oriented dramatic genres, including daytime and prime-time melodramas and programs such as *Finder of Lost Loves*.

The Equalizer

The double imbricated therapeutic problematic of *Finder of Lost Loves* is reproduced in *The Equalizer* but reconstrued in the terms of an urban thriller. In *The Equalizer* Robert McCall (played by Edward Woodward) compensates for his past as a career operative in "the Agency" (clearly meant to represent the CIA) by applying his professional skills to help defenseless victims of urban and corporate crime. He deploys the resources of his former profession in a good faith effort to rectify situations that cannot be handled through normal legal channels. In other words, he negotiates his own troubling past through the repetition each case represents. In his cases, he redresses individuals' experienced social ills rather than meddling in global social and political affairs. But he uses the methods he learned while professionally engaged in covert actions in the global arena to help individuals in the New York metropolitan area. In the process McCall serves a decisive therapeutic role in relation to his clients. For he not only solves the immediate, material, and often life-threatening problems that confront them but also often challenges them to resolve related personal conflicts. In this context it is not fortuitous that most of his cases involve couples and families.

Like Cary Maxwell, McCall offers a cure to his clients that he cannot provide for himself except through the displaced and inadequate repetition each case represents. For the very premise of the program is that he quit the Agency and began his work as an urban guerrilla for the good because of his profound personal and moral disgust with the work he had done for the Agency. This conflict is regularly narrativized in the course of the series. For example, in the episode entitled "Torn,"[10] McCall becomes involved in a domestic violence case and is at the same time confronted with the opportunity to capture a former Agency operative who betrayed him in the past. In the course of the episode, the narrative proceeds in terms of diversions and interruptions, as each investigation impinges on the other, forcing McCall to shift his focus of attention back and forth between the two cases.

The episode opens as a woman, Jessie Moore, is talking with a police detective about her husband, Mike, who has been in prison for wife abuse but is due to be released in one week. The detective explains that she is protected from her husband by a restraining order, but that the police cannot intervene unless the husband actually violates the conditions of his parole. McCall shows up to meet his client, Jessie's daughter Laura, who called him for help. He promises Jessie and Laura that he will protect them. In establishing this situation, it is made clear that the threat represented by Mike Moore has profoundly affected Jessie and Laura. The Moores were married for twelve years before Jessie ever filed formal charges against her husband. Jessie is quite helpless, fearful of her husband and unable to act on her own. Laura rarely talks or smiles, although she brings McCall into the case to protect her mother. Through the course of the episode McCall offers both of them counsel. In several scenes he urges Jessie to "go on with her life" and to assume control over her own fate. He also gives Laura advice about parents.

As the Moore case develops, McCall becomes involved in unofficial business for the Agency. His assistance is sought by Jason, the brash young director of the Agency's New York City office, a semiregular character on the program who has a continuing antagonistic relationship with McCall. McCall is initially irked by Jason's appeal for his help but changes his mind when he learns that the appeal is motivated by the fact that "Bryan" is coming to town. In flashback Bryan is shown to be a former fellow agent who violated security on a case McCall was overseeing in an unidentified besieged Eastern European city. (One assumes it is 1948 Berlin, 1956 Budapest, or 1968 Prague.) McCall was working with a woman, Angela, who is seen leading a group of children to a bus, probably orphans she is helping to get away from the fighting. Bryan's betrayal, despite assurances that Angela is being protected, lead to her apprehension by enemy forces and presumably to her death. In the present of the program, as McCall follows one of Jason's leads to track down Bryan, he learns that Mike Moore is about to be released from jail and has to go off to help Jessie and Laura. He thereby misses an opportunity to find Bryan, earning the scornful wrath of Jason.

The structure of missed opportunity erupts with full force in the denouement of the episode. McCall is at a heliport where Bryan is expected to arrive momentarily. On his way to the heliport, he receives a phone call from Mike Moore's parole officer informing him that Mike has been released from jail and is late for an appointment. As McCall continues to wait, an asynchronous sound and image montage presents a dramatic condensation of the two cases. Images from the earlier flashback are intercut with shots of Jessie, Laura, Jason, and McCall himself in extreme close-up. These images are accompanied on the soundtrack by a montage including Jason's verbal taunts in the present, Bryan's assurances about McCall and Angela's safety in the past, and Jessie's expressed concerns about Mike. This concatenation of past and present culminates in a repeated shot/reverse-shot construction, with Angela and Laura alternately holding the reverse field position in relation to McCall's gaze.

The formal parallelism between Angela and Laura in this

sequence suggests at once their absolute equivalence and absolute difference. This succinctly figures the ambiguity of the therapeutic problematic at the core of the program. For on the one hand they both participate as the reverse field of McCall's off-screen gaze, neither spatially present, but both equally inscribed in his consciousness as the images that close off, and stabilize, the onrush of memory. It is possible to argue that in this equivalence McCall's decision to resolve Laura's present situation in fact makes up for the past with Angela. But it is equally reasonable to suggest that this same formal structure proposes an absolute choice: one or the other, but never both together. This uncertainty of meaning is fore-grounded precisely because it is constructed through a highly self-conscious and stylized sound-image montage sequence.

At the end of this sequence, McCall gets into his car and drives off, abandoning the meeting with Bryan. He reaches the Moore apartment just in time to save Laura from Mike. Soon after this heroic rescue, Jason also catches up with McCall at the Moore apartment, to offer a disparaging assessment of McCall's work with regard to Bryan. In the process he taunts McCall, accusing him of responsibility for Angela's death. In response McCall suggests that Jason purposefully set him up to kill Bryan for personal reasons and declares his intention to find out why. In the final scene McCall visits with Jessie and Laura in a park overlooking the river, offering final counsel and consolation to both of his clients.

In this episode both cases represent disturbances in the do-main of interpersonal relations, intersecting in an interplay of repetition and difference, as each becomes the displaced supplement of the other for McCall. The Moore family is di-vided within itself, and McCall intervenes to protect the vic-tims while offering therapeutic counsel to ease them toward independence. In their case this also means giving up the tra-ditional nuclear family to function as a reformulated family unit. McCall serves a crucial role as mediator between Laura and Jessie, as well as provoking Jessie to break out of her general state of disabling panic and go on with her life.

In terms of the therapeutic process, it is significant that the idea of going on with one's life is central in episodes of both

Finder of Lost Loves and *The Equalizer*. It underscores the process of coming to grips with one's past in order to surmount it in the present: that was then; this is now. However the question of a total cure remains open, insofar as McCall cannot cure the father and restore him to the family. Indeed Mike Moore must return to prison. And McCall himself can only hold the position of father or therapist provisionally. In the final scene of the episode, he adopts a paternal function in relation to both Jessie and Laura, but the end of the episode terminates his relationship to these characters, as subsequent episodes elaborate different case histories.

Moreover, the Moore situation is only one issue in this episode and is imbricated in a network of interpersonal and dramatic conflicts focused on McCall. Bryan figures as the narrative instigator of these conflicts, as the fellow agent who betrayed McCall in the past and whose unexpected presence in New York provides the opportunity for revenge. McCall can either pursue Bryan to avenge Angela's death in the past or protect Laura and Jessie from Mike in the present. Achieving one of these goals will necessarily leave the other situation unresolved. Vengeance for Angela will result in a failed commitment in the present, temporally displacing and repeating the past failure, which would reduplicate and extend McCall's sense of guilt. But concentrating on the Moore case means that Bryan goes free, leaving the past unresolved. The equivalence and tension between the two cases is emphasized in the montage sequence as McCall waits at the heliport.

The tension of competing commitments is exacerbated in the present by Jason. While Jason and McCall are presumably allied, if only on this one case, strong parallels are drawn between Jason and Bryan. Both of them treat McCall with smug disdain, and both function as his adversaries within the Agency. They both give McCall partial and misleading information to turn his work to their own account. Moreover, the introduction of the Bryan case, which remains unresolved at the end, also introduces an open question with regard to Jason for McCall. Thus the resolution of the Moores' situation and the assurance of their safety leaves McCall's personal situation fragmented and incomplete. McCall can only go on with his life in the displaced repetition each case represents, and to successfully resolve his present cases sustains past, unresolved obsessions.

Midnight Caller

Like *The Equalizer*, *Midnight Caller* is a dramatic series in an urban setting. Its fictional premise combines elements of thriller/crime plots with a narrative context that immediately offers a setting for confessional discourse and its concomitant therapeutic effect. The hero of *Midnight Caller* is Jack Killian (played by Gary Cole), a former San Francisco policeman who quit his job after accidentally killing his partner while they were in pursuit of a criminal. In the first episode of the series, he is saved from wallowing in aimless self-pity by Devon King, the daughter of a prominent businessman who has recently taken over the management of one of her father's radio stations. She convinces Jack to host a late-night radio talk show. He proves to be successful in this new position, although it includes fending off phone calls and accusations pertaining to his role in his partner's death.

Like Cary Maxwell and Robert McCall, Jack Killian is able to offer a sympathetic ear and counsel to the late-night radio audience in San Francisco because of a wound in his past that cannot be healed. At the same time, as an ex-cop, Jack's range of expertise includes physical and investigative skills. In most episodes of the show he becomes embroiled in someone else's problems—someone he either knows from his past or presently encounters through the radio. He often has to carry out some kind of investigation and may find himself in life-threatening situations in the course of helping others with their problems. His own past is variably problematized across the episodes that comprise the series.

In one episode Jack's literal past figures slightly but is strikingly displaced onto a situation touched off by one of Jack's radio shows. The situation revolves around a forty-year-old unsolved murder, a retired but legendary police detective, and Devon King, who becomes a close personal friend to Jack over the course of the series. As the episode begins, Jack opens his midnight radio talk show by noting that it is the fortieth anniversary of a well-known, local unsolved murder case, known as the Red Rose Murders. A woman named Rose was found murdered along with an off-duty cop who had apparently come to her aid. As Jack talks, various listeners around the city are seen, including a journalist, Becka Nicholson, who expresses to her assistant the hope of solving the case and writing a best-selling book about it; the retired police detective, Sam Chase, whose partner was the cop killed, and who has never been able to solve the case; and an unseen caller who is moved to call in and confess to the killings as he listens to Jack: "I didn't mean to," he explains. "It was a terrible accident."

In this way, Jack's talk show incites a confession that sets the narrative in motion. This connection between the talk show and confession is made explicit when the retired cop shows up to ask Jack to help him follow up the confession. Jack writes it off as a crank call, explaining that he gets a dozen such calls a week. Chase explains that the confession included information that was known only to himself and the murderer—that the dead policeman was shot with his own gun.

The crime story offers a displaced version of Killian's own situation. The tragedy of losing a partner is shared by Killian and Chase, although their situations vary somewhat. As Chase says, "I'm not the only one here with a past. . . . No matter how lousy the truth is, kid, at least you know who shot your partner." The displacement and identity between Chase and Killian are also dramatized as issues of historical style, since the character of Chase is played in the manner of the hard-boiled detective. He smokes constantly (indeed we learn that he is dying of lung cancer), refers to women as "dames," and in general affects a tough-guy style associated with crime dramas of the 1940s and 1950s.

To reinforce this association, the crime is reenacted in a few brief flashbacks that are played out in black and white, specifically evoking the hard-boiled, film noir dramas of the 1940s. Yet for all this stylistic distancing to differentiate between the Red Rose Murders and Jack Killian's accidental shooting of his partner in the more recent past, the crime is narrativized as a problem of retribution by one policeman for the past murder of his partner, making up for a loss that is in fact unrecoverable. In these terms Chase's situation closely resembles Jack Killian's basic position in the program as a whole.

In this case, the crime story instigated by confession is also a family romance centrally engaging Devon's family history. For she learns that her father, Mel, was engaged to Rose, the woman who was murdered, and was with her just moments before she was killed. In the fiction of the program, her father has recently died. Her first appearance in this episode is a late-night meeting with her lawyer at her office discussing what she wants to do with the properties her father has left her, an extensive range of businesses and real estate. She learns about her father's past from Jack, as he pursues the Red Rose case with Chase, and confronts her mother, who explains that her father was a very private man. (In the program, Devon's parents were divorced while she was growing up.) Indeed the discovery of an alternative trajectory for her father's life, cut short by a murder, provokes a number of confrontations, and ultimately reconciliation, between Devon and her mother. Moreover, her father's business papers provide a clue that is essential in helping Killian and Chase locate the person who called and confessed to the murder on Jack's show.

Chase, Killian, and Devon finally track down the murderer, Ray Fontana, who has been living in a home for mentally disturbed patients for the past forty years. The director of the home explains that Ray suffered mental and emotional disorders after World War II and that Devon's father brought him there and paid for his care. Ray seems almost relieved when they confront him, and he tells them about the accidental deaths of both Rose and Chase's partner. Mel and Rose had just announced their engagement. Ray was happy for Mel but worried that Rose would abandon him in the same way Ray's wife had left him while he was away at war. Ray confronted Rose, and in the course of a scuffle she accidentally fell down a flight of stairs to her death. In a flash of delayed stress, Ray mistook the policeman, who had been attracted to the scene by the noise of the scuffle, for a Japanese soldier, turned the policeman's gun on him, shot, and ran off. Ray told Mel what he had done, and Mel promised to protect him. Indeed, Ray claims, Mel was his brother. Devon is startled by this revelation; she is certain that Ray is confused until he explains that he and Mel had the same mother and shows her old family photos including a young Mel King.

At this juncture, Chase wants to turn Ray over to the police. Killian argues that there would be no point and that they would probably return him to his current situation in any case. "You came to me for a favor," he tells Chase; "now I'm asking you for one. Let it be. Just let it be." Devon and her mother are brought together through the discovery of this new piece of the mystery concerning her father's past. They both visit Ray, and Devon promises to continue to take care of him. Later, Chase misses a meeting with Jack, and Jack accidentally learns that Chase is dying of lung cancer. He rushes to Ray's room, where he finds Chase with a gun to Ray's head. Killian talks Chase out of shooting Ray as revenge for his partner's death forty years earlier.

While this is the most overt therapeutic moment in the episode, in fact the whole narrative hinges on the complex imbrication of multiple irresolvable personal narratives based on losses in the past: Rose, Chase's partner, Killian's partner, and Devon's father. Every character is implicated in a network of relations that precludes resolution, even though a solution to the murder is found. Killian is at the center of this network, as the host of the talk show that provokes a confession—the first concrete lead in the unsolved murder in forty years—and as Devon's friend and employee. But in every case, conciliation in the present is premised on past losses.

Most obviously, for Chase to maintain his dignity and reputation as a legendary detective, he has to modify the very codes that define him as a hard-boiled-style detective from the 1940s. Specifically, he gives up the idea of seeing that his former partner's murder is avenged either by turning Ray over to authorities or by killing Ray himself.[11] Instead he follows Jack's advice and revises his goals in line with Killian's more contemporary, low-key style, and accepts having identified the killer as an adequate fulfillment of his obligation. Similarly, the very existence of Ray comes to light only as a direct function of Mel's death; and the therapeutic narrative thereby generated thus exists in direct proportion to an identifiable loss. For Ray is able to confess his role as murderer on Jack's show in the first place because Mel is dead (and because the anniversary date of the murder leads Jack to mention it at all). As he explains to Killian, Devon, and Chase, Rose recently told him that she and Mel were back together again, so he knew it was time to tell. Similarly, in the course of pursuing the investigation, Devon has access to Mel's personal papers, which include some documents concerning Ray, only because she is in control of her deceased father's estate.

Within this tight narrative web, the role of the mass media may initially appear to be accidental, if not incidental. It is merely a narrative convention, under the guise of coincidence, that leads Ray and Chase to listen to Jack's late-night show on the same night that he opens the program by raising the Red Rose Murders as a topic of discussion. But this very episode advances the position that the mass media provide, at least in contemporary culture, the structural and strategic conditions that enable the confessions at the center of therapeutic narratives. This is hinted at in the opening scene, as Jack introduces his subject by noting that past events become major media events on their anniversaries, even though there is nothing in a change of date that makes the past event more momentous per se. Having implicitly criticized this practice by the media, however mildly, he goes on to introduce the Red Rose Murders on his show, specifically because of the fortieth anniversary date.

Moreover, an important subplot in the episode involves one more person listening to Killian's program in the opening scene. Becka Nicholson decides that she can get her journalistic career back on track by solving the Red Rose Murders and writing a book about the case, as she had done some ten to fifteen years earlier with a famous kidnapping, the Baby

Laura case. Becka made her reputation with that case, based on the fact that the kidnapper sent her confessional letters at the newspaper where she worked, which she printed before turning over to the police. In the end, the child was never recovered, and the kidnapper was presumed to have been killed in a high-speed car chase with the police. Becka's investigation of the Red Rose Murders includes confrontations with Chase, Killian, and Devon. Killian discovers that her information on the Baby Laura case was largely fabricated by her, as the alleged kidnapper was a mob-connected figure who is in fact participating in the government's witness protection program and never really died. This information serves an important narrative function, as Killian uses it to bargain with Becka: he will not reveal her subterfuge in the past as long as she curtails her Red Rose investigation.

In the larger context of a program focused on a late-night radio talk show host, it is interesting that the credibility and reputation of another media figure—Becka Nicholson—is premised on her privileged access to confessional documents, fake or not. For the point is that her credibility and notoriety in the public eye hinge on the impression of authenticity carried by the confessional form of the kidnapper's notes. This is also the case with Jack Killian as a radio talk show host in the program, although he represents a scrupulous and legitimate version of a therapeutic agent.

A Profusion of Therapy

Finder of Lost Loves, *The Equalizer*, and *Midnight Caller* are different kinds of prime-time fiction: fantasy melodrama, urban thriller, and urban drama. Yet they share an underlying dramatic structure and symbolic problematic in their repeated enactments of a therapeutic cure overseen by a mediating authority figure. The protagonists in *Finder of Lost Loves* and *The Equalizer* are engaged by clients under the alibi of offering investigative or detective services. In *Midnight Caller* Killian's role as both a radio host and a former policeman leads him to get involved in the lives of others—

friends and strangers—as the media are centrally implicated in the flow of confession and therapy. Crucially, in all three shows the ability and willingness to direct a therapeutic cure is determined in direct proportion to the protagonist's lack, which is specifically delineated in the course of the programs, if not in every episode. This in turn provides viewers with multiple potential identifications and positions of knowledge in relation to the programs, a dispersion of positions that may be construed in terms of therapeutic discourse as it is rewritten in the course of the shows.

It is crucial to stress the potentiality of these positions insofar as there is no guarantee that any given viewer will recognize or occupy all of them. These positions are derived in relation to the ongoing narrative preoccupations of the programs and the mobilization of an unstable therapeutic discourse that provides familiar and recognizable positions within discourse for television viewers. On an episodic basis, the protagonist's stake in the therapeutic problematic may be more or less evident; and it may be directly or distantly implicated in the given weekly case. Thus the availability of multiple positions of identification and recognition is itself in flux through the course of a particular program. However, the delineation of these variable and unstable positions contributes to an understanding of how television's deployment of therapeutic relations impinges not only on dramatic strategies and narrative structure but also on viewing positions. In other words, therapeutic discourse as an aspect of fiction narrative television must be understood simultaneously as an ideological problematic and a mode of address.[12]

To understand this mode of address one cannot simply draw analogies between protagonists and clients within the fiction, therapists and patients, and television and its viewers with the assumption that one term in each set unilaterally exercises control over a curative process or speaks with the authoritative voice of dominant culture. For, as the analyses of *The Equalizer, Finder of Lost Loves*, and *Midnight Caller* indicate, such hierarchical control is immediately challenged by the recognition that weekly cases serve as therapy for the program protagonists, as symbolic compensatory repetitions for constitutive lacks, and indeed as the rationale for their fictional professions. From this perspective, the protagonist is the regular therapeutic subject who must undergo regulated and interminable repetition. This sets up a context for mobility within the positions provided by therapeutic discourse. Power is not exercised by occupying a specific position once and for all, but by the discourse itself, and the complicity of subjects who negotiate among the terms. Within these narratives power is not unilaterally held by the protagonists because they do not exert simple mastery over the therapeutic process. The very notion of fixed social and professional hierarchies is disturbed by the recognition that those figures who most readily occupy the positions affiliated with power are uneasily situated and may have to move aside and allow others, even their subordinates, to assume the functions of authority.

Indeed no one exercises definitive mastery within the therapeutic problematic, which nonetheless establishes a model of presumably hierarchical relations. Moreover, viewers may not only identify with program regulars or a specific client case but may also stand outside this dynamic in recognition of the double therapeutic problematic at the core of the programs. In this instance, viewing positions are not anchored by narrative identifications with a particular character or star, but instead hinge on the process of therapy to which fictional characters are subject. A viewer can assume the position of "therapist," recognizing the progress of multiple patients simultaneously, although unable to intervene directly in the narrative process that leads to terms of resolution, however provisional. Of course, part of the apparatus that impinges on any particular viewing act encourages, perhaps even facilitates, this position.[13] The slippages in identification within the therapeutic problematic disrupt the possibility of fixing individuals with specific positions of power within the therapeutic dynamic once and for all, while it sustains the established positions and terms of the discourse of therapy.

The variable identifications made available in these programs can be understood in terms of the mechanism of fantasy described by Elizabeth Cowie in her article "Fantasia."[14]

She elaborates on fantasy in psychoanalytic terms, stressing its status as a structure, the staging of desire rather than particular objects or goals. For Cowie fantasy offers a privileged approach to understanding the mobilization of the audience because it engages social reality and the unconscious simultaneously. "What is necessary for any public forms of fantasy, for their collective consumption," she explains, "is not universal objects of desire, but a setting of desiring in which we can find our place(s). And these places will devolve, as in the original fantasies, on positions of desire: active or passive, feminine or masculine, mother or son, father or daughter." [15] Cowie argues that original or primary fantasy encompasses multiple points of entry, "where the subject is both present *in* the scene and interchangeable with any other character." [16] In relation to the primary fantasy, narrative organizes material, along the lines of secondary elaboration in dreams.

> [Narrative restores] a minimum of order and coherence to the raw material and [imposes] on this heterogeneous assortment a facade, a scenario, which gives it relative coherence and continuity. A holding down, fixing, is performed in the production of a continuity, a coherence; the narrative seeks to *find* (produce) a proper place for the subject. . . . While subject-positions are variable the terms of sexual difference are fixed. It is the form of tension and play between the fixing of narrative—the secondary elaboration—and the lack of fixity of the subject in the original fantasies which would seem to be important, and not any already-given privileging of one over the other.[17]

This understanding of narrative and fantasy proposes that viewer identification is in flux across a field of fixed positions, in particular in terms of sexual difference. "While the terms of sexual difference are fixed, the places of characters and spectators in relation to those terms are not." [18]

Finder of Lost Loves, The Equalizer, and *Midnight Caller* conjoin sexual, familial, and therapeutic terms of difference —male/female, father/mother, professional/client, doctor/ patient, analyst/analysand—in playing out fantasy through narratives whose trajectories are modeled on the process of a therapeutic cure. Mobility among these established positions—a limited plurality—is not simply guided by individual choice but is worked out in relation to the particular dramatic, generic, and narrational perspectives offered in each episode on the one hand and in relation to the social formation of viewers on the other. Thus, for example, the narrative and representational conventions that construct sexual, racial, or ethnic difference within television may inflect a particular viewer's mode of engagement with a given episode.[19]

Through a range of prime-time dramatic fictions, therapy stands as a regime of power and a mode of understanding that can be seen as one of television's pervasive ideological forces. And within this discourse, no one individual wields definitive power. Rather all characters and viewers are situated as potential subjects of a discourse that itself offers a determining view of social and interpersonal relations. The power at work in confessional and therapeutic modes of discourse is more widely dispersed as it is decentered or destabilized. It by no means disappears. Moreover, while identity with familiar gender positions is construed in fluid terms, the fact of sexual difference, and differential relations to power based therein, hardly becomes moot. For it is striking that in all of these shows the protagonist remains a male figure with relative authority and associations with power, despite his lack.

Therapeutic and confessional modes of discourse have frequently been affiliated with female audiences, especially in forms of melodrama and women's fiction.[20] Yet insofar as therapy, confession, and therapeutic relations figure as pervasive influences on prime-time television in general, including urban thrillers and action shows such as *The Equalizer* and *Midnight Caller*, it becomes necessary to recognize their broad social efficacy, extending beyond the traditionally delimited range of programming for women. The multiplication of the therapeutic problematic within specific programs disperses the positions any single character or viewer may hold, as suggested in the discussion of fantasy. At the same time fantasy turns in on itself, as it is worked out in narratives whose underlying problematic involves finding one's place in a familial and social order. This process is exacerbated with the proliferation of therapeutic discourses through a range of television genres and programs. The potential for a plurality of identifications is balanced by increased repetition of the same positions within a discourse that overdetermines, and is overdetermined by, the family structure. The discourse of therapy constrains everyone who participates in it to turn to others in the effort to find one's place. Yet this process must be replayed over and over again, since one's place is never given once and for all, even though the positions one may assume are already given in advance.

Conclusion

The Simpsons in Therapy

The Simpsons is a half-hour animated situation comedy developed for the Fox network. Introduced in the 1989–90 television season, the program proved to be an immediate popular hit, so much so that in 1990–91 it aired opposite *The Cosby Show*, the monster hit of the late 1980s. Like characters in so many popular culture texts, including *Alf* (discussed in the Introduction), the Simpsons exploded beyond the confines of their own show into the larger text of American pop culture, appearing, among other places, on T-shirts, lunch boxes, and balloons, in toy stores as dolls and on board games, and even on MTV as stars of music videos. In fact, *The Simpsons* did not originate as a full-length, half-hour situation comedy in its own right, but first appeared on television as a feature within *The Tracy Ullman Show*, also a Fox network program. Success in this context spawned the more prominent position as a full-length situation comedy (though it still appears as a short-subject in reruns of *Tracy Ullman*, for example in 1991 on the Lifetime Channel).

The Simpsons is characterized by its slightly hip, and solidly irreverent, image of the American nuclear family, presenting the dark underside of the congenial families that typically populate the situation comedy. When compared to the families on other programs, the Simpsons come up short: the well-meaning parents are inept and unsuccessful in economic and careerist terms; the children are unprecocious or are ostracized in proportion to their particular talents, and they willfully talk back to their parents; and the family members share each other's company zoned out in front of the television. (It would not be unreasonable to assume that the Simpsons shop with the Home Shopping Club, at least every now and then.)

One of the social manifestations of their purported down-scale otherness within the world of television families, rejecting proper middle-class values and norms, is substantial public discussion of the appropriateness of the program's characters as role models for children. There was also a well-publicized uproar over T-shirts issued in 1990 featuring the son, Bart, labeled as an "underachiever" with a comic strip thought-balloon reading, "and proud of it, man." The T-shirt was, according to many newspaper stories, banned in a number of schools across the United States for fostering a bad message among the youth audience. Meanwhile, in response to these furors, the children positioned as the victims of this pop culture attack on dominant bourgeois values were defended by some as smart enough to recognize a joke when they see one.

In 1990 it was not surprising that this family, among others on television, underwent family therapy. The episode in question begins with the family unwillingly led by Homer (the father) to the annual family picnic given by his boss, owner of the local nuclear power plant. No one really wants to go, including Homer, who is perennially upstaged and humiliated by colleagues who seem to have perfect families. These families are characterized by one group in particular, who engage in apparently excessive, profuse expressions of affection, and cheerful cooperation: the son repeatedly hugs his father and says, "I love you Dad." Homer's response is anger and distress, as he wonders why his own family functions so differently from this apparent ideal. He goes so far as to play Peeping Tom to his neighbors in an effort to discover the truth of disharmony behind the facade of congenial domestic relations that surround him. But he ends up in a bar, drinking away his own feelings of familial inadequacy. In this state, he sees a commercial on the television at the bar for a family therapist, who guarantees his services: he will cure the family of its problems or give double his normal fee back for the failure of his services.

Homer immediately decides that his family needs therapy. He even hocks the family television to pay for therapy in spite of massive protests from his wife and children. The therapy session begins with efforts to provoke expressions of family tensions and hostility to be confronted and worked out by the family as group. But the Simpsons' rapid failure with the doctor's normal strategies requires an escalation in the form their therapy assumes, culminating in a form of aversion shock therapy, as the members of the family are wired to shock one another at will. Ideally, each person will react to emotional pain by inflicting physical pain in return. The idea is that when they see how much they hurt one another, they will realize how profoundly they really care for one another, leading to new family harmony. However, the members of the Simpson family start pressing the buttons right away, and they quickly increase the frequency and intensity of their shock attacks on one another. In response to one shock, they are either shocked right back or some other family member shocks them to punish them for hurting someone else. (All pain is physical; emotions are hardly the issue, even though the mother says, "I think we're making progress.") They use so much electricity that they cause a brownout; the doctor throws them out and gives them double their money back. With this newfound wealth, Homer decides to buy a brand new, and bigger, television rather than retrieving the old one from the pawn shop, winning expressions of affection from his wife and children.

In this episode, the linking of the family, television, and therapy could hardly be more explicit. Television is the instrument that sells Homer on the idea of family therapy in the first place. Only after trying therapy does he learn that in the final analysis watching television is a better form of therapy for the family. It is also healthier for the larger community, which suffers a power outage as a result of the Simpson family therapy session, although the owner of the nuclear power plant is delighted to see the plant operating at maximum capacity. Ironically, Homer himself is professionally committed to the production of electric power, as an employee of the local nuclear power plant.

If I were hoping to write a television episode to extend and confirm the arguments derived from watching television, situating the medium as a form of therapeutic practice, this is certainly one of the stories I might have told. The point is not that this is a good or bad lesson but that a logic of television as therapy has become sufficiently pervasive that the medium can write its own stories to both confirm and critique the television apparatus as a form of therapeutic practice, while inscribing therapy as a central structure within the consumerist appeals of the medium. Indeed the self-reflexive linking of television, consumer culture, and therapy in this particular episode can be considered as a sign of the importance of therapeutic discourse in the programming practices of contemporary American television at large. For self-reflexivity within the medium frequently supports the hegemonic mainstream, precisely in terms of simultaneous confirmation and critique.[1] In this light, it is useful to look more closely at the therapeutic dynamic at work in this episode of *The Simpsons*.

Who is the therapist here? The position of therapist is a circuit of shifting power rather than a singular site of authority. The doctor who advertises on television is the most literal therapist figure, but he is undone by the Simpson family and outdone by the medium that carries his message. Even at the start, he is something of a postmodern figure; rather than relying on the talking cure, or other versions of conventional verbal confession, he offers therapeutic methods that not only include drawing and soft mallets for beating one another to expel hostility but are also finally indebted to the age of electronic (re)production. In this context the Simpsons, strictly a made-for-TV family—objects of mechanico-electronic reproduction as animated figures—quite literally short-circuit the doctor's practice. In the process, they also threaten a loss of television reception throughout the city, a loss that can be understood as a version of therapeutic catastrophe.

As the one who makes decisions about when to sell and buy the family television, and when to go to therapy in the first place, Homer himself plays something of a misbegotten therapist, diagnosing the problems of his own family with reference to those of his fellow workers and neighbors. There are also, of course, the viewers who are privy to Homer's confessional ruminations and observations while watching their own television sets. The television apparatus instigates these trajectories, standing not as the therapist but as the apparatus that provokes and facilitates therapeutic exchange. Crucially, this includes literal exchanges within consumer culture, as the Simpsons first pawn their television for the money to afford therapy and then end up trading their old television in for a bigger and better model. The therapeutic experience is a definitive success for the Simpsons within the trajectory of therapy offered by television. The rewards of therapy are measured in the larger television set that brings them an improved vision of programming to renew the therapeutic experience; and the set itself embodies an image of an advance in their style of living.

Proliferating Information and Shrinking Sense[2]

The past five chapters have offered analyses of particular manifestations of therapeutic discourse in a variety of modes and genres of American television. These are exemplary instances of a discursive strategy that pervades the medium. Earlier I proposed that therapeutic and confessional discourse were closely linked and that they functioned as a narrative and narrational strategy within television. In other words, therapeutic discourse provides a ready-made and familiar narrative trajectory: the eruption of a problem leads to confession and diagnosis and then to a solution or cure. At the same time therapeutic discourse implies particular positions and relations in speech, situating those who participate as confessing subjects or as the authority(ies) who require(s) the confession.

In the context of television, therapeutic discourses assume a variety of narrative and narrational forms, encouraging recognitions and identifications in relation to a variety of positions. Therapeutic discourse is a strategy for generating narrative and narrational positions rather than a fixed structure. Its deployment does not guarantee specific textual results; instead it offers possibilities for stories, identifications, and positions that are ambivalent and contradictory. As a narrative strategy, therapeutic discourse projects stories as case histories, including the possibility of carrying both personal and social implications. The elaboration of narrative in terms of confession and therapy thus enables the production of a sense of context and history.

However, as has been demonstrated (for example in *The Equalizer* or *Finder of Lost Loves*), this history may itself take the form of nontransformative redundancy. This is a particular pressure exerted by series television as a form of popular narrative that must renovate itself on a weekly basis in relation to familiar, regular characters and genre/program conventions. Even in cases where transformation is more overtly figured, such as *The 700 Club*, repetition of the process—of confession, and of conversion—must take place again and again. As a narrative structure, then, therapy is figured as both transformative *and* repetitive. At the same time, as a narrational position, confession facilitates, even encourages, individuals to speak in their own voices, for themselves. And yet confessional subjects are often detached from speaking their own histories. Instead, narrative context is provided, and regulated, by an authority who positions the confessional subject, orienting what the subject will say and how the subject will speak in advance. In this sense, confessional discourse on television is not stable in its production of truth or in its delineations of power.

For Michel Foucault confession functioned as an agency of truth and power. It is a process of speech that inherently and immediately implicates power, in the relation of confessor to authority, a relation that in turn guarantees the truth of what is spoken: "a ritual in which the truth is corroborated by the obstacles and resistances it has had to surmount in order to be formulated."[3] Of course, television rewrites the rules of the confessional and therapeutic game. Through the course of different forms of television programming, positions within the confessional transaction at the heart of therapy are destabilized and dispersed. The position of authority and knowledge is not lost once and for all but subdivided and shared in provisional and variable ways among viewers and participants in the production of programming. Similarly, the position of confessor is subdivided and shared among a variety of speakers (and interlocutors). At the heart of this new therapeutic culture, everyone confesses over and over again to everybody else. In the process, television transforms ideas about the authenticity of one's own voice, especially in the singular first-person.

The forms of programming discussed offer a television version of cultural and social experiences that are—currently and historically—available in other forms. Therapy and advice shows reformulate conventional therapy conjoined with the literature of sexology and advice/agony columns and the conventions of radio call-in shows. The couples game shows model different versions of matchmaking (video dating, personal classified ads, traditional matchmakers), marriage counseling, and judicial court proceedings, along with game show conventions for competition. Television shopping draws on the catalogue (Sear's Wishbook), the mall, and the community auction, combined with the services of a personal shopper. Televangelism offers prayer and healing associated with church and revival meetings, reformulated through a range of television genres including news, talk shows, and melodrama.

Yet expressed in this way, it would seem that television merely provides simulated, and degraded, replacements of experiences that are, somehow, more "authentic" or valuable in their original or previous cultural manifestation than in their current deformed, consumerized expression on television. Although it is essential to recognize television's continuities with, and relations to, other modes and aspects of cultural and social practice (historical and contemporary), simple comparison along these lines fails to account for the complexity of television as a force for reformulating and adapting cultural and social practice. Such comparisons often mistakenly imply that earlier forms or practices are more authentic and valuable, especially in offering a personal, and face-to-face, encounter. However, it is essential to question for whom these experiences were (and are) valuable. More often than not, the valued prior formation is itself mythic or involves class and gender exclusions that have to be recognized as problematic in themselves. For example, it is difficult to privilege traditional forms of therapy and analysis in American society if one understands that access is frequently a question of economic and class privilege in the first place and if one understands the ways in which conventional psychoanalytic practice have operated at women's expense, at least in the United States, in the second place.[4]

Indeed, it is essential to recognize that, and how, the forms of social and cultural practice referenced by the programs discussed in this book are themselves fully in fee to patriarchal and consumer culture, although often in different terms than those proposed by television. Moreover, in simply formal and generic terms, none of these programs involves a straightforward reduplication of practices that can be found elsewhere in culture. Rather they all engage in complex recombinations of a variety of practices and genres. These generic and formal reconfigurations are brought out in the individual analyses of particular programs. As the exemplary mode of contemporary cultural expression, television significantly rewrites and transforms the cultural and social practices that it references and recombines. This is particularly acute in the case of therapeutic and confessional strategies.

The therapeutic strategy invites viewers to participate in any number of ways; that is its efficacy and its appeal. At the same time, it is intimately bound up with the functioning of consumer culture, which itself assumes a variety of forms. The entertainment values of all of the programs discussed, and therefore viewer willingness to watch on a regular basis, are connected to (though not necessarily singularly created by) the therapeutic strategies they engage. This occurs not only through the advertising and commercial appeals that are interspersed through the programs but also, crucially, through the class and lifestyle images they project. The flexibility of the therapeutic ethos is particularly striking, insofar as it is deployed to engage, even recruit, viewers for (and from) a wide range of class/lifestyle images within contemporary American consumer culture. Like television itself, therapy offers something for everyone, or can be tailored to fulfill a variety of needs and fantasies.

As an elaboration of these practices, new forms of therapeutic and confessional discourse can be traced in evolving television genres and in various mediated forms of confession via information technology. On television these include so-called infomercials and also reality-based programs such as *Rescue 911*, *Unsolved Mysteries*, and *America's Most Wanted*. The infomercial is a thirty- or sixty-minute program that exists in the generic terrain between shop-at-home television, the talk show, entertainment news/gossip, and educational or instructional programming. A particular product, which can be purchased by mail or phone, is discussed and demonstrated, most often along with personal testimony from people who have used it, for the bulk of the show. There is often a studio audience, and the hosts may include celebrities who have used the product in question and been transformed by it. This is especially the case with cosmetic items: teeth have been whitened for a brighter smile, or wrinkles have faded away. The programs are structured like typical and familiar forms of commercial programming, with advertising breaks that provide viewers with two-minute promotions for the product being discussed on the show, along with information about price and ordering procedures. Price and ordering information is by and large reserved for the commercial breaks, even though the whole program effectively functions as a commercial in the guise of informational chat about the product. This chat routinely includes confessional disclosures by those who have used the product.

Reality-based dramas are implicated in the therapeutic problematic in a number of ways. Their strategies of narration are closely linked to those deployed on *The 700 Club* in the course of the confessional, melodramatic narratives of individual conversion and salvation through CBN. The programs use voice-over narrators, but they include the voice of participants and victims of the stories they tell, along with re-enactments that frequently feature the actual people involved with the cases playing themselves. These same people are also presented as interview subjects, in a studio, after the fact, so to speak. In the course of retelling tales of life-threatening danger and heroic rescues in *Rescue 911*, the participants also speak for themselves, especially to describe how they felt at certain moments—say, as they helped rescue a drowning man from the bottom of the pool—or express how they value life more profoundly now that they have been through a life-threatening adventure. In such cases, the confessional voice is framed by a narrator and structurally encouraged to speak in terms of emotive and melodramatic conventions.

Moreover, with the proliferation of shows of this order in the late 1980s, there is a sense that participating as the confessional subject is part of the therapeutic ethos projected by television: telling one's story *on television* is part of the process of recovery (and repetition). At the same time this confers on participants a sense of celebrity. Their stories are told on national television, and they get to participate as actors and expert witnesses. In such instances the successful therapeutic trajectory is signified by the patient's accession to celebrity status via an appearance on television. In certain of these shows—notably *America's Most Wanted* and *Unsolved Mysteries*—there is also a sense of a socially therapeutic mission, as exposing unsolved crimes on television has led to the apprehension of a number of criminal suspects.

Confessional exchange is also at the center of a thriving industry for 900 and 976 phone services, which might be characterized as pay-per-chat telephone lines. There are an increasing variety of such services, for which television serves as the primary instrument of promotion via advertising.[5] These 900 and 976 lines charge by the minute (often substantial rates) for people to call and listen to others' prerecorded confessions and fantasies, to record their own confessions and fantasies, or to talk, often on party lines. While many of the services centrally involve and implicate sex, and are aimed at male callers,[6] there are also lines aimed at teen and female audiences, often featuring popular music groups, teen heart throbs, soap opera stars, or just an opportunity to talk. There is also a burgeoning industry in computer bulletin boards, where people with access to a computer and modem can leave personal, confessional messages to be shared with others with common interests. In the case of both pay-per-chat telephone and computer bulletin boards, the new information technology serves as a channel of confessional discourse, fully implicated in a therapeutic ethos that creates communities among individuals situated in their homes, in front of their television sets, on the telephone, or in front of their computer terminals. In other words, tracing the articulations of therapeutic discourse on television is only the beginning.

Television offers a double-edged intervention. It is perhaps more crass and thorough in its commodity/consumer operations than prior forms of therapeutic and confessional engagement, and apparently more totalizing. All viewers are always already inexorably caught up in the confessional mode and also in the consumer culture that it supports. But of course television is exceptionally blatant in proclaiming these interests; they are hardly hidden, even from the most purportedly naive viewer. In these terms, television's bluntness also allows for self-consciousness, of both viewers and programs. The medium thus carries the possibility of generating its own discourses of demystification. Yet one must be wary of too quickly assuming that demystification is the equivalent of a systemic critique. Analysis of the Home Shopping Club suggests that the ironic, self-critical, and potentially demystificatory tone that can be read through the course of its programming also carries assumptions about class distinction and the superiority of certain taste cultures.

At the same time, through the deployment of therapeutic and confessional strategies of discourse, viewers may perhaps participate in the production of programs more directly than they can in other forms of popular culture. (Radio is also open to audience participation in this way.) They speak in their own voices to help produce the texts of our multiply mediated, information/therapeutic culture. The audience is given the opportunity to speak—as expert, as authority, and as celebrity—even as their voices are channeled and contained to a great extent. Yet this channeling does not resemble forms of power and domination at stake in a dialogic interpersonal exchange. Instead, all voices are dispersed through and across contemporary technologies, information and financial exchanges, and conventions of entertainment in contemporary consumer culture. The voices of individuals are mobilized in the process. Indeed none of these systems would work properly without these confessional voices, whether they are fictional or not.

Therapeutic discourse in this sense supports a dispersion of subjectivity and meaning that has been seen to characterize the contemporary postmodern condition.[7] At the same time it provides familiar structures, however provisional, as reference terms of stability and reassurance. The therapeutic relation and positions of confession that constitute it, fluid and dispersed in practice, offer the appearance of a stable structure: one talks, the other listens. Moreover, the therapeutic relation readily inscribes the family structure, overdetermined by traditional gender roles: father, mother, son/daughter. In its current formation, the family is in turn inscribed within consumer culture, with its inextricable links to information/telecommunications culture. All of this emerges with clarity through the analysis of therapeutic discourse on television, explaining one of the dominant discursive practices in contemporary culture.

Understanding television's deployment of therapeutic and confessional discourse makes it possible to exploit the medium's own self-consciousness, its crass consumerism, so to speak, both for and against its own interests. The point is to recognize that speaking for oneself is not always what it seems. But it may be better than letting someone else have the last word, especially if one knows when refusing to speak is a way of claiming the last word.

Notes

INTRODUCTION

1. Doane, *The Desire to Desire*; Joyrich, "All That Television Allows"; Joyrich, "Critical and Textual Hypermasculinity"; and Modleski, "Femininity as Mas[s]querade."

2. In a later season, Alf moves into the woman's apartment briefly. With his refusal to go out and earn an independent living and his propensity to consume large quantities of food, he quickly wears out his welcome. Meanwhile, he misses the Tanner family crowd. Alf and the woman mutually decide he would be better off moving back in to the Tanner house. Throughout this time the woman never learns that Alf is an alien.

3. This aspect of the program is also commented on by Asimov, "ALF, You've Got Some Explaining to Do."

4. Coward, "Sexual Politics and Psychoanalysis"; Rubin, "The Traffic in Women"; and Silverman, *The Subject of Semiotics.*

5. Mellencamp, "Situation Comedy, Feminism, and Freud"; Morley, *Family Television*; Mulvey, "Melodrama In and Out of the Home"; and Spigel, "Television in the Family Circle."

6. Joyrich, "All That Television Allows"; Lears, "From Salvation to Self-Realization"; Lasch, *The Culture of Narcissism*; and Torres, "Melodrama, Masculinity, and the Family."

7. Foucault, *The History of Sexuality*, pp. 61–62.

8. Ibid., p. 61.

9. Masciarotte offers an analysis of the television talk show, focusing on Oprah Winfrey, in this vein, in "C'mon, Girl." Her work stresses the production of a mass or social subjectivity and the social implications of the formation of this new subjectivity as it emerges on *The Oprah Winfrey Show*. While Masciarotte approaches the program from a methodological and contextual framework that differs from the ap-

proach I have taken in this book, it is significant that she and I both recognize the current production of talk and confessional voices on television as reconfiguring subjectivity and truth. Masciarotte's project is to discern the difference in a particular show within a genre, from the ongoing generic tendencies; thus for her Oprah's show purveys a specific set of practices that differentiate it, finally, from other apparently similar programs such as *Donahue*. My interests include recognizing program specificities, but also seeing how confessional practices work across television, as an agency for producing new voices and new subjectivities that nonetheless remain in fee to consumer culture, voices that both constitute and evade the forces setting them in motion.

10. The connections between mass culture and consumerism are hardly original to television. For an analysis of the relation between the American film industry and consumer culture, see Eckert, "The Carole Lombard in Macy's Window"; also see White, "Ideological Analysis and Television."

11. This is in distinction to the emphasis on sex and/or orgasm in the 1960s and 1970s. In this regard, see Williamson, *Consuming Passions*, pp. 37–45, and Heath, *The Sexual Fix*.

12. Lears, "From Salvation to Self-Realization."

13. Berger, *Ways of Seeing*; Coward, *Female Desires*; and Williamson, *Consuming Passions*.

14. For example, see Marchand, *Advertising the American Dream*.

15. For example, see Palmer, *Confession Writer's Handbook*. This book provides a very brief historical overview, as well as guidelines for would-be confession writers. Given the association of female readers with confessional magazines, it is interesting that the founder of *True Story* in the early 1920s was Bernarr Macfadden, a leader of the muscular physical culture cult of the 1910s and publisher of *Physical Culture* and the *New York Evening Graphic*. He also started *True Confessions*, *True Detective Mysteries*, and *True Marriage Stories*, among other magazines. For more on Macfadden, see Ernst, *Weakness Is a Crime*.

16. Lears, "From Salvation to Self-Realization," p. 27.

17. Doane, *The Desire to Desire*; Joyrich, "All That Television Allows"; Modleski, "Femininity as Mas[s]querade"; Mulvey, "Melodrama In and Out of the Home"; and Spigel, "Television in the Family Circle."

18. Mulvey, "Melodrama In and Out of the Home," p. 98.

19. Mellencamp, "Situation Comedy, Feminism, and Freud," p. 80.

20. Joyrich, "All That Television Allows," p. 146.

21. Ibid., p. 147.

22. Allen, *Speaking of Soap Operas*; Brunsdon, "*Crossroads*"; Flitterman, "The *Real* Soap Operas"; Modleski, *Loving with a Vengeance*, esp.

pp. 85–109; Seiter, "Eco's TV Guide—The Soaps"; and Seiter, "Promise and Contradiction."

23. Joyrich's work extends soap opera research, arguing that melodrama is characteristic of television drama in general. Her position in "All That Television Allows" follows from that of Thorburn in "Television Melodrama." However, Joyrich's position is articulated in terms of postmodernism, consumer culture, and, most importantly, gender.

24. Flitterman, "The *Real* Soap Operas."

25. Feuer discusses the prime-time dramatic serial as the dominant form in the 1980s in "Melodrama, Serial Form, and Television Today." Among the prime-time dramatic series that adopted serial and melodramatic conventions in the 1980s are *Hill St. Blues*, *Chicago Story*, *St. Elsewhere*, *Bay City Blues*, *L.A. Law*, *Crime Story*, and *Wiseguy*.

26. Modleski, *Loving with a Vengeance*, p. 93.

27. Hobson, "Soap Operas at Work."

28. Modleski, *Loving with a Vengeance*, p. 107.

29. Torres has proposed that the prime-time domestic male melodrama may function therapeutically, with important implications for the representation of male and female sexuality within the family ("Melodrama, Masculinity, and the Family"). Her argument is made specifically with respect to the program *thirtysomething* and suggests that the program's therapeutic negotiation of sexuality, the family, and ideology are singular, or at least rare, in American television. While studies of this sort—narrowly focused on individual programs and genres—extend and provide some context for my own work, they cast a narrow view on the more pervasive presence and role of therapeutic and confessional discourse in American television. I am precisely against an analysis that suggests any individual program is singular in engaging therapeutic discourse and concomitant issues of gender, sexuality, and consumerism. I am, however, interested in how particular programs and program forms specify the therapeutic process.

30. This work is cogently summarized and explained in Silverman, *The Subject of Semiotics*. Also see Benveniste, *Problems in General Linguistics*

31. Of course Freud was well received in the United States, beginning with the lectures he gave at Clark University in the 1920s. His influence, in the form of "popular Freudianism," has been widely felt in women's magazines, films, and popular literature throughout the course of the twentieth century. Indeed, the historical links between the development of consumer culture and a therapeutic ethos may account for the establishment of a general social-cultural context receptive to the kinds of ideas Freud developed.

32. Baudrillard, *Simulations*; Baudrillard, *In the Shadow of the Silent Majorities*; Jameson, "Postmodernism and Consumer Cultures"; and Polan, "Brief Encounters."

33. Lyotard, *The Postmodern Condition*. This definition is applied to readings of popular culture in Collins, *Uncommon Cultures*. Also see Polan, "Brief Encounters."

34. Postmodern psychoanalysis does not conform to this model, nor do notions of interminable analysis. See, for example, Deleuze and Guattari, *The Anti-Oedipus*; Roustang, *Dire Mastery*; and Roustang, *Psychoanalysis Never Lets Go*.

35. Polan, "Brief Encounters," p. 178.

36. Benveniste, *Problems in General Linguistics*, and Silverman, *The Subject of Semiotics*. There is a clear relationship between Benveniste's formulation of *discours* as a linguistic mode, and Foucault's understanding of the confession, which is *discours* in Benveniste's sense. *Discours* undergirds my idea of therapeutic and confessional discourse; but I use discourse in a broader sense to suggest a whole field of signifying productivity.

37. Haraway, "A Manifesto for Cyborgs," p. 185.

38. Ibid.

39. Ibid., p. 187.

CHAPTER ONE

1. The following *TV Guide* articles, listed here in chronological order, were consulted in writing this chapter: Joanmarie Kalter, "No Problem Is Too Intimate for Your TV Therapist," June 4, 1983; Candy Justice, "Now TV Offers a Parenting Manual," July 28, 1984; John P. Docherty, M.D., "A Psychiatrist Looks at Prime Time," August 4, 1984; James E. Gardner, Ph.D., "Does Your Teen-ager *Need* a $95.00 Shirt—or Just Want One?," May 4, 1985; Teresa Kochmar Crout, "Your Therapy Could Be Watching *Dallas* or *Dynasty*," December 14, 1985; Willard Gaylin, M.D., "Prime Time on the Couch: A Psychiatrist Wonders What's Happening to Romantic Love," October 4, 1986; Louise Bernikow, "Is TV a Pal—or a Danger—for Lonely People?," October 25, 1986; David Hellerstein, M.D., "Can TV Cause Divorce?," September 26, 1987; Dr. Ruth Westheimer, "Dr. Ruth Advises: David—Quit Your Job! Maddie—Stop Playing Games!," October 24, 1987; Michael Leahy, "TV's Psychology Shows: More Hype Than Help?," November 21, 1987; Dr. Ruth Westheimer, "Dr. Ruth to The Golden Girls: How to Keep That Spice and Sparkle in Your Lives," April 30, 1988;

David Hellerstein, M.D., "Now the Psychiatrist Can Do More Than Just Listen," October 8, 1988; Gerald Goodman, Ph.D., "Successful Intimacy?: Watch *L.A. Law*'s Stuart and Ann," October 29, 1988; Dr. Joyce Brothers, "If You Want to Be a Better Parent . . . ," March 4, 1989; Robert Coles, M.D., "How Television's Stories Help Us," June 3, 1989; Dr. Susan Amsterdam, "Midlife Crises in Men: Are Women to Blame?," July 22, 1989; Dr. Joyce Brothers, "The Shows That'll Make You Feel Better," July 29, 1989; Dr. Joyce Brothers, "Why We Need to Laugh," November 11, 1989; Dr. Joyce Brothers, "How TV Adds Spice to Your Life," February 10, 1990.

2. In the late 1980s, in particular, this genre was highly visible in the broadcasting industry. Ads for such programs in the pages of *Broadcasting* include ones for *Strictly Confidential*, starring Dr. Susan Forward, author of the best-seller *Men Who Hate Women and the Women Who Love Them*; *Getting in Touch*, with Dr. David Viscott; and *Mr. Romance*. "At one point there were as many as six half-hour shows—either reenactments of therapy sessions or live sessions with an audience and a therapist—in the planning stages" (*Broadcasting*, January 19, 1987, p. 110).

3. This is not the full extent of Dr. Ruth's media career. She started on radio and became famous for her program *Sexually Speaking* before moving to television. In addition to these two programs, she has had other shows, both specials and regular series, on the Lifetime Channel.

4. Torres, "Melodrama, Masculinity, and the Family," cites two articles that discuss the use of taped episodes of *thirtysomething* in therapy: Patricia Hersch, "*thirtysomething*therapy," *Psychology Today*, October 1988, pp. 62–64, and Phoebe Hoban, "All in the Family: TV's *thirtysomething* Hits Home," *New York Magazine*, February 29, 1988, pp. 48–52. The specific context of these citations suggests that Torres sees this as a singular and symptomatic aspect of *thirtysomething* rather than as a tendency to be associated with television more broadly.

5. Crout, "Your Therapy," pp. 14–15.

6. Ibid., p. 15.

7. Ibid., p. 18.

8. Ibid.

9. Kalter, "No Problem Is Too Intimate," p. 6.

10. Ibid.

11. Brothers, "How TV Adds Spice to Your Life," and Gaylin, "Prime Time on the Couch."

12. Goodman, "Successful Intimacy?," and Hellerstein, "Can TV Cause Divorce?"

13. Hellerstein, "Can TV Cause Divorce?," p. 6.

14. Ibid., p. 7.

15. Bernikow, "Is TV a Pal?," p. 5.

16. Ibid., p. 6.

17. Ibid.

18. Leahy, "TV's Psychology Shows," p. 50.

19. Bernikow, "Is TV a Pal?," p. 5.

20. Justice, "Now TV Offers a Parenting Manual," p. 30.

21. Quoted in Leahy, "TV's Psychology Shows," p. 51.

22. For example, after the networks canceled *The Days and Nights of Molly Dodd*, Lifetime started showing reruns of the series and then began producing original episodes.

23. At least for the time being, sports programming, news, and public affairs are not centrally implicated in the therapeutic problematic. However, the airing of a number of documentaries germane to psychiatry and therapy was covered in *TV Guide* articles, becoming part of the discourse on television and therapy; see Hellerstein, "Now the Psychiatrist Can Do More," and Amsterdam, "Midlife Crises in Men." Also, in relation to sports, the emphasis on previews and postmortems of games, speaking with players and coaches, could certainly be analyzed in terms of the therapeutic problematic and confessional discourse.

24. Larry Angelo's function on the program is defined in terms of communications scholarship by Crow in "Conversational Pragmatics." A more sociologically oriented analysis is offered by Banks, "Listening to Dr. Ruth."

25. Her public stand on homosexuality has changed somewhat. Early on, she was quite critical of homosexuality and was criticized by the gay press for her position, which led to protests to advertisers, to Lifetime, and at her personal appearances. As a result, she became less critical, although her "neutrality" in some contexts could be taken in any number of ways. Homosexuality was not a frequent issue of discussion on *Good Sex!*, but was occasionally raised by callers. In these instances, Dr. Ruth would routinely—even formulaically—declare, "We do not know the aetiology of homosexuality." This statement could be interpreted as a refusal to take a firm stand about whether or not homosexuality is "natural." But it also leaves room for accepting homosexuality, no matter what its aetiology. By the time Dr. Ruth began to appear in syndication, AIDS had become a more visible problem; and she did assume a leading role in promoting AIDS education on television, including having Dr. Mathilde Krim, one of the leading specialists in this area, as one of her guests. The view of sex and relationships promoted on *Good Sex!* certainly presumed heterosexuality, the monogamous couple, and family relations as a norm.

26. For more detail on the structure of phone discussions on the program, see Crow, "Conversational Pragmatics."

27. Westheimer, "Dr. Ruth Advises," and Westheimer, "Dr. Ruth to The Golden Girls."

28. This is made explicit on another counseling show, *Couples*, which is discussed in Chapter 2.

29. Interestingly, this is the same information that callers provide when they talk on the Home Shopping Club, discussed in Chapter 3.

30. See Crow, "Conversational Pragmatics."

31. Ibid., pp. 475–78.

CHAPTER TWO

1. "The relationship monster has truly exceeded all expectations" (Coward, *Female Desires*, p. 131).

2. This phrase comes from the program itself, in its solicitations for contestants.

3. It is not that this genre is "original" to the 1980s, but rather that it is becoming far more common. Thus, in the first four months of 1987, *Broadcasting* included ads for, or brief articles about, four new shows in this genre that were being promoted for the fall season. Since the mid-1980s, new counseling shows have regularly appeared on cable and in syndication. This includes a range of different programs starring Dr. Ruth Westheimer and, in 1991, *The Barbara DeAngelis Show*. See Chapter 1 for a more thorough discussion of counseling as a form of therapeutic practice on television.

4. McNeil, *Total Television*, p. 171 (entry on *Divorce Court*).

5. This is extended in *Studs*, a version of the couple dating/confession game show that premiered after this analysis was done. *Studs* suggests the durability of the format's basic appeal and compounds the ways in which couples are formed in unstable mobility, identified via multivocal confessions, discussed in this chapter.

6. This is not strictly the case with *Couples*. The "pair" in analysis on this program is usually a heterosexual romantic couple but may also be two siblings, a parent and children, or some such combination.

7. For critical perspectives on the family and gender, and on the construction of gender in relation to the family as a symbolic force, see Eisenstein, "The Sexual Politics of the New Right"; Harding, "Family Reform Movements"; McIntosh, "The Family in Socialist-Feminist Politics"; and Rubin, "The Traffic in Women."

8. It can be argued that the "first impression" as a kind of superfi-

cial recognition has been a crucial construction in the development and operation of consumer culture. Most advertising relies on the immediacy of brand name recognition; and television commercials emphasize the effectivity of products in unforeseen and spontaneous narrative contexts. For example, if you use the spray cologne Impulse, a stranger may suddenly give you flowers—the cologne will, in other words, generate a flamboyant and desirable first impression, instantaneously igniting romance and passion.

9. The choosers on the show are not always female, though they are disproportionately so; thus in my description I refer to the chooser as "she" and treat the choice pool as male. I do so simply to avoid contortions in writing, and not to simplify the show or the implications of the show's assumptions about gender.

10. Again, this is not strictly true but has been simplified for the sake of description. The show does include people who agree to go out with someone selected from a videotape pool by the studio audience with the expectation that they will come back after the date to discuss it on the show. This is done on rare occasions with "celebrities" and sometimes at the end of the week to "close off" the process of the production of "suspense" as viewers wait to learn who the chooser selected from the choice pool or who the audience voted for.

11. If, after appearing on the show, the chooser elects to go out with whomever the audience plurality supports, the program will pay for a second date. But the chooser is not constrained to follow the audience's advice. Thus, if the date was a success but the studio audience voted for someone else from the choice pool, it is unlikely (but not impossible) that the chooser will reject her or his original choice to follow the audience's advice. Similarly, if the date was unsuccessful and the audience voted for the initial object-choice, the chooser is unlikely to follow their recommendation. Even in cases where the first date was unsuccessful and the audience selects a different object-choice, the chooser is free to reject their suggestion (this occurs, for example, when the chooser feels the audience choice is unacceptable based on having previously seen the whole tape).

12. Over time, the studio audience has become increasingly raucous, using loud hooting to express support and derision. This collective voice undercuts itself at the same time that its presence indicates an important consolidating function. Other aspects of the show have similarly shifted in tone over time. The conversations among Woolery and the two parties involved in the date have always been highly directed. But as the show has aged, the nature of the discussion as well as its pacing have indicated more aggressive pre-scripting, as the daters often

start to respond to a question from Woolery before he has even finished asking it.

13. Over time, this program underwent modification and at least two changes in set dressing. One version of the set featured two intertwined neon circles above each couple, abstracting two entwined wedding rings. Given the binary structure of the show, these also evoked the abstract symbols for male and female, without the arrow or cross to specify the sex of the participants.

14. Baudrillard, *Simulations*, p. 152.

15. Haraway, "A Manifesto for Cyborgs"; see also Baudrillard, *Simulations*.

16. Foucault, *The History of Sexuality*, pp. 61–62.

17. Haraway, "A Manifesto for Cyborgs," discusses stress in this way.

18. All quotes from the program were transcribed by the author from off-the-air videotapes (air checks) of the program.

19. These particular examples come from Levine, *Divorce Court*, which offers narrative summaries of "25 actual cases" from the TV show. For more on daytime courtroom dramas, including consideration of *Divorce Court*, see Petro, "Criminality or Hysteria?"

20. Foucault, *The History of Sexuality*, p. 61.

21. I do not want, here, to get embroiled in debates about pornographic representation. For two analyses of pornography, see Ross, *No Respect*, chap. 6, and Williams, *Hard Core*. Among works on questions of female sexuality, including pornography, are Snitow, Stansell, and Thompson, *Powers of Desire*, and Vance, *Pleasure and Danger*.

CHAPTER THREE

1. For a variety of perspectives on how television negotiates meaning in institutional and textual terms, see, among other sources, Fiske and Hartley, *Reading Television*; Schulze, *"Getting Physical"*; and White, "Ideological Analysis and Television." Also see the essays in Mellencamp, *Logics of Television*, and Seiter et al., *Remote Control*.

2. "Home Shopping," *Business Week*, December 15, 1986; Gill, "The Rise and Rise of HSN," *Esquire*, April 18, 1987; Wilkins, "A Visit to 'The Home Shopping Club,'" *Film Comment* 23, no. 2 (March–April 1987); Morgenson, "Fabulous Fads That Fizzled?," *Forbes*, February 23, 1987; Dorfman, "Overnight Sensation," *New York*, June 16, 1986.

3. *Channels*, June 1987, esp. pp. 25–30.

4. All of the stations owned by HSN are UHF. As HSN was growing, federal regulations regarding broadcast station ownership allowed a

single entity (individual, partnership, or corporation) to own twelve AM radio, twelve FM radio, and twelve television outlets. The total audience reached by any set of twelve television stations was not allowed to exceed 25 percent of the nationwide audience. However, an exception was made for UHF TV on the principle that UHF (channels 14–83) signals tend to be weaker than, and thus not to travel as far as, VHF (channels 2–13) signals. In recognition of this signal imbalance and attendant implications of smaller audiences, UHF audiences were figured at 50 percent of the total toward the nationwide 25 percent quota. In other words, with UHF stations, only half of the audience in the market is counted. Theoretically, an all-UHF network with twelve television stations could broadcast to half of the television viewing audience in the United States. The rules regarding station ownership are subject to periodic review and revision. It is also important to note that on its broadcast stations, HSN includes regular public service programs several times a day, running as long as fifteen minutes, as part of the requirements for holding a broadcast license.

5. In the fall of 1987, HSN offered a syndicated variant of its service, the Home Shopping Overnight Service; see "Home Shopping Hits Syndication."

6. In a *TV Guide* review of a number of different shop-at-home television services, HSN is criticized for this "high pressure" tactic. Feldon, "Join This Home Shopping Expedition."

7. Flitterman, "The *Real* Soap Operas," p. 94, makes this point with regard to the advertisements that play during daytime soap operas.

8. The concept of televisuality, especially in relation to 1980s American television, is developed by Caldwell, "Televisuality."

9. Bourdieu, *Distinction*.

10. Wilkins, "A Visit to the 'Home Shopping Club,'" and "Home Shopping."

11. Feldon, "Join This Home Shopping Expedition," p. 32.

12. These perspectives have been elaborated by Doane, *The Desire to Desire*; Joyrich, "All That Television Allows"; and Modleski, "Femininity as Mas(s)querade."

13. Wilkins, "A Visit to the 'Home Shopping Club,'" p. 71.

14. Desmond, "How I Met Miss Tootie," p. 346.

15. In the spring of 1987, HSN worked with GTE and AT&T to improve its phone systems. The company claimed it was losing "well in excess of $1 million per day" in sales because callers were getting busy signals. A company spokesman suggested that as many as 50 percent of customer calls were not getting through. See "Telephone Trouble."

16. Gunning, "The Cinema of Attractions."

17. Ibid., p. 58.

18. Issues of connoisseurship and upward mobility are also raised in Desmond, "How I Met Miss Tootie."

19. Schor, *Reading in Detail.*

20. Ibid., p. 4.

21. Ibid., p. 97.

22. Modleski, "Femininity as Mas(s)querade"; Joyrich, "All That Television Allows"; Bowlby, *Just Looking*; Benson, *Counter Cultures*; and Biggart, *Charismatic Capitalism.*

23. Most likely, hosts are given the name of repeat callers as the call is switched to them by the sales operator, but this is unacknowledged on the air.

24. Desmond, "How I Met Miss Tootie."

CHAPTER FOUR

1. These introductory teasers are compiled from a variety of shows, aired between summer 1986 and spring 1987. The analysis of *The 700 Club* offered in this chapter is based on consistent viewing, taping, and note-taking over a period of roughly two years, starting in 1986, with intermittent viewing following the period of concentrated analysis. Since that period, the actual hosts of the show, excepting Pat Robertson, have changed. However, the basic tactics, strategies, and appeals deployed by the program remain substantially the same as during the period of focused analysis.

2. Winfrey, "Sanitized Success," p. 5. Pat Robertson purchased a defunct UHF television station in Virginia Beach, Virginia, in 1961. A few years later he asked 700 people to make a ten dollar monthly pledge to cover the yearly operating costs of running the station. *The 700 Club*, which started in 1966, was named in honor of the donors who had sustained the station during its early years. Bruce, *Pray TV*, p. 39, and Armstrong, *The Electric Church*, pp. 106–7.

3. It is important to stress the heterogeneity of the Christian community, even within the evangelical Christian Right. Not all evangelicals would endorse Pat Robertson's organization or his particular range of practices and beliefs. Differences within the religious Right became all the more crucial in the wake of a series of scandals within the televangelical community in the late 1980s, most prominently involving Jim and Tammy Bakker and Jimmy Swaggart.

4. Sociologically based accounts of viewers of evangelical programming in general and *The 700 Club* in particular include Abelman,

"Motivations for Viewing *The 700 Club*," and Clymer, "Survey Finds Many Skeptics Among Evangelists' Viewers." The audience is also discussed in most of the book-length studies of religious and evangelical television; a number of sources are give in n. 7, below.

5. In some ways my approach to *The 700 Club* constitutes an aberrant decoding in that it neither assumes prior religious commitments nor implies the necessity of future faith: it is willfully desacralized. But it also therefore presumes no prior judgment in the sense that I do not take *The 700 Club* (or any televangelical program) to be an abuse or a perversion of either religion or television. Rather, I construe *The 700 Club* and the CBN as manifestations of a religious subculture whose institutional and philosophical imperatives intersect with contemporary media culture. These intersections in turn ground my reading of the program.

As a television viewer, especially as a cable subscriber, I am given access to the Family Channel, along with millions of other viewers. In this sense I am an intended viewer of the program, if not the ideal viewer addressed by the show and the network. At the same time, the program does embrace an evangelical mission, addressing nonadherents in the hope of converting them. In this sense, despite my nonreligious inclinations, I might indeed be considered one of the program's ideal viewers. I endeavored to exploit this prefigured disjunction in position to the fullest degree as a reading strategy.

I should also note that work on this chapter, from initial conception through publication, spans the years of scandals within the televangelical community. In retrospect, as many prominent figures have faded from the public eye, and all evangelical programming has been scaled back, we can more clearly see the subcultural elements of televangelical culture.

6. In early 1987, scandals in the televangelical community, notably focused on the Bakkers and Oral Roberts, brought massive media attention. This attention included cover stories in *Time*, *Newsweek*, and *U.S. News & World Report*, as well as extensive coverage in major newspapers and magazines and in broadcast journalism.

7. The phrase "evangelical upsurge" comes from Judis, "The Charge of the Light Brigade." Others who have dealt with the issue of televangelism include Horsfield, *Religious Television*; Hoover, *Mass Media Religion*; Bruce, *Pray TV*; Frankl, *Televangelism*; Capps, *The New Religious Right*; LeSage, "Why Christian Television Is Good TV"; McLaren, "Televangelism as Pedagogy and Cultural Politics"; and Hadden and Swann, *Prime-Time Preachers*.

8. The global activities of televangelists are discussed in a number of places, including Hadden and Swann, *Prime-Time Preachers*; Bruce, *Pray TV*; and a special issue of *Covert Action Information Bulletin* ("The Religious Right").

9. The difference between paid-time and sustained-time programming is explained in Horsfield, *Religious Television*.

10. These charges are discussed by Horsfield, *Religious Television*.

11. Ads aired during *The 700 Club* are always for the CBN organization and its activities. However, during other programming the Family Channel includes the same kind of commercial advertising found throughout American television.

12. Many people have noted that within American television this pluralism extends to the conservative perspective far more easily than it accommodates that of the Left. The success of televangelism, especially on cable, is often pointed to as evidence of this fact.

13. "We Care," a public relations pamphlet mailed by CBN in fund-raising in 1986.

14. *Hazel, Father Knows Best, The Flying Nun, Dobie Gillis*, and *Burns and Allen* are all situation comedies from the 1950s and 1960s; *The Big Valley* is a western series from the late 1960s; and *Remington Steele* is a detective series from the 1980s.

15. White, "Television: A Narrative—A History."

16. This sample, which is not atypical, is taken from the Providence, Rhode Island, edition of *TV Guide*, April 1987. The CBN show at this time, *Hardcastle and McCormick*, is an action-adventure/crime series from the 1980s. *Airwolf* is an action-adventure show also from the 1980s. The other programs listed include a medical drama (*Marcus Welby, M.D.*), situation comedies (*Sanford and Son, The Honeymooners, M*A*S*H*, and *Barney Miller*), a game show (*Wheel of Fortune*), a reality courtroom drama (*The People's Court*), and a news magazine (*Entertainment Tonight*).

17. White, "Television: A Narrative—A History."

18. The quote is taken from a fund-raising letter sent out by CBN in 1987, but the same kinds of phrases and rhetoric are common on the program.

19. This perspective is not, strictly speaking, all that different from the one that pervades news, public affairs, and talk shows, in which the world is cast in terms of multiple, local crises. For theoretical considerations of television in terms of crisis, catastrophe, and time, see Doane, "Information, Crisis, Catastrophe," and Mellencamp, "TV Time and Catastrophe."

20. The quote is from a television commercial soliciting for CBN phone counselors and encouraging viewers to become supporting members of The 700 Club.

21. The text is taken from a television commercial to encourage membership.

22. The text is taken from a CBN fund-raising letter (March 1987) to support the Lives in Crisis campaign.

23. Some of these stories are repeated in Robertson's *Beyond Reason*.

24. The text is taken from a television commercial on CBN for prayer-counselor lines.

25. From "Family Relationships," an undated pamphlet distributed by CBN.

26. Ibid.

27. Ibid.

CHAPTER FIVE

1. The year 1985 also witnessed the release of a film entitled *That Was Then; This Is Now*, based on the S. E. Hinton novel for young adults. (The film was written by, and starred, Emilio Estevez.) It was in production as *Finder of Lost Loves* was airing, and it was released shortly after the episodes I discuss in detail were broadcast. This suggests that the phrase itself had a general currency during the period, even achieving the status of instant banality. My analysis of the phrase contributes to a theoretical understanding of the linguistic and narrational mechanisms that enabled the phrase to circulate so readily.

2. See Silverman's discussion of Benveniste in *The Subject of Semiotics*, pp. 43–53.

3. Benveniste, "The Correlations of Tense in the French Verb" (*Problems in General Linguistics*, pp. 205–15).

4. The dialogue in the scene is as follows:

Cary: Go ahead and fight; but you've already lost the girl.
Mike: What are you talking about?
Cary: She's packing.
Mike: (To Thad) Was this your idea?
Cary: No, it was yours, when you decided it was more important to blame Thad for your problems than go on with your life.
Thad: Now wait a minute Cary. He's got a lot to blame me for.
Cary: Granted. But he also owes you a lot. You brought Beth here.
Mike: He cost me my marriage!

Cary: That was then; this is now. She's always loved you Mike. Do you want to do something about that? Or stay in this rut you've dug yourself?

5. In their final scene Linda asks Evan why he has been so angry. This dialogue follows directly from her question:

Evan: At our fate. I'm a minister. You're a madam. The only thing we can do . . .
Linda: . . . is to continue as we are.
Evan: Well I'll think of you. And I'll dream of you. And I'll pray for you. And someday you might even find what you're looking for.
Linda: That I never will.
Evan: Why do you say that?
Linda: Because what I'm looking for is you.

6. Barthes, *S/Z*, pp. 18–20.

7. I refer here to both psychoanalysis and psychology to indicate the generalized therapeutic strategies engaged by the narrative, drawing on a range of traditions.

8. The term "family romance" comes from Freud and refers to fantasies of parental origin that develop as a child grows up and tries to establish independence in relation to parental authority. In the family romance scenario the child may imagine that he has been adopted, or lost, and that his real parents are more elevated or noble than the adults who are raising him. As the child comes to understand sexuality and reproduction, the imaginary elevation of his parents focuses on the father. Freud, "Family Romances."

In *Origins of the Novel* Marthe Robert proposes that the family romance, culminating in Oedipus, undergirds the modern novel: "During the whole of its history the novel has derived the violence of its desires and its irrepressible freedom from the Family Romance; in this respect it can be said that this primal romance reveals, beneath the historical and individual accidents from which each particular work derives, more than simply the psychological origins of the genre; it is the genre, with all its inexhaustible possibilities and congenital childishness, the false frivolous, grandiose, mean, subversive and gossipy genre of which each of us is indeed the issue . . . and which, moreover, recreates for each of us a remnant of our primal love and primal reality" (p. 31).

9. In one episode Cary situates himself as a prime client for a Maxwell-style cure which he simultaneously rejects. He is explaining to Daisy why he holds back from expressing his (unnamed) feelings for her: "I guess I'm scared if I let go of one feeling, I don't know what other feelings may come tumbling out."

10. The episode first aired February 12, 1986.

11. In terms of generic antecedents, the strength of this code is most clearly expressed in the film *The Maltese Falcon* (1941). The importance of the hard-boiled detective as a prototype for Chase is stylistically elaborated in the program not only in the way the character plays the role but also in the inclusion of a few, brief black-and-white sequences depicting the murder, narrated in voice-over by Chase.

12. This distinction is elaborated by Morley in *The "Nationwide" Audience*: "The concept 'ideological problematic' designates not a set of 'contents' but rather a defined space of operation, the way a problematic selects from, conceives and organizes its field of reference. This then constitutes a particular agenda of issues which are visible or invisible, or a repertoire of questions which are asked or not asked. . . . The concept of 'mode of address' designates the specific communicative forms and practices of a programme which would constitute what would be referred to in literary criticism as its 'tone' or 'style.' . . . The mode of address establishes the form of the relation which the programme proposes to/with its audience" (p. 139).

13. See Chapter 1, where I discuss *TV Guide* articles that promote the association of television viewing and therapeutic strategies of discourse.

14. Cowie, "Fantasia."

15. Ibid., p. 87.

16. Ibid., p. 101.

17. Ibid., p. 102.

18. Ibid.

19. The particulars of specific reader relations to television are beyond the scope of this study. The matter is discussed in many other places, including Ang, *Watching Dallas*; Ang, *Desperately Seeking the Audience*; Hall, "Encoding/Decoding"; Liebes and Katz, *The Export of Meaning*; Lull, *Inside Family Viewing*; Morley, *The "Nationwide" Audience*; Press, *Women Watching Televison*; and the essays in Seiter et al., *Remote Control*.

20. See, among others, Coward, *Female Desires*, esp. pp. 135–42 and 175–204; Modleski, *Loving with a Vengeance*; and Radway, *Reading the Romance*.

CONCLUSION

1. This kind of both/and logic, whereby the assertion of two positions leads to a cancellation of meaning, is discussed in Mellencamp, *High Anxiety*.

2. This phrase—in full, "We are living in a world of proliferating information and shrinking sense"—comes from Baudrillard, "The Implosion of Meaning in the Media," p. 137.

3. Foucault, *The History of Sexuality*, p. 62.

4. Chesler, *Women and Madness*.

5. The connection of these services to marketing research is discussed in Schwoch, White, and Reilly, *Media Knowledge*, pp. 117–19. Chapter 6 in this book addresses questions of telecommunications technologies in everyday life and their implications for consumerism, commodification, information, and privacy in contemporary life.

6. McCarthy, "Metaphors of Connection," makes a compelling argument for linking issues of gender to telecommunications precisely at the site of these phone services and their television commercials.

7. See, among many others, Baudrillard, *In the Shadow of the Silent Majorities*; Virilio, *Speed and Politics*; and Poster, *The Mode of Information*.

Bibliography

Abelman, Robert. "Motivations for Viewing *The 700 Club*." *Journalism Quarterly* 65, no. 1 (Spring 1988): 112–18.

Allen, Robert C. *Speaking of Soap Operas*. Chapel Hill: University of North Carolina Press, 1985.

Amsterdam, Susan. "Midlife Crises in Men: Are Women to Blame?" *TV Guide*, July 22, 1989, pp. 18–21.

Ang, Ien. *Desperately Seeking the Audience*. New York: Routledge, 1991.

————. *Watching Dallas*. Translated by Della Couling. New York: Methuen, 1985.

Armstrong, Ben. *The Electric Church*. Nashville: Thomas Nelson, 1979.

Asimov, Isaac. "ALF, You've Got Some Explaining to Do." *TV Guide*, August 15, 1987, pp. 26–29.

Banks, Jane. "Listening to Dr. Ruth: The New Sexual Primer." In *Talking to Strangers: Mediated Therapeutic Communication*, edited by Gary Gumpert and Sandra Fish Norwood, pp. 71–84. Norwood, N.J.: Ablex, 1990.

Barthes, Roland. *S/Z*. Translated by Richard Miller. New York: Hill and Wang, 1974.

Baudrillard, Jean. "The Implosion of Meaning in the Media and the Implosion of the Social in the Masses." In *The Myths of Information: Technology and Postindustrial Culture*, edited by Kathleen Woodward, translated by Mary Lydon, pp. 137–48. Madison, Wis.: Coda Press, 1980.

————. *In the Shadow of the Silent Majorities*. Translated by Paul Foss, Paul Patton, and John Johnston. New York: Semiotext(e), 1983.

————. *Simulations*. Translated by Paul Foss, Paul Patton, and Philip Beitchman. New York: Semiotext(e), 1983.

Benson, Susan Porter. *Counter Cultures: Saleswomen, Managers, and Customers in American Department Stores, 1890–1940*. Urbana: University of Illinois Press, 1986.

Benveniste, Emile. *Problems in General Linguistics*. Translated by Mary Elizabeth Meek. Coral Gables: University of Miami Press, 1971.

Berger, John. *Ways of Seeing*. New York: Penguin, 1973.

Bernikow, Louise. "Is TV a Pal—or a Danger—for Lonely People?" *TV Guide*, October 25, 1986, pp. 4–6.

Biggart, Nicole Woolsey. *Charismatic Capitalism: Direct Selling Organizations in America*. Chicago: University of Chicago Press, 1989.

Bourdieu, Pierre. *Distinction: A Social Critique of the Judgment of Taste*. Cambridge: Harvard University Press, 1984.

Bowlby, Rachel. *Just Looking: Consumer Culture in Dreiser, Gissing, and Zola*. New York: Methuen, 1985.

Brothers, Joyce. "How TV Adds Spice to Your Life." *TV Guide*, February 10, 1990, pp. 13–14.

———. "If You Want to Be a Better Parent. . . ." *TV Guide*, March 4, 1989, pp. 22–25.

———. "The Shows That'll Make You Feel Better." *TV Guide*, July 29, 1989, pp. 12–15.

———. "Why We Need to Laugh." *TV Guide*, November 11, 1989, pp. 18–20.

Bruce, Steve. *Pray TV: Televangelism in America*. New York: Routledge, 1990.

Brunsdon, Charlotte. "*Crossroads*: Notes on Soap Opera." In *Regarding Television*, edited by E. Ann Kaplan, pp. 76–83. Frederick, Md.: University Publications of America, 1983.

Caldwell, John Thornton. "Televisuality: The Emergence and Performance of Visual Style in American Television." Ph.D. dissertation, Northwestern University, 1991.

Capps, Walter H. *The New Religious Right: Piety, Patriotism, and Politics*. Columbia: University of South Carolina Press, 1990.

Chesler, Phyllis. *Women and Madness*. Garden City: Doubleday, 1972.

Clymer, Adam. "Survey Finds Many Skeptics Among Evangelists' Viewers." *New York Times*, March 31, 1987, A1.

Coles, Robert. "How Television's Stories Help Us." *TV Guide*, June 3, 1989, pp. 18–21.

Collins, Jim. *Uncommon Cultures: Popular Culture and Post-Modernism*. New York: Routledge, 1989.

Covert Action Information Bulletin 27 (Spring 1987). Special issue on "The Religious Right."

Coward, Rosalind. *Female Desires: How They Are Sought, Bought, and Packaged*. New York: Grove Press, 1985.

―――. "Sexual Politics and Psychoanalysis: Some Notes on Their Relation." In *Feminism, Culture, and Politics*, edited by Rosalind Brunt and Caroline Rowan, pp. 171–87. London: Lawrence and Wishart, 1982.

Cowie, Elizabeth. "Fantasia." *m/f* 9 (1984): 71–104.

Crout, Teresa Kochmar. "Your Therapy Could Be Watching *Dallas* or *Dynasty*." *TV Guide*, December 14, 1985, pp. 14–18.

Crow, Brian. "Conversational Pragmatics in Television Talk: The Discourse of *Good Sex*." *Media Culture and Society* 8 (1986): 457–84.

Deleuze, Gilles, and Felix Guattari. *The Anti-Oedipus: Capitalism and Schizophrenia*. Translated by Robert Hurley, Mark Seem, and Helen R. Lane. New York: Viking, 1977.

Desmond, Jane. "How I Met Miss Tootie: *The Home Shopping Club*." *Cultural Studies* 3, no. 3 (October 1989): 340–47.

Doane, Mary Ann. *The Desire to Desire: The Woman's Film of the 1940s*. Bloomington: Indiana University Press, 1987.

―――. "Information, Crisis, Catastrophe." In *Logics of Television: Essays in Cultural Criticism*, edited by Patricia Mellencamp, pp. 222–39. Bloomington: Indiana University Press, 1990.

Docherty, John P. "A Psychiatrist Looks at Prime Time." *TV Guide*, August 4, 1984, pp. 3–6.

Dorfman, Dan. "Overnight Sensation." *New York*, June 16, 1986, pp. 18–20.

Eckert, Charles. "The Carole Lombard in Macy's Window." *Quarterly Review of Film Studies* 3 (1978): 3–21.

Eisenstein, Zillah. "The Sexual Politics of the New Right: Understanding the 'Crisis of Liberalism' for the 1980s." *Signs* 7, no. 3 (Spring 1982): 567–88.

Ernst, Robert. *Weakness Is a Crime: The Life of Bernarr Macfadden*. Syracuse: Syracuse University Press, 1990.

Feldon, Leah. "Join This Home Shopping Expedition." *TV Guide*, July 4, 1987, pp. 30–32.

Feuer, Jane. "Melodrama, Serial Form, and Television Today." *Screen* 25 (January–February 1984): 4–16.

Fiske, John, and John Hartley. *Reading Television*. London: Methuen, 1978.

Flitterman, Sandy. "The *Real* Soap Operas: TV Commercials." In *Regarding Television*, edited by E. Ann Kaplan, pp. 84–96. Frederick, Md.: University Publications of America, 1983.

Foucault, Michel. *The History of Sexuality*. Vol. 1. Translated by
Robert Hurley. New York: Pantheon, 1978.
Frankl, Razelle. *Televangelism: The Marketing of Popular Religion*.
Carbondale: Southern Illinois University Press, 1987.
Freud, Sigmund. "Family Romances." In *The Standard Edition of
the Complete Psychological Works*, vol. 9, edited by James Strachey.
London: Hogarth, 1959.
Gardner, James E. "Does Your Teen-ager *Need* a $95.00 Shirt—or
Just Want One?" *TV Guide*, May 4, 1985, pp. 35–37.
Gaylin, Willard. "Prime Time on the Couch: A Psychiatrist Wonders
What's Happening to Romantic Love." *TV Guide*, October 4, 1986,
pp. 5–8.
Gill, Mark. "The Rise and Rise of HSN." *Esquire*, April 18, 1987,
p. 70.
Goodman, Gerald. "Successful Intimacy?: Watch *L.A. Law*'s Stuart
and Ann." *TV Guide*, October 29, 1988: 32–35.
Gunning, Tom. "The Cinema of Attractions: Early Film, Its Spectator,
and the Avant-Garde." In *Early Cinema: Space Frame Narrative*,
edited by Thomas Elsaesser, pp. 56–62. London: British Film Insti-
tute, 1990.
Hadden, Jeffrey K., and C. E. Swann. *Prime-Time Preachers: The
Rising Power of Televangelism*. Reading, Mass.: Addison-Wesley,
1981.
Hall, Stuart. "Encoding/Decoding." In *Culture, Media, Language*,
edited by Stuart Hall, Dorothy Hobson, Andrew Lowe, and Paul
Willis, pp. 128–38. London: Hutchinson, 1981.
Haraway, Donna. "A Manifesto for Cyborgs." In *Coming to Terms:
Feminism, Theory, Politics*, edited by Elizabeth Weed, pp. 173–204.
New York: Routledge, 1989.
Harding, Susan. "Family Reform Movements: Recent Feminism and
Its Opposition." *Feminist Studies* 7, no. 1 (Spring 1981): 57–75.
Heath, Stephen. *The Sexual Fix*. New York: Schocken, 1984.
Hellerstein, David. "Can TV Cause Divorce?" *TV Guide*, Septem-
ber 26, 1987, pp. 4–7.
———. "Now the Psychiatrist Can Do More Than Just Listen." *TV
Guide*, October 8, 1988, pp. 14–15.
Hobson, Dorothy. "Soap Operas at Work." In *Remote Control: Tele-
vision, Audiences, and Cultural Power*, edited by Ellen Seiter, Hans
Borchers, Gabriele Kreutzner, and Eva-Maria Warth, pp. 150–67.
New York: Routledge, 1989.
"Home Shopping Hits Syndication." *Broadcasting*, May 4, 1987, p. 59.

"Home Shopping: Is It a Revolution in Retailing—or Just a Fad?" *Business Week*, December 15, 1986, pp. 62–69.

Hoover, Stewart M. *Mass Media Religion: The Social Sources of the Electronic Church*. Newbury Park, Calif.: Sage, 1988.

Horsfield, Peter. *Religious Television: The American Experience*. New York: Longman, 1984.

Jameson, Fred. "Postmodernism and Consumer Cultures." In *The Anti-Aesthetic: Essays in Postmodern Culture*, edited by Hal Foster, pp. 111–25. Port Townsend, Wash.: Bay Press, 1983.

Joyrich, Lynne. "All That Television Allows: TV Melodrama, Post-modernism and Consumer Culture." *Camera Obscura* 16 (1988): 129–54.

————. "Critical and Textual Hypermasculinity." In *Logics of Television: Essays in Cultural Criticism*, edited by Patricia Mellencamp, pp. 156–72. Bloomington: Indiana University Press, 1990.

Judis, John B. "The Charge of the Light Brigade." *The New Republic*, September 29, 1986, pp. 16–19.

Justice, Candy. "Now TV Offers a Parenting Manual." *TV Guide*, July 28, 1984, pp. 28–30.

Kalter, Joanmarie. "No Problem Is Too Intimate for Your TV Therapist." *TV Guide*, June 4, 1983, pp. 4–6.

Lasch, Christopher. *The Culture of Narcissism: American Life in an Age of Diminishing Expectations*. New York: W. W. Norton, 1979.

Leahy, Michael. "TV's Psychology Shows: More Hype Than Help?" *TV Guide*, November 21, 1987, pp. 48–53.

Lears, T. J. Jackson. "From Salvation to Self-Realization: Advertising and the Therapeutic Roots of the Consumer Culture, 1880–1930." In *The Culture of Consumption: Critical Essays in American History, 1880–1980*, edited by Richard Wightman Fox and T. J. Jackson Lears, pp. 1–38. New York: Pantheon, 1983.

LeSage, Julia. "Why Christian Television Is Good TV." *The Independent* 10 (May 1987): 11–20.

Levine, Robert. *Divorce Court*. New York: Dell, 1986.

Liebes, Tamar, and Elihu Katz. *The Export of Meaning: Cross-Cultural Readings of Dallas*. New York: Oxford, 1990.

Lull, James. *Inside Family Viewing: Ethnographic Research on Television's Audiences*. New York: Routledge, 1990.

Lyotard, Jean-François. *The Postmodern Condition*. Minneapolis: University of Minnesota Press, 1984.

McCarthy, Anna. "Metaphors of Connection: Women and Technology in 'Pornophony' Advertising." Unpublished seminar paper, Northwestern University, 1990.

McIntosh, Mary. "The Family in Socialist-Feminist Politics." In *Feminism, Culture, and Politics*, edited by Rosalind Brunt and Caroline Rowan, pp. 109–29. London: Lawrence and Wishart, 1982.

McLaren, Peter. "Televangelism as Pedagogy and Cultural Politics." In *Popular Culture, Schooling, and Everyday Life*, edited by Henry Giroux and Roger I. Simon, pp. 147–73. Granby, Mass.: Bergin and Garvey, 1989.

McNeil, Alex. *Total Television*. New York: Penguin, 1984.

Marchand, Roland. *Advertising the American Dream: Making Way for Modernity, 1920–1940*. Berkeley: University of California Press, 1985.

Masciarotte, Gloria Jean. "C'mon, Girl: Oprah Winfrey and the Discourse of Feminine Talk." *Genders* 11 (Fall 1991): 81–110.

Mellencamp, Patricia. *High Anxiety: Catastrophe, Scandal, and Age*. Bloomington: Indiana University Press, 1992.

———. "Situation Comedy, Feminism, and Freud: Discourses of Gracie and Lucy." In *Studies in Entertainment: Critical Approaches to Mass Culture*, edited by Tania Modleski, pp. 80–95. Bloomington: Indiana University Press, 1986.

———. "TV Time and Catastrophe, or *Beyond the Pleasure Principle* of Television." In *Logics of Television: Essays in Cultural Criticism*, edited by Patricia Mellencamp, pp. 240–66. Bloomington: Indiana University Press, 1990.

———, ed. *Logics of Television: Essays in Cultural Criticism*. Bloomington: Indiana University Press, 1990.

Modleski, Tania. "Femininity as Mas[s]querade: A Feminist Approach to Mass Culture." In *High Theory/Low Culture: Analyzing Popular Television and Film*, edited by Colin McCabe, pp. 37–52. New York: St. Martin's, 1986.

———. *Loving with a Vengeance: Mass-Produced Fantasies For Women*. New York: Methuen, 1982.

Morgenson, Gretchen. "Fabulous Fads That Fizzled?" *Forbes*, February 23, 1987, pp. 40–48.

Morley, David. *Family Television: Cultural Power and Domestic Leisure*. London: Comedia, 1986.

———. *The "Nationwide" Audience*. London: British Film Institute, 1980.

Mulvey, Laura. "Melodrama In and Out of the Home." In *High Theory/Low Culture: Analyzing Popular Television and Film*, edited by Colin McCabe, pp. 80–100. New York: St. Martin's, 1986.

Palmer, Florence. *Confession Writer's Handbook*. Cincinnati: Writer's Digest, 1975.

Petro, Patrice. "Criminality or Hysteria?: Television and the Law." *Discourse* 10 (1988): 48–61.

Polan, Dana. "Brief Encounters: Mass Culture and the Evacuation of Sense." In *Studies in Entertainment: Critical Approaches to Mass Culture*, edited by Tania Modleski, pp. 167–87. Bloomington: Indiana University Press, 1986.

Poster, Mark. *The Mode of Information: Poststructuralism and Social Context.* Chicago: University of Chicago Press, 1990.

Press, Andrea L. *Women Watching Television: Gender, Class, and Generation in the American Television Experience.* Philadelphia: University of Pennsylvania Press, 1991.

Radway, Janice. *Reading the Romance: Women, Patriarchy, and Popular Literature.* Chapel Hill: University of North Carolina Press, 1984.

Robert, Marthe. *Origins of the Novel.* Translated by Sacha Rabinovich. Bloomington: Indiana University Press, 1980.

Robertson, Pat. *Beyond Reason: How Miracles Can Change Your Life.* New York: Bantam, 1986.

Ross, Andrew. *No Respect: Intellectuals and Popular Culture.* New York: Routledge, 1989.

Roustang, François. *Dire Mastery: Discipleship from Freud to Lacan.* Translated by Ned Lukacher. Baltimore: Johns Hopkins University Press, 1982.

———. *Psychoanalysis Never Lets Go.* Translated by Ned Lukacher. Baltimore: Johns Hopkins University Press, 1983.

Rubin, Gayle. "The Traffic in Women: Notes on the 'Political Economy' of Sex." In *Toward an Anthropology of Women*, edited by Rayna R. Reiter, pp. 157–210. New York: Monthly Review Press, 1975.

Schor, Naomi. *Reading in Detail: Aesthetics and the Feminine.* New York: Methuen, 1987.

Schulze, Laurie Jane. "*Getting Physical*: Text/Context/Reading and the Made-for-Television Movie." *Cinema Journal* 25, no. 2 (Winter 1986): 35–50.

Schwoch, James, Mimi White, and Susan Reilly. *Media Knowledge: Popular Culture, Pedagogy, and Critical Citizenship.* Albany: State University of New York Press, 1992.

Seiter, Ellen. "Eco's TV Guide—The Soaps." *Tabloid* 5 (Winter 1982): 35–43.

———. "Promise and Contradiction: The Daytime Television Serial." *Film Reader* 5 (Winter 1982): 150–63.

Seiter, Ellen, Hans Borchers, Gabriele Kreutzner, and Eva-Maria

Warth, eds. *Remote Control: Television, Audiences, and Cultural Power*. New York: Routledge, 1989.

Silverman, Kaja. *The Subject of Semiotics*. New York: Oxford University Press, 1983.

Snitow, Ann, Christine Stansell, and Sharon Thompson, eds. *Powers of Desire: The Politics of Sexuality*. New York: Monthly Review Press, 1983.

Spigel, Lynne. "Television in the Family Circle: The Popular Reception of a New Medium." In *Logics of Television: Essays in Cultural Criticism*, edited by Patricia Mellencamp, pp.73–97. Bloomington: Indiana University Press, 1990.

"Telephone Trouble." *Broadcasting*, May 4, 1987, p. 8.

Thorburn, David. "Television Melodrama." In *Television: The Critical View*, 2nd ed., edited by Horace Newcomb, pp. 536–53. New York: Oxford University Press, 1979.

Torres, Sasha. "Melodrama, Masculinity, and the Family: *thirtysomething* as Therapy." *Camera Obscura* 19 (1989): 86–106.

Vance, Carole S., ed. *Pleasure and Danger: Exploring Female Sexuality*. Boston: Routledge and Kegan Paul, 1984.

Virilio, Paul. *Speed and Politics: An Essay on Dromology*. Translated by Mark Polizzotti. New York: Semiotext(e), 1980.

Westheimer, Ruth. "Dr. Ruth Advises: David—Quit Your Job! Maddie—Stop Playing Games!" *TV Guide*, October 24, 1987, pp. 27–28.

———. "Dr. Ruth to The Golden Girls: How to Keep That Spice and Sparkle in Your Lives." *TV Guide*, April 30, 1988, pp. 10–13.

White, Mimi. "Ideological Analysis and Television." In *Channels of Discourse: Television and Contemporary Criticism*, edited by Robert C. Allen, pp. 134–71. Chapel Hill: University of North Carolina Press, 1987.

———. "Television: A Narrative—A History." *Cultural Studies* 3, no. 3 (October 1989): 282–300.

Wilkins, Mike. "A Visit to the 'Home Shopping Club.'" *Film Comment* 23, no. 2 (March–April 1987): 70–74.

Williams, Linda. *Hard Core: Power, Pleasure and the Frenzy of the Visible*. Berkeley: University of California Press, 1989.

Williamson, Judith. *Consuming Passions: The Dynamics of Popular Culture*. New York: Marion Boyars, 1987.

Winfrey, Lee. "Sanitized Success: FAM Limits Preaching, Offers 75% Secular Slate." *Chicago Tribune*, September 5, 1989, sec. 5, p. 5.

Index

ABC, 145

Acquired immune deficiency syndrome (AIDS), 125–26, 127–28, 190 (n. 25)

Advertising, 82, 191–92 (n. 8); therapeutic strategies, 12, 13, 180; on soap operas, 16; on couples shows, 66; as programming, 84; creativity in, 88; for 900-number phone services, 182; on CBN Family Channel, 197 (n. 11)

Advocate, The, 126

Alf, 1–6, 10, 23, 173, 185 (n. 2)

All New Dating Game, The, 53; as revival of original program, 54, 55; confessional discourse on, 56, 67–68; competitive format, 57–59, 60, 62, 192 (n. 9); technological fictionality, 64

America's Most Wanted, 181, 182

Angelo, Larry, 36–37, 40, 41, 42, 44–45

Ankerberg, John, 120

Asimov, Isaac, 45

Ask Dr. Ruth, 25–26

Audience, television, 46, 57, 71, 73, 114, 121, 128, 194 (n. 4); in studio, 8, 9, 58, 60, 61, 67, 68, 118, 181; and women, 15,

35, 171, 182; and melodrama, 15, 171; and therapeutic transaction, 19, 35, 50, 51, 137, 171, 183; and confession, 51, 67, 78–79, 171, 182, 183; and consumer culture, 66, 82, 83, 84, 89, 94, 95, 97, 101, 102; and sexuality, 76, 78–79, 80; and programming, 82, 83, 200 (n. 12); and class, 90–92, 100; and religion and religious programming, 114–25 passim, 131; and fantasy, 117, 182; and youth, 174, 182

Bakker, Jim, 112, 113, 195 (n. 3), 196 (n. 6)

Bakker, Tammy, 195 (n. 3), 196 (n. 6)

Baudrillard, Jean, 65–66

Benveniste, Emile, 21, 145, 146, 188 (n. 36)

Bible, 115; *700 Club* doctrine of, 123, 130, 134; tithing in, 133; gender roles in, 143

Book, The, 115

Brackelmanns, Walter, 35–36, 53, 69–72, 74–75

Breuer, Josef, 20

Broadcasting, 85, 191 (n. 3)

Macfadden, Bernarr, 186 (n. 15)
Maltese Falcon, The, 200 (n. 11)
Maniac Mansion, 120
Marketing, 65, 76, 116, 120
Marriage: therapy shows and, 30; couples shows and, 61, 62, 77–78; *The 700 Club* and, 126, 142, 144
Masciarotte, Gloria Jean, 185–86 (n. 9)
Mass culture, 3, 11; women in, 2, 14; therapeutic discourse in, 13, 52; capitalism and, 21; home shoppers and, 91; CBN and, 111. *See also* Consumer culture; Popular culture; Taste culture
Mass media: in *Alf*, 3, 6; home shopping and, 91; in *Midnight Caller*, 166, 167–68
Media culture, 8–10, 45, 118–19
"Media therapy," 33
Mellencamp, Patricia, 14–15
Melodrama, 187 (nn. 23, 29); in soap operas, 15; prime-time, 16; in courtroom drama, 72; in *The 700 Club*, 125, 130, 142, 143
Middle class, 174; and morality of dating shows, 77–79, 80, 81; home shopping and, 90; CBN and, 120
Middle East Television, 115
Midnight Caller, 146, 162–68, 170, 171
Mode of address, 7, 108, 168, 200 (n. 12)
Modleski, Tania, 17–18
Moonlighting, 34–35
Moral Majority, 113
Morley, David, 200 (n. 12)
MTV, 173

Mulvey, Laura, 14

NBC, 1
New Newlywed Game, The, 53, 54, 56, 57, 64, 193 (n. 13); confessional discourse, 62, 68, 77, 79–80
New York, 85
Nickelodeon, 121

Old Time Gospel Hour, The, 113
Operation Blessing, 115, 118
Operation Good Shepherd, 116, 117–18
Oprah Winfrey Show, The, 185–86 (n. 9)

Pay-per-chat telephone, 182–83
Perfect Match, 53, 57, 62, 63, 66, 68
Perry, Mark, 126–27, 128
Perry, Shireen, 126–27
Polan, Dana, 21
Politics, 113, 123–24
Popular culture, 2, 45, 113, 173, 183. *See also* Consumer culture; Mass culture; Taste culture
Pornography, 80
Postmodernism, 11, 15; defined, 21; philosophy, 21; therapeutic discourse and, 21, 22, 23–24, 184; dating shows and, 65
Prime time: melodrama, 16; contrast of soap operas to, 16, 18; therapeutic approach to, 36; fictional drama, 146, 156, 167, 171
Protestantism: self-denial, advertising and, 12; fundamentalist, 111, 130, 144; evangelical, 112

opment of, 112–14; scandals in, 113, 120, 195 (n. 3), 196 (nn. 5, 6)

Television: as therapy, 6–7, 25, 26, 27–36, 44, 176–77, 180–81, 182; therapeutic discourse in, 7, 11, 17, 20, 22–24, 50, 52–53, 177–84; role of confession in, 8–11, 19–20, 67, 137, 166, 177, 178–79, 182–83, 184; domestic ideology, 14–15; programming patterns, 16–17, 52, 82, 83, 109, 176; psychoanalysis and, 18–19; postmodernism and, 21, 22–23; fictional characters, 25, 27, 34–35, 43; commodification of viewers, 82–83; station ownership, federal regulations, 193–94 (n. 4). *See also* Audience, television; Cable television; Commercial television

TelShop, 86

Therapeutic discourse: in *Alf*, 3, 6, 10; role of consumerism in, 6–7, 10, 12, 13, 85, 108, 137, 184; centrality in television programming, 7, 11, 17, 20, 22–24, 32, 34, 50, 52–53, 176, 177–84, 187 (n. 29); role of the family in, 7, 21, 23, 81, 172, 184; as narrative strategy, 8, 11, 177–78; role of confession in, 8–11, 13, 19–20, 67, 137, 166, 177, 178–79, 182–83, 184; in home shopping, 10, 85, 105–6, 108; as communication, 11, 23; in advertising strategies, 12, 13, 180; psychoanalysis and, 12–13, 18–19, 20; association with women, 17, 35, 171, 184; postmodernism and, 22,

23–24, 184; *TV Guide* articles and, 25, 26–27, 32–34, 44, 50; in *Good Sex!*, 38, 40–44, 50; in couples shows, 52–53, 76–77, 81; in *The 700 Club*, 112, 137, 144; in prime-time dramas, 146–47, 152, 154–55, 156–58, 160–61, 165, 167–69, 171, 172. *See also* Confessional discourse; Therapy

Therapy, 12–13, 20; postmodernism and, 21; television as, 25, 26, 27–36, 44, 176–77, 180–81, 182; in *The Simpsons*, 174–75, 176–77; access to, 180. *See also* Therapeutic discourse

Therapy (counseling) programs, 25–26, 35–36, 51, 179, 189 (n. 2), 191 (n. 3); *TV Guide* articles on, 26–27, 33–35, 190 (n. 23); for couples, 54, 70

thirtysomething, 187 (n. 29)

Torres, Sasha, 187 (n. 29)

Tracy Ullman Show, The, 173

TV Guide: on television as therapy, 25, 26, 27–33, 36, 38, 43, 44, 50; on therapy shows, 26–27, 33–35, 190 (n. 23); on home shopping channels, 85, 194 (n. 6)

UHF TV, 193–94 (n. 4)

Unsolved Mysteries, 181, 182

USA Network, 121

Vamos, Mark N., 82

Viscott, David, 34, 189 (n. 2)

Voyeurism, 50, 75, 93

Westheimer, Ruth: *TV Guide* articles, 25, 34–35; television sex counseling, 25–26, 35–

37, 38–50, 137; media career, 36, 41, 189 (n. 3), 191 (n. 3); authority credentials, 37–38, 45; and homosexuality, 47, 190 (n. 25)

Women, 36; in mass culture, 2, 14; as consumer, 5, 14, 15, 85, 99–100, 106–7, 108; television and domesticity, 14–15; soap opera genre and, 15–16, 17, 18; in couples shows, 79– 80; family role of, 108, 123, 143, 144; therapeutic discourse associated with, 171; psycho-analysis and, 180

Woodward, Edward, 157

Woolery, Chuck, 9, 53, 59, 65, 192–93 (n. 12)

Working class, 90–91, 92–93, 100, 103, 105, 106

WTBS, 121